FRETBOARD
PhD

FRETBOARD PhD
by Ashkan Mashhour

ISBN: 978-1-939619-08-2

Cover & interior design, typesetting, music engraving,
artwork, prepress: Ashkan Mashhour

For inquiries, feedback, and suggestions, or to stay informed of new
titles and promotions, please contact:
ashkan@cheatsheetmusic.com

For updates and the latest information, visit:
pelemeleworks.com

pelemeleworks.com

ABOUT THE AUTHOR

Ashkan Mashhour is the author of the books *Guitar Fingers: Essential Technique in Pictures* and *Intervallic Fretboard: Towards Improvising on the Guitar*. He has also developed a range of music instructional products for guitar and other instruments. Ashkan has held R&D and project management positions in the field of RF and digital communications in the wireless and semiconductor industries. He has studied guitar privately and at Orange Coast College, California. Ashkan is an Electrical Engineering graduate of ENST Bretagne, France, and University College London, UK.

·················

ACKNOWLEDGEMENTS

This book is the result of a journey that has its roots in lessons I took with guitarist Dave Murdy, over a decade ago. The assignments he gave me jogged my mind and made me question my understanding of the fretboard. This led to a first book, written with Dave, titled *Intervallic Fretboard*. Now with a lot more experience under my belt, as well as feedback, questions, and suggestions from readers the world over, *Fretboard PhD* has a different focus and is dedicated to the study of the fretboard. So I'm indebted to Dave for igniting in me the quest to make sense of the fretboard puzzle and to find pathways that work for me. Hopefully, this book will help the light bulb go off for others too!

Thanks also go to Mark Wein, formerly of Premier Music, where I was lucky to be one of the first "victims," and to Jay Simper of Musicians Institute, whose groove on the bass guitar is only rivalled by his sense of humour. Thank you to Eddie Oropeza and John Pollard for bygone "guitar conversations" and for unwittingly inspiring a couple of points discussed in the book.

A number of organisations have been very supportive over the years, in particular staff at Guitar Techniques and Guitarist magazines and folks at Elixir Strings, amongst many others. These "others" include Jon Bloomer at Guitar Noize, Ivan Chopik at Guitar Messenger, Gary Cooper at Guitar Interactive, as well as Dunlop and MakeMusic.

And to my parents, Azy and Vahid, of course.

Ashkan Mashhour

TABLE OF CONTENTS

PREFACE

To the layman watching a guitarist play, the fretboard is a simple piece of wood riddled with metal wire. It doesn't mean anything at all. Yet, the trained guitar player manages to make music out of it. As you learn more about the guitar, you will unveil the fascinating world that the fretboard conceals…at first sight.

Fretboard PhD focuses solely on the study of the fretboard, with an emphasis on intervals. Its goal is to take you to a point where you intimately understand how the fretboard works, from its physical layout to the bridges that connect it to music theory. With this fretboard knowledge, you are able to form a mental picture of the fretboard that will allow you to navigate the fretboard freely and assertively. Whether you choose to cherry-pick every single note you play, or let the visual nature of the guitar guide your fingers, or operate anywhere in between, you will at all times "know what you're doing."

The book is written for the curious and committed guitarist who wants to further his understanding of the fretboard. The material is taught with hundreds of supporting examples and diagrams to illustrate and cement the concepts being covered. Knowledge of basic music theory is a prerequisite. The book is organised in a progressive manner: chapters are fairly independent but gradually build the big picture in a logical sequence. A brief summary of each chapter follows.

- **Chapter 1: Seeing the fretboard**
  This introductory chapter lays out the goals of the book and the importance of intervals in understanding the fretboard, followed by a refresher on fretboard-specific notation.

- **Chapter 2: Intervals**
  This music theory chapter covers the topic of intervals in great detail and highlights a number of conventions used in this book and elsewhere. The subject matter applies to any instrument.

- **Chapter 3: Interval addition**
  This chapter formalises the process of adding two intervals together. Several methods are described and for each, numerous examples hand-hold the reader through an addition, every step of the way. The chapter can be skipped in a first reading.

- **Chapter 4: Tuning**
  This chapter attempts to explain why the guitar is tuned the way it is and elaborates on some of the implications of its tuning.

- **Chapter 5: Note names**
  Note names on the fretboard are a vital step in labelling the fretboard map. All the necessary diagrams are provided here to become fully confident at naming the notes on the fretboard and mapping them to a pitch on the music staff.

- **Chapter 6: Fretboard geometry**
  This chapter puts intervals through their paces and presents string intervals as the fabric of the fretboard.

It follows with key properties resulting from the fretboard's layout. You may need to read or review Chapter 3 beforehand.

- **Chapter 7: Fretboard transforms**
  This short chapter addresses the important topic of transposition on the guitar and other transposition-like transforms.

- **Chapter 8: Fretboard mirror**
  This chapter introduces the concept of mirroring and presents several applications of this out-of-the-box fretboard trick.

- **Chapter 9: Anchoring**
  The anchoring principle is an essential approach to navigating the fretboard. It crystallises fretboard knowledge into a bite-sized and actionable method to derive chords, scales, and what have you, anywhere on the fretboard, with little to no shape/pattern memorisation.

- **Chapter 10: The CAGED system**
  The chapter on CAGED revisits this well-known fretboard partitioning system, with an emphasis on intervals.

- **Chapter 11: Harmonics**
  The last chapter on harmonics provides a comprehensive explanation of how harmonics work and are laid out on the guitar neck. It takes the mystery out of these mysterious bell-like sounds but also gives invaluable insight into string motion, pitch, tuning, etc.

- **Appendices**
  Complete interval shape charts, Intervals Wheel cutouts, and remarks on the placement of fret markers wrap up the book.

The material on intervals and interval addition is not instrument specific and can be studied independently. The harmonics chapter is a topic of its own and can also be studied by itself. It gets a little technical at times. Parts of these chapters can be challenging—arm yourself with patience, it's worth it.

Some readers may find it easier to get acquainted with the concept of anchoring through a system like CAGED first and then move backwards to full-fledged anchoring. CAGED sets boundaries within which you must operate (shapes to build from), but anchoring allows you more freedom and autonomy, which coincidentally can make the approach harder to apprehend.

The book can be used without a guitar in hand, though it helps to project on the actual instrument the diagrams you see on paper and the mental picture you learn to form.

In short, we will map the fretboard, label our map, and extract the underlying relationships that make the 6-string world go round! We say we *play* guitar—it shouldn't feel like labour, it should be fun and fulfilling. Despite the hard work and sweat, the more you know about the fretboard, the more fun it gets.

---

*For additional information on the book and any updates, please visit: www.**pelemeleworks**.com*

If you have a question, comment, suggestion, or find an error to report, you are welcome to **get in touch** through the website. Should you **write a review of the book** (on Amazon or elsewhere), please do share the link with me. Thank you!

1 SEEING THE FRETBOARD

When you speak, do you think about each sentence, each word, each letter, how they sound or look, what they mean, the rules of grammar, spelling, etc., or do you just speak your mind and the words seem to pour out? As a guitar player, how do you "see" the fretboard, the notes, how do you connect theory with what you play, etc.? How do other guitar players see these things? Have you ever made a conscious effort to understand how you process what you've learnt about guitar playing? This introductory chapter aims to heighten your awareness of how you see and think about the fretboard—a brief but necessary guitarist's introspection! We will touch upon a variety of ways of approaching the fretboard. In particular, we will spend some time on viewing the fretboard through intervals, a road less travelled. The last part of the chapter is a refresher on fretboard notation or how the fretboard looks like on paper. We close the chapter by making a statement for a state of mind: the questioning guitarist!

1.1 What do you see?

I'd like to start by asking you a simple question. If I say "C minor chord in 3rd position," what is the first picture that instantly pops in front of you? Your answer might be in Figure 1.1.

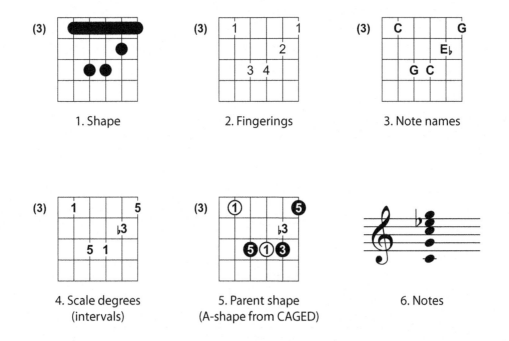

Figure 1.1 *What do you see?*

Most of us see at least #1, while few may answer #6, and many will see a combination. There are many ways to "see" the fretboard and what works for one person may not be suitable for another. By the time you're through with this book, you should be comfortable with #1–5, in particular #4.

"How do you see the fretboard?", "What do you think when you play?", "How do you connect the fretboard to music theory?", are questions that many guitarists or teachers don't verbalise or articulate the answers to—it sort of just happens. Entering a guitarist's mind is like pulling teeth and we always see what comes out of it but hardly ever know what goes on inside! I encourage you to ask guitar players around you these questions to understand how others approach the guitar neck.

If you haven't really paid attention to what you think when you play the guitar, pick up your guitar, close your eyes, empty your mind, and start playing. In your mind's eye, do you picture your fingers? Do you see where they are on the fretboard? Do you see any of the representations of Figure 1.1? It's unlikely that your mind just goes blank but for some, the answer may not be in Figure 1.1! Occasionally, someone may not click with a visual approach to the guitar and feel more at home with an aural approach to the instrument (hear pitch, play by ear). The question to ask that person would be "what do you hear?" in order to enter their mind's ear. Another person may have an acute tactile sense of the instrument (with the guitar in hand, muscle memory). There is no right or wrong. Most of us though rely mainly on a visual representation of the fretboard—this doesn't mean that we must look at the fretboard, but that we picture it before our eyes.

With no understanding of what is going on, shapes (#1) can get your feet wet playing something. Fingerings (#2) are simply the next stage and go hand in hand with shapes. Now, you become aware of which finger frets what. Depending on context (what precedes or follows), or if only part of the shape is played, you learn that the suggested fingering may no longer apply and there may be several fingering options you can use. Note names (#3) are a sure bet, but if you play the "same" thing elsewhere, note names change (e.g., G major chord and A major chord). Scale degrees (#4), closely related to intervals, are a versatile and powerful tool if you learn to tame them. A shape system that breaks up the fretboard into smaller sections (#5), like the CAGED system, can be as effective as you want it to be (e.g., see them as simple dot markings or recognise scale degrees within). Classical and jazz guitarists are perhaps more proficient with notes (#6) than anyone else. Note and pitch recognition are a far stretch from the visual nature of the guitar but they're the common language of music and are well worth our time, especially if we must read music.

You're given the tools to build a mental picture of the instrument and tie it in with music theory. It is your decision how you want to approach the fretboard and which representation of the fretboard you want to steer your thinking towards. You will be at ease with several, if not all of these representations, but will eventually gravitate towards one that is in sync with how your mind works.

1.2 The power of intervals

What is the motivation for intervallic thinking on guitar? Teaching the guitar is predominantly note and/ or shape based. Unfortunately, intervals are often overlooked or come second. For this reason, viewing the fretboard through intervals is unsettling for those who have had little exposure to intervals. But that initial jolt is soon overcome to take advantage of the benefits of this complementary approach to the guitar.

In music, we encounter several entities: notes on the music staff (with an associated pitch), note names, scale degrees (or the position of a note with respect to a reference), and intervals (the distance between two notes). On guitar, we also encounter a few other creatures: shapes (dots on the fretboard) and fingerings. The two pillars of music—harmony and melody—rely on chords and scales, both of which can be defined as a collection of notes separated by specific intervals. **In Western music, the mother of all of these entities— the "standard" they are compared to—is the major scale.** The major scale is made of seven notes. The relationship between these notes is invariable and can be represented as follows:

- Consecutive notes of the scale are separated by whole step / half step intervals: **1–1–½–1–1–1–½**
- Notes of the scale are expressed in scale degrees (- = ½ step): **1--2--3-4--5--6--7-8**

These are formulas depicting the major scale in different ways: the first formula captures the separation between two consecutive notes of the scale, in steps (step = whole tone); the second formula captures the separation between each note in the scale and the tonic 1, as scale degrees. Both are intervallic representations of the major scale and from now on, we'll mostly use the scale degree representation. An eighth note 8 is added to the scale to capture the distance between the seventh note and the octave, 8 = 1 + octave.

Other entities are measured against the major scale formula. For example, the natural minor scale formula is 1--2-♭3--4--5-♭6--♭7--8, the dominant 7th chord formula is 1–3–5–♭7. In other words, the scale degree representation instantly reveals what distinguishes an entity from the major scale (♭3, ♭6, and ♭7 in the natural minor scale and ♭7 in the dominant 7th chord). This proves that scale degrees are an all-purpose tool for representing these musical entities. Let's see if there are other benefits for the guitarist, with the following example where a G major scale and an A major scale are represented in multiple ways.

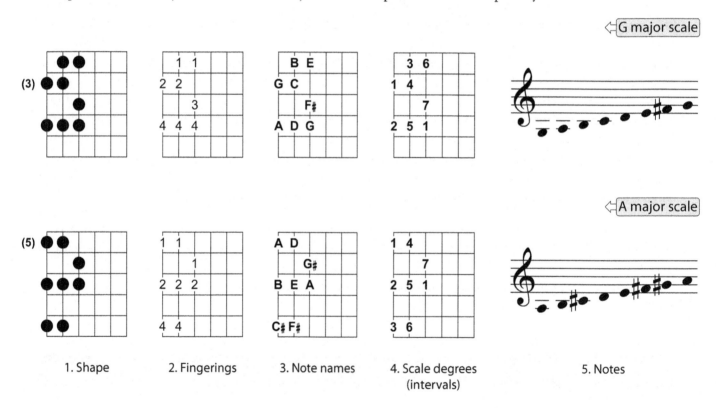

Figure 1.2 *Comparison: intervals vs. other representations*

What observation can we make from Figure 1.2? The only representation that doesn't change is the one with scale degrees. If we were to learn shapes, fingerings, note names, or notes on the staff for the G major and the A major scales, we would memorise one of each for each scale. But if we learnt the major scale as a formula, it would apply to G major, A major, and any other major scale or key! That's a tremendous simplification.

In tonal harmony, each note has a role to play—a function—in relation to the other notes (this applies to chords built on that note too). This role has to do with the notion of tension and release. Hence we refer to the *harmonic function* of that note and talk more generally of functional harmony.[1] The role is captured by the position of the note with respect to others, namely its scale degree. In fact, each major scale degree is given a name, which indicates its function.

Table 1.1 *Note function*

Scale degree	1	2	3	4	5	6	7
Function	Tonic	Supertonic	Mediant	Subdominant	Dominant	Submediant	Leading

In some playing situations (e.g., playing over chord changes), we go after specific notes, known as *target notes*. Those are easily identified by their scale degree in relation to a reference note. For example, the Dorian mode (1--2-♭3--4--5--6-♭7--8) can be underlined by its natural 6th, setting it apart from the minor scale.

If I were to draw an analogy with fields most of you are familiar with, I would say that *intervals are to music what variables are to maths or programming.* Intervals / scale degrees steer you towards more thinking and less memorisation.[2] If you have neglected intervals so far, there are substantial benefits in viewing the fretboard through them (e.g., one reference, one formula in all keys, exposure of note function, easy note manipulation). I encourage you to start adding this component to your approach to the fretboard. **One of the goals of this book is to enable you to know, for every note you play, its scale degree with respect to the reference note you have chosen.**

NOTE In equal temperament, there are 12 notes. But there are 15 keys: 7 sharp keys, 7 flat keys, and 1 key with no sharps/flats (key of C). Three of these seven sharp and flat keys are enharmonic keys (equivalent), effectively reducing the number of keys from 15 to 12.

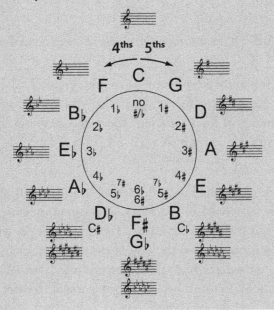

---

1. The topic of functional harmony is outside the scope of this book. Just retain: each note has a role within a musical context.
2. I have mingled the terms interval and scale degree intentionally. They are not the same. We'll discuss how they relate in the Intervals chapter.

1.3 Fretboard notation

This book relies almost exclusively on fretboard diagrams to convey the concepts at work. This section details notation and symbols used in the book and associated concepts that you will be coming across throughout.

> **NOTE**   A *fretboard* has frets. A *fingerboard* may or may not have frets. A violin has a fingerboard, not a fretboard. For guitar, we use these terms interchangeably. No one would even blink if you called it a *neck*.

▬▬ *Fretboard diagrams*

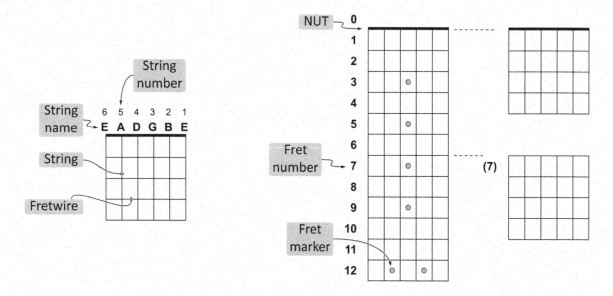

Figure 1.3 *Fretboard diagram: 1- chord box; 2- neck diagram*

The fretboard or a section of the fretboard is represented as a grid (Figure 1.3). If you are a right-handed player, place your guitar vertically on a music stand, facing you. What you see is exactly the fretboard representation about to be described. Horizontal grid lines represent the metal fretwire. Vertical grid lines represent the strings. Strings are numbered from left to right: 6 5 4 3 2 1. In standard tuning, these correspond to strings E A D G B E, respectively.

All the lines of the grid have the same thickness. Some publications will display thicker vertical lines for thicker gauge strings (low E string would be thickest), and sometimes use colour or a shade of grey to distinguish string and fretwire, but this is not standard. The topmost line, when thicker, represents the nut (*fret 0*). Frets are indicated by their number on the side of the diagram, or by fretboard inlays/dots right on the diagram itself. Fret numbers are written in Arabic numerals [e.g., 7 or (7) for fret 7] or Roman numerals (e.g., VII for fret 7). The fret and the fret number refer to the actual fretwire but in practice, they also refer to the space between that fretwire and the preceding fretwire (e.g., fret 1 is the first metal wire right after the nut but also designates the space between the nut and that wire). Unlike the real fretboard, fret spacing is usually uniform on the diagram.

Fretboard diagrams can represent a small chunk of the fretboard (typically 4 or 5 frets wide) when dealing with chords, an entire fretboard (typically 12 or 15 frets wide, up to 24), or anything in between. If no nut bar or position is indicated, the diagram is a snapshot of the fretboard and could be located at any fret. The information written on the diagram would then be *transposable* or moveable to other parts of the fretboard.

Fretboard diagrams can be drawn vertically or horizontally (flipped 90 degrees) as shown in Figure 1.4.

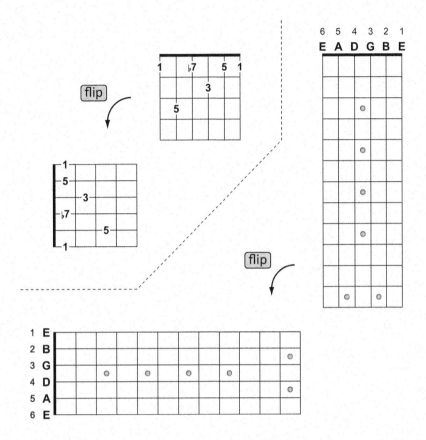

Figure 1.4 *Vertical & horizontal fretboard diagrams*

From time to time, there is a need to represent the entire neck, from nut to bridge. Figure 1.5 simply prolongs the strings all the way to the bridge.

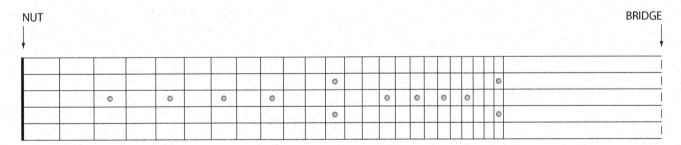

Figure 1.5 *Full neck from nut to bridge*

Diagrams always represent a right-handed guitar. Therefore, in this book, "left hand" refers to the fretting hand and "right hand" refers to the picking/plucking hand. Unfortunately, left-handed players will have to get used to reading right-handed diagrams. Specific literature designed for left-handed players is available but the vast majority of transcriptions are for right-handed players.

> **NOTE** Lefties ahoy! A vertical representation of the fretboard can be interpreted as a left-handed guitar diagram. If you are left-handed, look at the vertical diagram as though you were looking through the back of the neck instead of looking at the front of your guitar. What you see on the diagram is exactly what you would be seeing through the back of the neck, had the fretboard been see-through! Unfortunately, this neat trick no longer works when the diagram is horizontal.

▬▬ *Notation symbols*

Let's take a peek at the labels we will be writing on a fretboard diagram. There are four families of symbols populating a fretboard diagram (Figure 1.6 shows a D7 chord diagram with each type of label). These are:

- DOT MARKING
- FINGERING
- NOTE NAME
- SCALE DEGREE

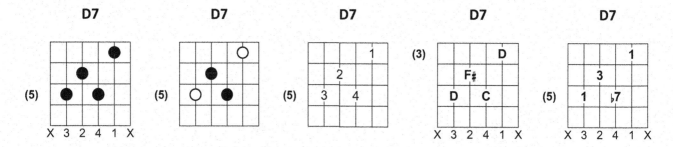

Figure 1.6 *Fretboard notation symbols: 1 & 2- dot marking; 3- fingering; 4- note name; 5- scale degree*

A **dot marking** is a black disc representing a fretted note at the fret/string it is positioned on. The dot marking can also be a white-filled disc and represent the root or fundamental/tonic of a chord or scale. **Fingering** is placed directly on the fretboard diagram, on the fret/string being depressed. In the context of chords, fingering is commonly placed outside the diagram, above or below the chord diagram. Fingering represents left hand finger numbers (1: index; 2: middle; 3: ring; 4: pinkie; T: thumb; 0: open string). **Note name** is self-explanatory. A **scale degree** label is the degree of the note with respect to the major scale of another note (labelled 1, if displayed). It can represent a note in a scale or a chord tone: the quantity is the interval number and the quality is ♭, ♮ (nothing), or ♯. The scale degree label shares some attributes of the interval.

Some of these notations can be combined: for example, several are shown here with added fingerings below the chord diagram; discs can be filled with fingering or scale degree information to reinforce the visual. The position indicates fret 5 but the chord is really played in 3rd position, therefore, another good choice for the position indicator is fret 3. Any fret indication is fine to tell which part of the fretboard is being shown.

You choose the notation based on the information you want to convey (Table 1.1). Dot marking is by far the most common notation. It is visually the most impactful but the dots alone carry no other information than which frets/strings must be depressed, they don't even tell you which fingers to use! The other three notation forms not only tell you which frets to depress, they also give you one more piece of information. Fingering is the next most common notation form, followed by note names. Scale degree / intervallic notation is less frequent but carries information that is arguably worth its weight in gold. By "information," I mean information that connects the fretboard and the music.

Table 1.1 *Notation "payload"*

Least to most amount of information						
Dot marking	➡	Fingering	➡	Note name	➡	Scale degree

NOTE Right hand fingering is not provided on fretboard diagrams. If such indication is supplied, you will find it on the music staff or tablature. It makes sense because right hand fingering depends heavily on the music (order in which the notes are played, pace, desired effect or articulation/expression, etc.).

With time and experience, these notations will "speak" to you (some more than others) and you will learn to "see" the fretboard through the notation that suits your thinking best with context.

▬▬ *Position*

<u>DEFINITION</u>

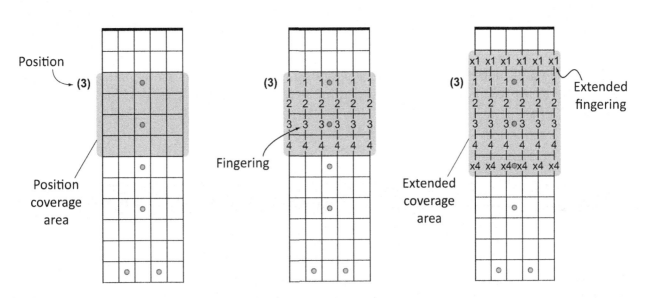

Figure 1.7 *Position & position extension (3rd position)*

While a fret number indicates a specific location along the guitar neck, a *position* is a section of the fretboard, spanning four adjacent frets, on all strings. A position covers a total of 4 frets × 6 strings = 24 notes. It is so called because when you place your left hand on the neck, you assign each finger to one fret. The leftmost fret is assigned the index finger (finger 1) and is the position number. The middle finger (finger 2) is assigned the next fret up, the ring finger (finger 3) the following fret, and the little finger or pinkie (finger 4) is assigned the next fret. Without moving your hand, your fingers have easy access to the fret they are assigned to, on all strings. Figure 1.7 shows position 3 and the fret assignments for each finger. Position 3 spans frets 3–6. In N^{th} position, finger 1 is assigned to fret N, finger 2 to fret $N+1$, 3 to $N+2$, and 4 to $N+3$.

When in N^{th} position, little effort is required to stretch the index finger in order to grab fret $N-1$. Likewise, the pinkie can be stretched to grab fret $N+4$. This is called *position extension* and covers a total of 6 frets × 6 strings = 36 notes. The extended index and the extended pinkie are marked x1 and x4, respectively. The same figure shows the extended position 3, spanning frets 2–7. Extending the index is usually easier than extending the pinkie.

In a position, the thumb stays put. If you must move the thumb, then it is likely you have moved positions.

We can still talk of a position when the former rules are slightly bent. Fingers 2 and 3 can also extend and reach for neighbouring frets to the ones they're assigned to. They'd be marked x2 and x3. In 3-note-per-string scales, it is tempting to define the position by the fret assigned to the extended index x1. In chords, it is common for several fingers to fret strings on the same fret. Usually, the position is still defined by the (non-extended) index finger. Simply put, when you think of a position, think of a *hand position* and the number of frets your hand can cover with reasonable stretching.

OPEN POSITION

The *open position* is the section of the fretboard spanning frets 0–4. Fret 0 is the nut: it corresponds to the open strings and doesn't require the index finger, which can take care of fret 1 instead. So the open position is in fact position 1, with the added open strings. That is 4 frets × 6 strings + 6 open strings = 30 notes.

POSITION PLAYING

Position playing or *playing in position* refers to placing your left hand on the given section of the fretboard with each finger assigned the frets of that position. For instance, playing in 5th position means fingers 1, 2, 3, 4, are assigned frets 5, 6, 7, 8, respectively. As an example, pentatonic/blues scale boxed shapes are notorious for position playing.

Note that 3-note-per-string playing spans several positions. In practice, we constantly shift positions, extend positions, play in between positions. Position playing is merely a framework we don't have to religiously confine ourselves to.

1.4 The questioning guitarist

Why this, why that?…Why not? The philosophy of this book and a healthy approach to the instrument is best explained through a few examples and I urge you to read this paragraph again after you have finished the Tuning chapter. In that chapter, we could have stopped at "The guitar is tuned to E A D G B E." but look at how much there is to learn by asking a few simple questions about tuning! As we do for the tuning, we can ask ourselves similar questions about other fretboard characteristics. For example, we can wonder why the scale length for guitar is typically 25", give or take. Why not longer, why not shorter? A starting point for the answer is to look at other instruments: What sound do you get from the bass guitar? The ukulele? How does it alter your holding the instrument? In a similar fashion, we can ask many other questions: Why string gauge is what it is? Why not use a thicker high E string? Why are bass guitar strings so thick compared to the guitar? Can thicker strings bend easily? Why are lower strings made of a core with wire wound around it? Why is the width of the fretboard around 1¾" for electric and 2" for classical guitars? Why does the fretboard become wider near the bridge? Why is the fretboard's surface curved (fretboard radius)? Why are some headstocks straight, some bent at an angle (tilted back)? Why does string action rise from the nut towards the bridge? Why does fretwire come in various sizes (width and height)? Why is the pitch of strings in ascending order (from string 6 to 1)? Why not reverse this order? Why does the material or gauge of a pick affect the sound produced by the string when all it does is to set the string in motion? Would pickups sound different if they could be placed near the nut as opposed to near the bridge? Why do all strings have the same length? The endless list goes on and on. We won't attempt to answer these questions here. What matters is the process of being inquisitive and curious about the guitar; it will boost your grasp of the instrument.

INTERVALS

I ntervals are an essential building block at the heart of this book. Even though basic music theory is a prerequisite, in this chapter, we cover what you need to know as far as intervals go. We start with standard definitions before introducing several key conventions used in this book. The chapters on intervals and interval addition are music theory chapters and apply to all instruments.

2.1 Interval

▬▬ *Definition*
An *interval* or tonal distance is defined as **the difference in pitch between two notes**.

When the notes of an interval are played <u>one after another</u>, it is called a *melodic interval*. If the lower pitch is played first, followed by the higher pitch, it is an *ascending interval*. If the higher pitch is played first, followed by the lower pitch, it is a *descending interval*. When both notes of an interval are played <u>at the same time</u>, it is called a *harmonic interval* and sometimes a *double-stop*.[1] Figure 2.1 shows an ascending interval (P4, we'll see what that means later) and the same interval but descending. The interval P4 is then shown as a harmonic interval, with the two notes sounding at once (stacked on top of each other on the staff).

MELODIC INTERVALS   **HARMONIC** INTERVAL

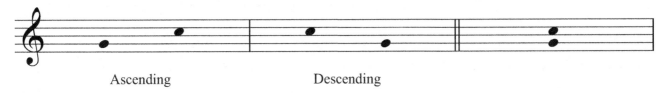

Ascending   Descending

Figure 2.1 *Interval types*

In an equal temperament system, each consecutive note is separated by a fixed-size interval called a *semitone*. The semitone is the smallest interval we will have to deal with in written music.

▬▬ *Interval name and notation*
An interval's size is measured by the number of scale tones it contains and determines the interval *quantity*.

---
1. Yet another, less common name for an interval is the *dyad*. This is more relevant in the context of chords where its three-note counterpart, the *triad*, is a common term.

To obtain this quantity, which is an integer number N, measure the distance between the bottom note (lower pitch) and the top note (higher pitch) of the interval: simply count through the music alphabet A B C D E F G. When counting, include the bottom note "1" and the top note. The number of scale tones contained within an interval is the same whether it is measured from the lower or the upper note of the interval. If you count on the staff, each line and each space counts as one.

The interval quantity is a coarse measure and alone, it doesn't fully define the interval. The interval *quality* further and fully qualifies the interval. If the top note belongs to the major scale of the bottom note (it is diatonic), then the quality of the interval is *perfect* (P) or *major* (M). If the top note does not belong to the major scale of the bottom note, then the interval is either *minor* (m), *augmented* (A or +), or *diminished* (d, dim, or °). Caution: counting and belonging to the major scale is always referred back to the bottom note of the interval (number 1), not to the top note. These rules can be summarised as:

- If the top note is **diatonic** to the major scale of the bottom note, the interval is **perfect** or **major**. Perfect or major is determined by the interval's quantity: perfect is 1, 4, 5, 8; major is 2, 3, 6, 7.
- If the top note is **raised by a semitone**[2] (with respect to a diatonic note), the interval is **augmented.**
- If the top note is **lowered by a semitone**, the interval is **minor** when lowered from major, and the interval is **diminished** when lowered from perfect or minor.

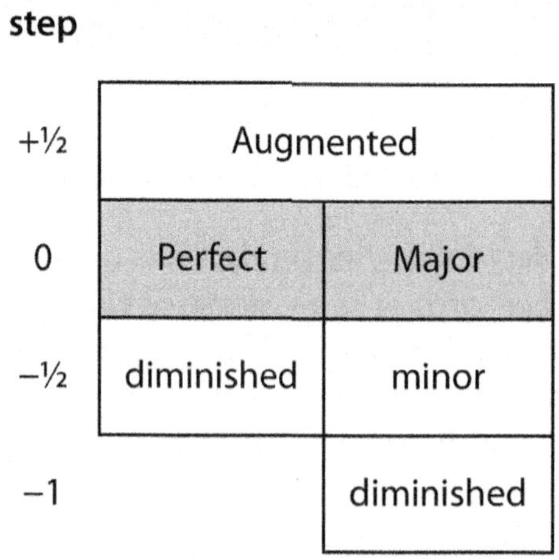

step

+½	Augmented	
0	Perfect	Major
−½	diminished	minor
−1		diminished

Figure 2.2 *Interval quality*

The complete name of the interval is spelt: **QualityQuantity**. For example, a major 6th interval is written M6, a diminished 7th is written d7 or °7.

Table 2.1 shows the interval quantity and the number of scale tones/degrees it contains, the number of whole tones and semitones the interval contains, along with the interval quality. For each interval quantity, there are several possible qualities. For example, a 5th can be perfect (spans 7 semitones), diminished if it's lowered by a half step (spans 6 semitones), or augmented if it's raised by a half step (spans 8 semitones). Intervals formed between the tonic and diatonic notes are in the darker cells: P1, M2, M3, P4, P5, M6, M7, P8.

An interval can be stretched further. A major or perfect interval can be made one whole tone larger. It is then called a *doubly augmented interval* (AA or ✻). A minor or perfect interval can be made one whole step smaller. It is then called a *doubly diminished interval* (♭♭). These are less common and are not indicated in Table 2.1, but you can easily fill in the appropriate cells.

---

2. Terminology: semitone = ½ whole tone = half step = ½ whole step.

Table 2.1 *Interval quantity & quality*

NUMBER OF TONES / SEMITONES	NUMBER OF SCALE TONES	Unison 1	Second 2	Third 3	Fourth 4	Fifth 5	Sixth 6	Seventh 7	Octave 8
0	0	P1	d2						
	1	A1	m2						
1	2		M2	d3					
	3		A2	m3					
2	4			M3	d4				
2½	5			A3	P4				
	6				A4	d5			
3½	7					P5	d6		
	8					A5	m6		
4½	9						M6	d7	
	10						A6	m7	
5½	11							M7	d8
5 + ½ + ½	12							A7	P8

Figure 2.3 goes through the process of naming four intervals. In bar 1, first count the number of letters between the bottom and the top note: G A B C, that's 4 notes, so the quantity is 4. Does the top note C belong to the bottom note G's major scale? Yes, it does, so the quality is perfect (column 4, row 5 in Table 2.1). Thus, this is an ascending P4 interval. Bar 2 shows the same notes, starting with the top note C. We can tell straight away it's a descending P4 interval because we just worked out the ascending interval. You can count from top to bottom note if you like but you must go through the music alphabet backwards (C B A G, not C D E F G). Bar 3 is a harmonic interval. From G to C, we count 4 but C♯ does not belong to G major (C does), so it's not a perfect 4th but an A4. Last, bar 4 shows G to E♭. We count 3 notes (E F G), so it's a 3rd. The top note G belongs to the bottom note E♭'s major scale so it's a descending M3.

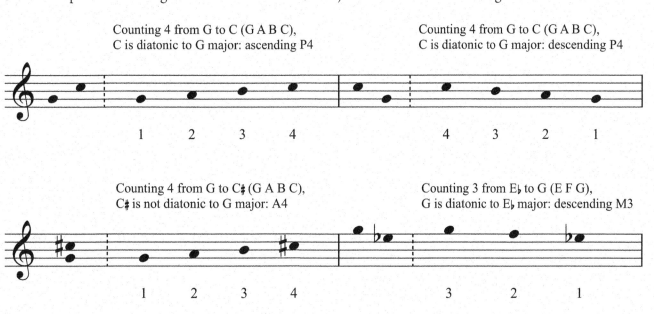

Counting 4 from G to C (G A B C),
C is diatonic to G major: ascending P4

Counting 4 from G to C (G A B C),
C is diatonic to G major: descending P4

1   2   3   4   4   3   2   1

Counting 4 from G to C♯ (G A B C),
C♯ is not diatonic to G major: A4

Counting 3 from E♭ to G (E F G),
G is diatonic to E♭ major: descending M3

1   2   3   4   3   2   1

Figure 2.3 *Naming an interval: finding quantity then quality*

Numerically, an interval is measured by comparing the pitch of the top note with the pitch of the bottom note, and is given either as a frequency ratio (no unit) or in *cents*. We will talk more about this in the Harmonics chapter.

Diatonic and chromatic intervals

Remember from music theory that a note that belongs to the major scale is diatonic to that scale and that a note that does not belong to the major scale is chromatic. For example, the note D belongs to the C major scale so the note D is diatonic but D♯ does not belong to C major so D♯ is a chromatic note, it is not diatonic to the C major scale. A similar principle applies to intervals.

In naming an interval, we said that if the top note belongs to the major scale of the bottom note, the interval is either major or perfect. Like many aspects of music theory, intervals are traced back to the major scale. If an interval can be found inside the major scale—between any two notes of the major scale—the interval is *diatonic*. If an interval cannot be found inside the major scale, the interval is *chromatic*. Figure 2.4 shows all intervals between the tonic of the major scale and the other six degrees within that scale (here the G major scale). That's only a subset of all diatonic intervals in the major scale! To obtain them all, repeat the diagram by making each note of the major scale the tonic. Table 2.2 does just that and lists all possible intervals that exist within the major scale. These diatonic intervals are: **P1**, **m2**, **M2**, **m3**, **M3**, **P4**, **A4**, **d5**, **P5**, **m6**, **M6**, **m7**, **M7**, **P8**. Any other interval would be chromatic (not found inside the major scale). Those diatonic intervals increase in size by one semitone each (except A4 and d5 that are of the same size), ranging a full octave from 0 to 12 semitones.

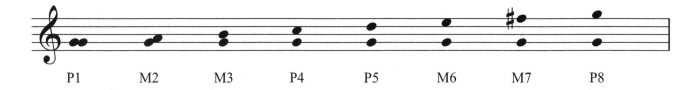

Figure 2.4 *Intervals between the tonic and other major scale degrees*

Table 2.2 *Diatonic intervals of the major scale*

Starting degree of major scale / mode		Scale formula	Intervals formed with tonic							
1	Ionian / major scale	1--2--3-4--5--6--7-8	P1	M2	M3	P4	P5	M6	M7	P8
2	Dorian	1--2-♭3--4--5--6-♭7--8	P1	M2	m3	P4	P5	M6	m7	P8
3	Phrygian	1-♭2--♭3--4--5-♭6--♭7--8	P1	m2	m3	P4	P5	m6	m7	P8
4	Lydian	1--2--3--♯4-5--6--7-8	P1	M2	M3	A4	P5	M6	M7	P8
5	Mixolydian	1--2--3-4--5--6-♭7--8	P1	M2	M3	P4	P5	M6	m7	P8
6	Aeolian / minor scale	1--2-♭3--4--5-♭6--♭7--8	P1	M2	m3	P4	P5	m6	m7	P8
7	Locrian	1-♭2--♭3--4-♭5--♭6--♭7--8	P1	m2	m3	P4	d5	m6	m7	P8

The table reads like so: row 3 shows all possible intervals between the notes of the major scale and the 3rd degree of the major scale. If we make the 3rd degree the tonic (1) and start counting from the new tonic, the scale formula is that of the Phrygian mode. Looking at the entire table, we can see for instance that the only A4 interval occurs between the 4th degree and the 7th degree of the major scale (or between the tonic and the 4th degree of the Lydian mode).

> **NOTE** Do not mix up the concept of *diatonic interval* with *the top note of the interval belonging to the bottom note's major scale*. There is a subtle difference. For example, in the m3 interval C–E♭ (where C is the bottom note and E♭ the top note), E♭ does not belong to the C major scale but m3 is a diatonic interval. In other words, the note E♭ is not diatonic to the C major scale (E♭ is not found in the C major scale) but the interval C–E♭ is diatonic (m3 can be found in the major scale).

For notes, the concept of diatonic/chromatic can be extended beyond major scale harmony. For instance, we say G♯ is diatonic to A harmonic minor. The same can be done with intervals.

Enharmonic intervals

In Table 2.1, you might have noticed that in a same row, you can encounter an interval name in one column and a different interval name in the next column. For example, in row 3 (3 semitones), column 2 shows the interval A2, but column 3 shows the interval m3. Both intervals are made of 3 semitones (same size), but why do they have different names? Why aren't they both called A2, or why aren't they both called m3?

Let's return to the analogy with scale degrees inside the major scale. You know from music theory that A♯ is the same note as B♭, and that B♯ is the same note as C; they are enharmonic equivalents.[3] Yet, we choose to spell the same note differently, depending on its function. Why is that? Let's take the scale of G major. In that scale, B is the 3rd degree and C is the 4th degree. We don't call B♯ the 4th degree, because its harmonic function is the 3rd degree of the scale (G--A--B-C). C is the 4th degree of the scale. Yet B♯ and C sound the same, they are the same pitch. Likewise, the interval G to B♯ and the interval G to C sound the same. G–B♯ interval quantity is 3 and G–C interval quantity is 4. B♯ does not belong to the G major scale (B does). Looking at Table 2.1, we see that G–B♯ is one semitone larger than G–B, it is therefore an augmented 3rd; G–C is in the same row but in column 4. C does belong to the G major scale. It is therefore a perfect 4th.

Intervals that sound the same but are spelt differently are called *enharmonic intervals*. Enharmonic intervals contain the same number of semitones. Figure 2.5 gives examples of enharmonic intervals in each bar except the last bar where it's all the same interval.

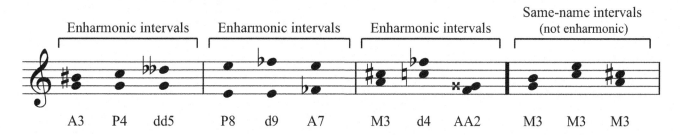

Figure 2.5 *Examples of enharmonic intervals*

---

3. This applies to an equal-temperament tuning system where a sharp and a flat are of the same size (the octave is divided into 12 equal intervals: the semitone or half step). In other tuning systems, B♯ isn't quite C!

■■■ *Simple and compound intervals*

An interval that is smaller than an octave is a *simple interval*. An interval that extends beyond an octave is a *compound interval*. Remember the following rules:

- For every octave you add to a simple interval, **add 7** to the interval quantity.
- To reduce a compound interval to a simple interval, **subtract 7** from the compound, as many times as necessary for the difference to be smaller than 8.
- Interval **quality is unchanged** when expanding or reducing an interval in octaves.

Some examples: The compound of a P4 and an octave P8 is a P11: $4 + 7 = 11$. The compound of a m3 and two octaves P15 is a m17: $3 + 2 \times 7 = 17$ (the minor quality is unchanged). The compound interval M13 is reduced to a simple interval of a M6 like so: $13 - 7 = 6$. The compound A9 is reduced to A2: $9 - 7 = 2$. Figure 2.6 shows a simple interval and two compounds built on it. Here, we are adding octaves to an interval; we will talk about interval addition in the next chapter. The most common compound intervals are the 9th (2nd), 11th (4th), 13th (6th), and the octave 8th (1 or unison).

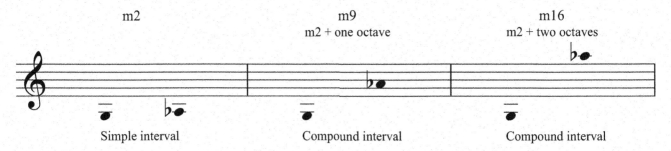

Figure 2.6 *Simple and compound intervals*

In practice, we mostly talk in terms of simple intervals, even though we may be referring to a compound interval. For example, we say we play the 4th of the G major scale, whether we play it as is, an octave above, or two octaves above. You wouldn't hear anyone call those notes the 11th or the 18th of the G major scale. In the context of chords, it's a different story, and compound intervals are part of the language. For example, in a G13 chord, whether the 13th is in the same octave as the root (6th), in the octave above (13th), or in the octave below (minor 3rd—that's an inversion, we'll get to that in a minute), it's still called the 13th.

■■■ *Inversion*

An interval is *inverted* by either raising the lowest pitch an octave, or lowering the highest pitch an octave. Figure 2.7 shows how this plays out. Remember the following rules for interval quality when inverting an interval: M becomes m, m becomes M, P remains P, A becomes d, d becomes A.

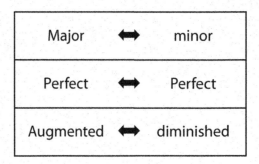

Major	⬌	minor
Perfect	⬌	Perfect
Augmented	⬌	diminished

Figure 2.7 *Inversion (quality)*

The sum of the quantities of a simple interval and its inversion always **adds up to 9**. As an example, for a major 6th and its inversion a minor 3rd, that sum equals: $6 + 3 = 9$. You can think of an interval and its inversion as complements of one another, adding up to form an octave. The inversion of an inversion is the original interval (m3 is the inversion of M6 and M6 is the inversion of m3).

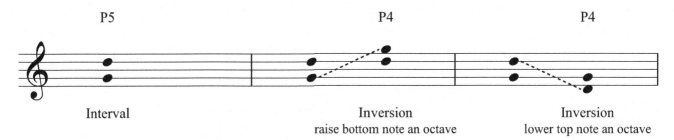

Figure 2.8 *Inversion (interval P5 and its inversion P4)*

Whether the inversion takes place by raising the bottom note or lowering the top note, in the newly inverted interval, the bottom note is now what used to be the top note in the original interval. In Figure 2.8, D was the top note of P5, it is now the bottom note of P4.

> **DID YOU KNOW?**   Enharmonic intervals A4 and d5 are commonly known as the *tritone* (TT). The tritone is made of 3 whole tones (6 semitones)—hence its name—and is the halfway point in an octave (12 semitones). The tritone is the only interval that remains unchanged, size-wise, when inverted. Its name, however, does change: A4 ↔ d5.
> A4 = 2 whole tones + 1 diatonic semitone + 1 chromatic semitone; d5 = 2 whole tones + 2 diatonic semitones.
> Diatonic semitone: the semitone between two notes of different names. Chromatic semitone: the semitone between two notes of the same name. For example, C–C♯ is a chromatic semitone but B–C and C♯–D are diatonic semitones.

Some examples of intervals and their inversion: M3 ↔ m6, m2 ↔ M7, P5 ↔ P4, d5 ↔ A4, P1 ↔ P8. An interesting observation is that no interval is inverted by swapping the two pitches (e.g., G3–D4 cannot be inverted to D4–G3 because whichever way you look at it, D4–G3 is the same interval as G3–D4).

2.2 Interval and scale degree

In musician talk, you often hear "a scale with a minor third (m3)" when they mean a flat third (♭3rd) scale degree or "a dominant chord with a sharp ninth (♯9th)" when they could say an augmented ninth (A9) interval. It's all understood but why are we mixing interval and scale degree terminology? Are they the same? It's important to have a clear picture of how intervals relate to scale degrees, especially when inversions are involved.

■■■■ *Similarities and differences*

An interval expresses the distance in pitch between two notes. A scale degree indicates the position of a note within the major scale, with respect to the tonic—in some ways, it is also a measure of the distance between that note and the tonic (just like an interval). In fact, when the tonic is the bottom note of the interval, the interval and the scale degree bear a strong resemblance.

In Figure 2.9, the interval G3–D4 is a P5 and D is the 5th degree of the G major scale. If D4 is lowered by a half step, the interval G3–D4♭ is a d5 and D♭ is the ♭5th degree in the G major scale. Now let's raise D4 an octave to D5. The interval G3–D5 is a compound interval of P12 and D is the 12th degree with respect to the tonic. We can discard the octave information and refer to D as the 5th degree of the scale. Again, interval and scale degree look alike. What if D4 is lowered an octave to D3? The interval G3–D4 is now inverted to D3–G3, it's no longer a P5 interval, it's now a P4. But D3 is still the 5th degree of the scale! That's where interval and scale degree start to look different.

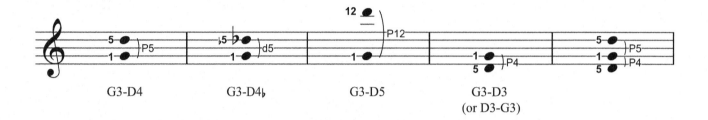

G3-D4   G3-D4♭   G3-D5   G3-D3
                                       (or D3-G3)

Figure 2.9 *Interval & scale degree: pretend look-alikes*

In Section 2.1, I implied that intervals are directionless: whether you look at the interval G3–D4 standing on G3 or whether you look at the interval D4–G3 standing on D4, it's the same interval and they have the same name: P5 (let's ignore ascending/descending in a melodic interval). It makes sense because either way, the distance in pitch between the two notes is identical. Just like numbers, you wish there was some sort of a "+" sign when going up from G to D and a "−" sign when going down from D to G, to capture direction! However, when we look at the scale degree for that same P5 interval, going up is different from going down. If I go up a P5 from note 1, I end up on scale degree 5. But if I go down a P5 from note 1, I end up on scale degree 4. Table 2.3 illustrates this. Remember that when measuring an interval, the top note is always referred back to the major scale of the bottom note (1), so making the top note (1) does not change the name of the interval.

Table 2.3 *Interval & scale degree comparison: rising/falling pitch*

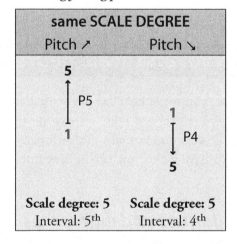

When we deal with scales and chords, we frequently use formulas. For example, for the minor scale, we point to the formula 1--2--♭3--4--5-♭6--♭7--8 (scale degrees). We can also refer to the intervals separating each consecutive degree 1–½–1–1–½–1–1 (whole tone / semitone). Likewise, for chords, for the dominant

7th chord, we point to the formula 1–3–5–♭7 (chord tones). We can also refer to the intervals stacked up to build the chord M3–m3–m3. Written that way, it is difficult to compare scale degree formula and intervallic formula. That's because we are comparing apples and oranges: the scale formula references every note back to the tonic but the intervallic formula references each note to its neighbour. A benefit of scale degrees is that they can be compared: both the minor scale formula and the 7th chord formula are scale degrees referenced back to the major scale. It is difficult to compare the intervallic formulas of the scale and the chord! However, if instead of 1–½–1–1–½–1–1, I write the minor scale formula with intervals referred back to the tonic P1–M2–m3–P4–P5–m6–m7–P8, then it starts to look like the scale degree formula 1--2-♭3--4--5-♭6--♭7--8.

An interesting relationship exists between interval and scale degree. We'll articulate it through an example. We have the note G3 which serves as our reference pitch in the key of G. In this key, E is the 6th degree. When E is at a higher pitch than G, the interval's name is the same as the scale degree. So G3–E4 forms a M6 interval, and E4 is the 6th degree. The likeness is even more obvious if I call M6 (major 6th) a 6th. When E is at a lower pitch than G, the name of the interval's inversion is the same as the scale degree. So G3–E3 forms a m3 interval, the inversion of a 6th. Again, this is all the more obvious if I call m3 (minor 3rd) a ♭3rd. This brings us to the next section.

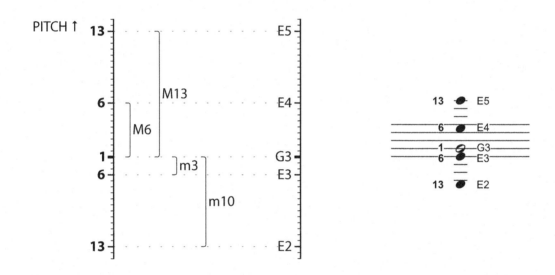

Figure 2.10 *Interval & scale degree naming: pitch rises (same name) / pitch drops (inversion name)*

■■■ *The inversion rule*

From the perspective of the harmonic function of a note, the scale degree is most valuable. We'll illustrate this statement through an example. Let's say we play two notes E3 and G3 (part of a scale, a chord, or an arpeggio). First, we think in the key of E: E is the tonic (1) and G is the flat third degree (♭3). Then, we play the same notes but in the key of G: now G is the tonic (1) and E is the sixth degree (6). Instead of looking at interval E3–G3 standing on the bottom note E3, we flip our point of view (not the interval) and look at it standing on the top note G3. You may think this is an inversion but it's not: the notes stay where they are, only how we think of each note changes (in fact, if you try to invert the interval as in Figure 2.11-2, you wind up with different pitches). If we had been thinking in terms of intervals, whether we were in the key of E or the key of G, it wouldn't matter, E3–G3 would always be a m3 interval; we would not immediately recognise the role of the notes E and G in those keys.

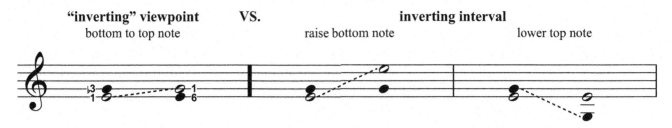

Figure 2.11 *Inverting viewpoints vs. inversion*

This benefit of scale degrees is even more apparent in the context of a chord. In Figure 2.12, we look at what becomes of a major triad if we change viewpoints, and instead of having the bass note as the root, we make the middle and then the top note the root. We end up with other chords, with a different function. The note names are the same, the intervals separating chord tones are the same, only the scale degree (chord tone) captures our changing viewpoint.

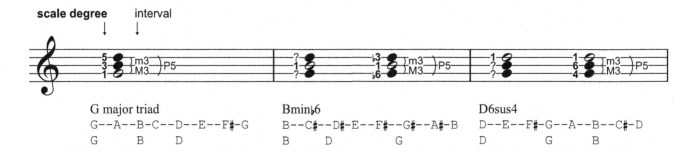

Figure 2.12 *Triad where each note becomes the root*

NOTE   Do not confuse *ascending and descending intervals* with *an interval and its inversion*. In the ascending and descending intervals, both notes remain at the same pitch. When inverting an interval, the top note is lowered an octave or the bottom note is raised an octave.

Figure 2.13-1 shows the interval of M6 separating the tonic 1 and its scale degree 6. If the roles are flipped (but the pitch of each note remains the same) and the tonic 1 becomes the top note, the bottom note is then the ♭3 in the scale of this new tonic. The interval separating the two notes is still M6. m3 (♭3) is the inversion of M6. This leads to the rule in Figure 2.13-2: we'll call this the **inversion rule**. If an interval X is viewed from the top note as the tonic 1, its bottom note's scale degree is the interval X̄ (inversion of X). This shorthand notation for inversions is explained in the next section.

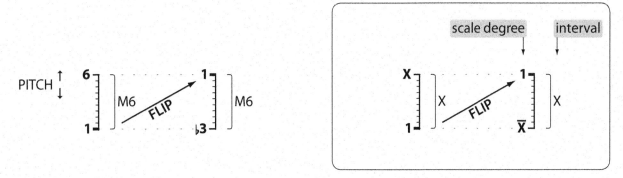

Figure 2.13 *Inversion rule: 1- example; 2- rule for scale degree X*

The complement rule

The relationship between scale degree, interval, and inversion leads to a useful property we will exploit later in the book. We're going to work with simple intervals, and discard any octave information from scale degrees or intervals we encounter. Figure 2.14-1 shows the intervals separating the tonic 1 and its scale degree 6, and the tonic 1 and its scale degree 6 an octave below. These intervals are respectively a M6 and its inversion a m3. This leads to the rule in Figure 2.14-2: we'll call this the **complement rule**. Any scale degree X between 1 and 8 forms interval X with the tonic and interval $\overline{X}$ (inversion of X) with the octave 8.

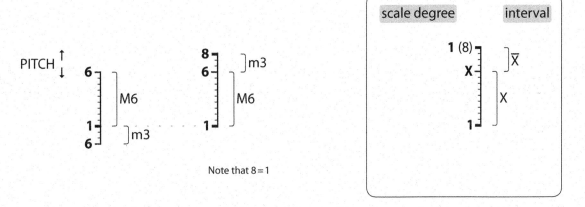

Figure 2.14 *Complement rule: 1- example; 2- rule for scale degree X*

Relative intervals

By definition, an interval gets its name from the top note's position within the bottom note's major scale (bottom note is labelled scale degree 1). We discussed inverting this viewpoint and labelling the top note 1; we learnt that the interval remains the same but the bottom note's scale degree becomes the inversion's name (e.g., in Figure 2.11, the bottom note is labelled 6, the inversion of the interval m3). We can extend this idea: if we label a note in an interval with any scale degree, what is the other note's scale degree? Let's take the example of the interval G3–D4. This can be labelled with scale degrees 1–5, but also 4–1, ♭6–♭3, 2–6, 3–7, etc. All are P5 intervals, but we changed the reference point, it's no longer the bottom note. In the 2–6 label, this is in reference to the F major scale (F is 1), of which G is the 2nd degree and D the 6th degree. When we label intervals like so, we'll call them *relative intervals*.

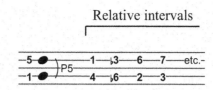

Figure 2.15 *Examples of relative intervals for P5 (G3–D4)*

You've been working with relative intervals without realising it. To find the diatonic intervals in Table 2.2 or the chord inversions in Figure 2.12, that's what you did!

The ability to recognise relative intervals is an important skill because between unfamiliar scale degrees sometimes lies a familiar interval. For instance, a major 7th chord is made of 1–3–5–7 (chord tones), or 3rd–♭3rd–3rd (stacked intervals). What if you don't play the root 1? What's left in the chord? 3–5–7. If you recognise these relative intervals as ♭3rd and 3rd, then it will dawn on you that it's no other than 1–♭3–5, a minor triad. There's more! How about 1–♭3–5–♭7? That's a minor 7th chord. What if instead of the root, you start counting from the ♭3 chord tone? You see ♭3–5 (major 3rd), 5–♭7 (minor 3rd), ♭7–1 (major 2nd). These are the intervals separating the following chord tones: 1–3–5–6, a major 6th chord. You just figured out that a minor 7th chord and a major 6th chord are *homonyms*.[4] Wait, there's more. A 7th chord is 1–3–5–♭7. The interval between 3–♭7 is a tritone (♭5 or d5), the most unstable diatonic interval. Yet, you don't see 1–♭5 or 1–♯4 in the formula, it's hidden to the untrained eye.

2.3 Conventions used in this book

■■■■■ *Fundamental, tonic, root*

Lexically speaking, the *fundamental* refers to a frequency quantity and designates the lowest frequency of a note in its harmonic series, the *tonic* refers to the first scale degree of a scale, the *root* refers to the lowest pitch in a chord in its non-inversion form or an arpeggio. In practice, fundamental and tonic are used interchangeably. Root is reserved for chords (or intervals) but you might see it in scales too.

■■■■■ *Signed interval*

I mentioned before that an interval's name doesn't capture a sense of direction (except in melodic intervals where this transpires as ascending and descending). We'll restore direction by introducing a "–" sign (minus sign) when the interval is descending in pitch and leave the interval unchanged when it is ascending in pitch (implicit "+" sign). We won't use this convention much except in interval subtraction and when necessary to emphasise direction or relative position of scale degrees.

■■■■■ *Intervals spelt as scale degrees*

I write intervals like scale degrees, with accidentals when necessary, and will rarely be using the P, M, m, d, A, etc., shorthand notation (except in this chapter). The parent scale is the major scale of the lower note of

---

4. *Chord homonyms* are chords built with the same chord tones but named differently, like Fmin7 and A♭6. It is a misleading term because homonym implies same name.

the interval and the scale degree that gives the interval its name is the top note. For example, P3 is written 3, m3 is ♭3, P4 is 4, A4 is ♯4, AA5 is ×5, A9 is ♯9. This makes sense because a scale degree forms an interval between two notes: the fundamental (1) and the scale degree. For example, the 4th degree of the scale, when viewed with respect to the fundamental 1, is a P4 interval (4 with this notation). This is quite intuitive and you'll get used to it fast. A benefit of this notation is that it mimics the notation used in scale and chord formulas (e.g., 1--2-♭3--4--5-♭6---7-8 for harmonic minor or 1–3–♯5 for an augmented triad). In a sense, it's a "shorterhand" notation!

This notation clearly differentiates intervals formed between: 1- the tonic and diatonic notes, 2- the tonic and non-diatonic notes.

- If the interval is **natural**—it is only a number (1, 2, 3, etc.)—the top note belongs to the major scale of the bottom note. The interval's quantity is the number *N* and the interval's quality is P or M.
- If the interval is **altered**—it contains ♭/♯ signs—the top note does not belong to the major scale of the bottom note. The interval's quantity is the number *N* and the interval's quality is m, d, or A.

To write the quality of an interval, symbols P, M, m, A, d, AA, dd, are no longer used. In this new notation system, the quality of an interval is amongst the following symbols: ♮ (none), ♯, ♭, ×, ♭♭.[5] The interval quantity is unchanged and is the same number as in standard notation. Table 2.4 shows how interval quality in standard interval notation maps to interval quality in this new notation. It also tells you that depending on the scale note, accidentals may have different meanings. For example, ♭3 means m3 but ♭5 means d5. This is because the interval formed between the fundamental and diatonic scale note 3 is major but the interval between the fundamental and diatonic scale note 5 is perfect. Or, if I write a 4th, I mean P4, but if I write ♯4, I mean A4. When I write 7, it is M7, but if you see ♭7, it is m7. Got it? It's a common notation (and not new at all).

Table 2.4 *Interval quality: standard notation vs. new notation*

step		
+½	Augmented	
0	Perfect	Major
−½	diminished	minor
−1		diminished

➡

step				
+½	♯			
0		♮ (none)		♮ (none)
−½		♭		♭
−1				♭♭

▬▬▬ *Always simple intervals*

Compounds are important but for our purposes in this book, we mostly care about the function of a note, so whether it is several octaves away doesn't affect our understanding. In order to avoid lugging around large numbers, we will stay within an octave and use simple intervals as much as possible. If we have a compound interval, we reduce it to a simple interval (except in specific situations such as chord extensions). That being said, be aware when an interval is a compound, even though you treat it like a simple interval!

NOTE We routinely discard octaves in note names, scale degrees, and even chord tones (except chord extensions). In daily usage, an E is an E on the instrument, not an E2 or an E4; the 3rd of a major chord is the 3rd, not the 10th, whether it's played in the same octave or an octave above the root. So this convention is nothing extraordinary.

---

5. By ♮ (none), I mean to strip away any accidental in front of the interval number.

2.4 Interval stability

To wrap up this chapter, we'll touch upon stability. Even though it has nothing to do with the fretboard, it matters to keep this facet of intervals in mind because it further describes the musical meaning and purpose of the interval (e.g., in composition). Here is a brief incursion into this topic.

Intervals fall into one of two categories: *consonant* (stable) or *dissonant* (unstable). A consonant interval is quite complete and content by itself. But a dissonant interval sounds incomplete or unfinished. It exhibits tension and gives the impression that it wants to go somewhere: it wants to resolve, to release the tension. You have to hear it to sense it, and sometimes compare one interval to another to truly get a feel for its stability. To make matters more subjective, some intervals can be ambiguous (e.g., a P4 interval is generally considered consonant but can be viewed as dissonant when used above the bass) and inversions can alter our perception of the interval. Stability can be traced back to the *harmonic series* (overtone series). The following tables show generally accepted stability charts of intervals and single notes (in major scale harmony).[6]

Table 2.5 *Interval stability*

CONSONANT intervals							DISSONANT intervals
perfect		imperfect				mixed	
P1	P5	M3	m6	M6	m3	P4	All other intervals

Table 2.6 *Scale tone stability (diatonic tones of the major scale)*

Stable to unstable (active) tone ⟶							
1	5	3	2	6	4	7	All chromatic tones
Common resolution							
			1↙2	5↙6	3↙4	7↗1	↗ or ↙ to the nearest diatonic tone

DID YOU KNOW? The chromatic notes of the major scale outline…a major pentatonic scale (e.g., C major's chromatic notes form F♯ major pentatonic). One man's wrong notes are another man's good ones!

To conclude on intervals, it is beneficial to become familiar with and eventually be able to recognise the sound of intervals. We torture intervals in all kinds of ways in this book but don't cover this aspect. Ear training, combined with the visual recognition of intervals both on the music staff and on the fretboard, will help you in many ways in your musical development. So while your brain is at work playing these intervals on your guitar, awaken your ears to them too.

---

6. 1, 3, 5 are deemed stable tones but some are "more stable" than others. How does that affect their movement/activity? The tonic 1 is rock solid where it is and sounds final. Unlike other tones that resolve to a close-by diatonic tone, the 3rd and the 5th have a tendency to move to the tonic to find closure. Stability is a complex topic and has given rise to various interpretations over time. My personal inkling is that stability is part objective, part subjective, part acquired, and part circumstantial. For a primer, see Nancy Scoggin's *Barron's AP Music Theory, 2nd Edition* (2014) and Jack Perricone's *Melody in Songwriting* (2000).

INTERVAL ADDITION

I f intervals are fairly new to you, you may want to skip this chapter for now and come back to it later. Interval addition is not intuitive and many find it hard to understand. I will take you step by step through the process, but keep in mind it is not the addition you are accustomed to in the decimal system.[1] Interval addition is an aid to help you stack up intervals and ascertain the size of the resulting interval. With time, you will know a lot of the results of an interval addition by heart, like your addition and multiplication tables, so if you feel it is a tough nut to crack, don't worry, you can do without it.

3.1 Interval addition

▬▬ *Why it matters*

Interval addition is a topic that arouses curiosity. Students are often confused when adding intervals because it doesn't behave like the addition we know (addition in base 10). Interval addition has applications within general music theory such as stacking up intervals in chords or dealing with tonal distance and harmonic function. It's also useful for working your way around the fretboard with string intervals (we'll get to that shortly). In this chapter, we examine three methods of adding intervals: *lookup table*, *carry*, and *intuitive*. At first, the explanation of interval addition is somewhat overwhelming and formal, making the process look mechanical and far from instantaneous. Over time, you will learn to break down intervals through shortcuts and perform the operation quickly and mentally. So don't let the next pages you are about to read intimidate you and work through the examples diligently, at your own pace.

To illustrate the value of interval addition in chords, let's simply consider tertian harmony where chords are built by stacking up intervals of a 3rd. Knowing what intervals adding a 3rd (major or minor or any other quality) to a 3rd, 5th, 7th, 9th, 11th, produces is the foundation for building chords. For example, a ♭3rd added to a 3rd gives a 5th, a 3rd added to a 5th produces a 7th. Chord extensions are also derived that way: a ♭3rd added to a ♭7th gives a ♭9th. So adding any kind of a 3rd to an interval forms the basis for many chords.

▬▬ *Rules and notation*

Here is a selection of reminders on intervals and rules governing interval addition, along with their notation and symbols, as used in this book (the "shorterhand" notation!).

The addition methods described in this chapter assume that the intervals being added are **simple intervals only**. *If an interval is a compound, you must first reduce it to a simple interval and then add the corresponding number of octaves back to the addition result.*

---

1. If you put two and two together…you're not going to get four!

Table 3.1 *Rules & notation*

Interval rules and notation	Examples
quantity of interval X = qn(X) or ♮X quantity is integer part of X	qn(♭3) = 3
quality of interval X = ql(X) = accidental quality is among: none or 0 (♮), ♯, ♭, 𝄪, 𝄫	ql(♭3) = ♭
X is written ql(X)qn(X)	a minor 3rd or m3 is written ♭3
addition symbol: + subtraction symbol: –	2 + 3 = ♯4; 5 – 2 = 4
X is ascending interval; –X is descending interval (applies to melodic and harmonic intervals)	G3–B3 = 3; B3–G3 = –3
identity: X + 1 = X, zero for intervals is the unison 1	♭2 + 1 = ♭2
commutativity: X + Y = Y + X	2 + ♭3 = ♭3 + 2
inversion of X = $\overline{X}$ X + $\overline{X}$ = 8 (octave) inversion of inversion of X = $\overline{\overline{X}}$ = X linearity of inversion: $\overline{X + Y}$ = $\overline{X}$ + $\overline{Y}$ (if discarding compound)	X = 2, $\overline{X}$ = ♭7 2 + ♭7 = 8 X = 5, $\overline{X}$ = 4, $\overline{\overline{X}}$ = 5 $\overline{2 + 4}$ = $\overline{5}$ = 4 = $\overline{2}$ + $\overline{4}$ = ♭7 + 5 (♭7 + 5 = 11 compound, same as 4 simple interval)
qn(X + Y) = qn(X) + qn(Y) – 1	qn(5 + ♯2) = qn(5) + qn(♯2) – 1 = 5 + 2 – 1 = 6; 5 + ♯2 = ♯6
compound: qn(X + 8) = qn(X) + 7; ql(X + 8) = ql(X)	♯5 + 8 = ♯12 (♯5th + one octave), 5 + 15 = 19 (5th + two octaves)
interval + inversion: qn(X) + qn($\overline{X}$) = 9	qn(6) + qn(♭3) = 6 + 3 = 9
there is no 0 interval, unison is 1, octave is 8	
tritone (♯4 or ♭5) divides an octave in two	♯4 + ♭5 = 8, ♯4 and ♭5 are each 6 semitones
when adding accidentals (e.g., as carries): ♯ = –♭ or ♯ + ♭ = 0 ♯ + ♯ = 𝄪; ♭ + ♭ = 𝄫 ♮X + accidental = accidental X	♭3 + ♯5 = 3 + 5 ♯3 + ♯5 = 3 + 𝄪5 4 + ♯ = ♯4
X – X = 1 (unison)	4 – 4 = 1
interval subtraction is not commutative: X – Y = –(Y – X)	2 – 7 = –(7 – 2) = –6

NOTE   When adding intervals, be careful not to mistake an enharmonic interval for the result. It's easy to lose track of the interval quantity, especially in mental calculation. For example, a ♯4th + 3rd equals a ♯6th, not a ♭7th! When in doubt, run a quick sanity check to confirm that: **qn(X + Y) = qn(X) + qn(Y) – 1.**

▬▬ *Lookup table addition: semitones*

An obvious way to add two intervals is to add their semitone equivalents. This is a straightforward but cumbersome method to carry out mentally. It requires a pen, a piece of paper, and the lookup table!

SEMITONE ADDITION: Add intervals X and Y and find interval Z = X + Y.

1. Convert X and Y to semitones, according to Table 3.2.* The number of semitones is s(X) and s(Y).

2. The number of semitones in Z is s(Z) = s(X) + s(Y). If 12 ≤ s(Z), then s(Z) = s(Z) – 12 (discarding octave information so we can use the table).

3. Convert the value back to an interval, using Table 3.2:
   - Row is: s(Z).
   - Column is: qn(Z) = qn(X) + qn(Y) – 1. If 8 ≤ qn(Z), then qn(Z) = qn(Z) – 7.
   - Name the interval.

* In the table, read row 0 for zero semitone and column 1 for unison.

Table 3.2 *Reminder: interval quantity & quality*

semitones \ quantity	1	2	3	4	5	6	7	8
0	1	♭♭2						
1	♯1	♭2						
2		2	♭♭3					
3		♯2	♭3					
4			3	♭4				
5			♯3	4				
6				♯4	♭5			
7					5	♭♭6		
8					♯5	♭6		
9						6	♭♭7	
10						♯6	♭7	
11							7	♭8
12								8

Let's work through some examples using this method. For this, we'll rely on Table 3.2, which is a copy of the same table in the Intervals chapter.

Add a 2nd and a 3rd (X = 2, Y = 3), or 2 + 3 = ?

1. s(2) = 2 semitones, s(3) = 4 semitones. In the table, the row for a cell gives the number of semitones.
2. s(2 + 3) = s(2) + s(3) = 2 + 4 = 6. And 6 < 12 so s(2 + 3) is unchanged.
3. Convert back to an interval:
   Row: s(2 + 3) = 6.
   Column: qn(2 + 3) = qn(2) + qn(3) – 1 = 2 + 3 – 1 = 4. And 4 < 8 so qn(2 + 3) is unchanged.
   In row 6, column 4, readout is: ♯4 (or A4).

Add a 6th and a 5th (X = 6, Y = 5), or 6 + 5 = ?

1. s(6) = 9, s(5) = 7.
2. s(6 + 5) = s(6) + s(5) = 9 + 7 = 16. And 12 ≤ 16 so s(6 + 5) becomes s(6 + 5) = 16 – 12 = 4.
3. Convert back to an interval:
   Row: s(6 + 5) = 4.
   Column: qn(6 + 5) = qn(6) + qn(5) – 1 = 6 + 5 – 1 = 10. And 8 ≤ 10 so qn(6 + 5) = 10 – 7 = 3.
   In row 4, column 3, readout is: 3 (or M3). Add an octave to restore compound information discarded in step 2: 3 becomes 10.

Add a 5th and a 4th (X = 5, Y = 4), or 5 + 4 = ?
1. s(5) = 7, s(4) = 5.
2. s(5 + 4) = s(5) + s(4) = 7 + 5 = 12. And 12 ≤ 12 so s(5 + 4) = 12 – 12 = 0.
3. Convert back to an interval:
   Row: s(5 + 4) = 0.
   Column: qn(5 + 4) = qn(5) + qn(4) – 1 = 5 + 4 – 1 = 8. And 8 ≤ 8 so qn(5 + 4) = 8 – 7 = 1.
   In row 0, column 1, readout is: 1 (or P1). Add an octave to restore compound information discarded in step 2: 1 becomes 8.

Add a 4th and a 4th (X = 4, Y = 4), or 4 + 4 = ?
1. s(4) = 5, s(4) = 5.
2. s(4 + 4) = s(4) + s(4) = 5 + 5 = 10. And 10 < 12 so s(5 + 4) is unchanged.
3. Convert back to an interval:
   Row: s(4 + 4) = 10.
   Column: qn(4 + 4) = qn(4) + qn(4) – 1 = 4 + 4 – 1 = 7. And 7 < 8 so qn(4 + 4) is unchanged.
   In row 10, column 7, readout is: ♭7 (or m7).

Add a ♭7th and a 7th (X = ♭7, Y = 7), or ♭7 + 7 = ?
1. s(♭7) = 10, s(7) = 11.
2. s(♭7 + 7) = s(♭7) + s(7) = 10 + 11 = 21. And 12 ≤ 21 so s(♭7 + 7) = 21 – 12 = 9.
3. Convert back to an interval:
   Row: s(♭7 + 7) = 9.
   Column: qn(♭7 + 7) = qn(♭7) + qn(7) – 1 = 7 + 7 – 1 = 13. And 12 ≤ 13 so qn(♭7 + 7) = 13 – 7 = 6.
   In row 9, column 6, readout is: 6 (or M6). Add an octave to restore compound information discarded in step 2: 6 becomes 13.

Add a 3rd and a 6th (X = 3, Y = 6), or 3 + 6 = ?
1. s(3) = 4, s(6) = 9.
2. s(3 + 6) = s(3) + s(6) = 4 + 9 = 13. And 12 ≤ 13 so s(3 + 6) = 13 – 12 = 1.
3. Convert back to an interval:
   Row: s(3 + 6) = 1.
   Column: qn(3 + 6) = qn(3) + qn(6) – 1 = 3 + 6 – 1 = 8. And 8 ≤ 8 so qn(3 + 6) = 8 – 7 = 1.
   In row 1, column 1, readout is: ♯1 (or A1). Add an octave to restore compound information discarded in step 2: ♯1 becomes ♯8.

Add a ♯4th and a ♭2nd (X = ♯4, Y = ♭2), or ♯4 + ♭2 = ?
1. s(♯4) = 6, s(♭2) = 1.
2. s(♯4 + ♭2) = s(♯4) + s(♭2) = 6 + 1 = 7. And 7 < 12 so s(♯4 + ♭2) is unchanged.
3. Convert back to an interval:
   Row: s(♯4 + ♭2) = 7.
   Column: qn(♯4 + ♭2) = qn(♯4) + qn(♭2) – 1 = 4 + 2 – 1 = 5. And 5 < 12 so qn(♯4 + ♭2) is unchanged.
   In row 7, column 5, readout is: 5 (or P5).

▬▬▬ *Carry addition: quantity & quality*

This is a fast and easy method based on working out the quantity and the quality separately. It can be performed mentally without difficulty.

CARRY ADDITION: Add intervals X and Y and find interval Z = X + Y.

1. Quantity of X + Y: qn(X + Y) = qn(X) + qn(Y) − 1. Keep compounds in the result.

2. Assessment of X and Y carry.
    - If 4 ≤ qn(X), carry ♭.
    - If 4 ≤ qn(Y), carry ♭.

3. Assessment of X + Y carry.
    - If **4** ≤ qn(X + Y) ≤ 7, carry ♯.
    - If **8** ≤ qn(X + Y) ≤ 10, carry ♯♯.
    - If **11** ≤ qn(X + Y), carry ♯♯♯.

4. Quality of X + Y: ql(X + Y) = ql(X) + ql(Y) + carry from step 2 + carry from step 3.
    In the scale degree notation form, quality is amongst: none/0 (♮), ♯, ♭, ✗, ♭♭.

5. Z = ql(X + Y)qn(X + Y). This includes compound information.

The carries look more impressive than they are! What is happening is that every time an interval (X, Y, or the sum X + Y) rises beyond certain thresholds, we add a carry. These threshold numbers are 4, 8, and 11. You will recognise that these are exactly scale degrees following a half step in the major scale formula spanning two octaves: 1--2--3-**4**--5--6--7-**8**--9--10-**11**--12--13--14-15. This is no surprise because these half steps are precisely why we can't use the regular addition we are all familiar with (decimal system) to add intervals.

A few examples (same as before) will help the process sink in:
Add a 2ⁿᵈ and a 3ʳᵈ (X = 2, Y = 3), or 2 + 3 = ?
1. qn(2 + 3) = qn(2) + qn(3) − 1 = 2 + 3 − 1 = 4.
2. qn(2) = 2 and 2 < 4, no carry. qn(3) = 3 and 3 < 4, no carry.
3. qn(2 + 3) = 4 and 4 ≤ 4 ≤ 7 so carry ♯.
4. ql(2 + 3) = ql(2) + ql(3) + 0 (no carry step 2) + ♯ (carry step 3) = 0 + 0 + 0 + ♯ = ♯.
5. Z = ql(2 + 3)qn(2 + 3) = ♯4.

6 + 5 = ?
1. qn(6 + 5) = qn(6) + qn(5) − 1 = 6 + 5 − 1 = 10.
2. 4 ≤ 6, so carry ♭. 4 ≤ 5, so carry ♭. That's a total of two carries ♭♭.
3. qn(6 + 5) = 10 and 8 ≤ 10 ≤ 10 so carry ♯♯.
4. ql(6 + 5) = ql(6) + ql(5) + ♭♭ (carry step 2) + ♯♯ (carry step 3) = 0 + 0 + ♭♭ + ♯♯ = 0.
5. Z = ql(6 + 5)qn(6 + 5) = 10.

5 + 4 = ?
1. qn(5 + 4) = qn(5) + qn(4) − 1 = 5 + 4 − 1 = 8.
2. 4 ≤ 5, so carry ♭. 4 ≤ 4, so carry ♭. That's a total of two carries ♭♭.
3. qn(5 + 4) = 8 and 8 ≤ 8 ≤ 10 so carry ♯♯.
4. ql(5 + 4) = ql(5) + ql(4) + ♭♭ (carry step 2) + ♯♯ (carry step 3) = 0 + 0 + ♭♭ + ♯♯ = 0.
5. Z = ql(5 + 4)qn(5 + 4) = 8.

4 + 4 = ?
1. qn(4 + 4) = qn(4) + qn(4) − 1 = 4 + 4 − 1 = 7.
2. 4 ≤ 4, so carry ♭. 4 ≤ 4, so carry ♭. Total carry ♭♭.
3. qn(4 + 4) = 7 and 4 ≤ 7 ≤ 7 so carry ♯.

4. ql(4 + 4) = ql(4) + ql(4) + ♭♭ (carry step 2) + ♯ (carry step 3) = 0 + 0 + ♭♭ + ♯ = ♭.
5. Z = ql(4 + 4)qn(4 + 4) = ♭7.

♭7 + 7 = ?
1. qn(♭7 + 7) = qn(♭7) + qn(7) − 1 = 7 + 7 − 1 = 13.
2. 4 ≤ 7, so carry ♭. 4 ≤ 7, so carry ♭. Total carry ♭♭.
3. qn(♭7 + 7) = 13 and 11 ≤ 13 so carry ♯♯♯.
4. ql(♭7 + 7) = ql(♭7) + ql(7) + ♭♭ (carry step 2) + ♯♯♯ (carry step 3) = ♭ + 0 + ♭♭ + ♯♯♯ = 0.
5. Z = ql(♭7 + 7)qn(♭7 + 7) = 13.

3 + 6 = ?
1. qn(3 + 6) = qn(3) + qn(6) − 1 = 3 + 6 − 1 = 8.
2. 3 < 4, no carry. 4 ≤ 6, carry ♭. Total carry ♭.
3. qn(3 + 6) = 8 and 8 ≤ 8 ≤ 10 so carry ♯♯.
4. ql(3 + 6) = ql(3) + ql(6) + ♭ (carry step 2) + ♯♯ (carry step 3) = 0 + 0 + ♭ + ♯♯ = ♯.
5. Z = ql(3 + 6)qn(3 + 6) = ♯8.

♯4 + ♭2 = ?
1. qn(♯4 + ♭2) = qn(♯4) + qn(♭2) − 1 = 4 + 2 − 1 = 5.
2. 4 ≤ 4, carry ♭. 2 < 4, no carry. Total carry ♭.
3. qn(♯4 + ♭2) = 5 and 4 ≤ 5 ≤ 7 so carry ♯.
4. ql(♯4 + ♭2) = ql(♯4) + ql(♭2) + ♭ (carry step 2) + ♯ (carry step 3) = ♯ + ♭ + ♭ + ♯ = 0.
5. Z = ql(♯4 + ♭2)qn(♯4 + ♭2) = 5.

▬▬▬ *Intuitive addition: shortcuts*

The previous methods are somewhat mechanical ways of adding intervals and don't give much insight into relative distances, i.e., the actual intervals you are manipulating. You are smarter than that! This next method relies on your knowledge of the major scale, its constituent intervals (diatonic intervals), and a few tricks. It is more free-form—there are several ways to get to the result—and with experience, you will get pretty quick at it. We want to shift the process of adding intervals from pen & paper into our head. For this, we will use some shortcuts.

- **The major scale formula is: 1--2--3-4--5--6--7-8.** The information I want you to take away from this is the semitone distance between neighbouring scale degrees (two semitones between 1 and 2, two semitones between 2 and 3, one semitone between 3 and 4, and so on). Another piece of information you will learn over time is distance between non-neighbouring scale degrees (relative intervals: two whole tones between 1 and 3, two whole tones between 4 and 6, two whole tones between 5 and 7, and so on).

- **The tritone** divides the octave in half. It is made of 6 semitones, or 3 whole tones. You can view it as ♯4 or ♭5. The tritone puts a midpoint in our octave, reducing the addition problem to a shorter span: we can compare an interval with the tritone (TT) instead of the unison (1) or the octave (8).

- **The inversion** (complement rule) of an interval reduces a large interval to a small interval. We can add the inversions instead and invert the result.

These shortcuts are summarised in Figure 3.1.

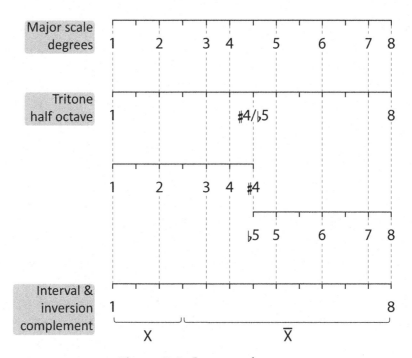

Figure 3.1 *Intuitive shortcuts*

What can we do with all this? Let's take some of the examples we added mechanically and put them through our intuitive interval-crunching machine.

Let's add a 2ⁿᵈ and a 3ʳᵈ (X = 2, Y = 3).
Here, we use our knowledge of the major scale intervals. First, instead of starting with 2, we start with 3, just because 2 is smaller and easier to bounce around. We have a major 3ʳᵈ to which we add a major 2ⁿᵈ (two semitones). We know that 3 + one semitone is 4, and 4 + one semitone is ♯4. Done. Be careful, not ♭5; remember the rule qn(X + Y) = qn(X) + qn(Y) – 1. What we really did here is to add one diatonic semitone to 3 to get to 4 and one chromatic semitone to 4 to get to ♯4.

Add a 4ᵗʰ and a 4ᵗʰ (X = 4, Y = 4).
4 + 4, that's a little difficult with major scale intervals because the intervals are large. Enter the tritone TT. We know that the tritone is ♯4. Well, 4 is just one semitone short of ♯4. We have 4 twice so we are two semitones short of two tritones added together. And we know that two tritones added together is an octave. So we are two semitones short of an octave. Knowing our major scale intervals, the separation between the 7ᵗʰ degree and the octave 7-8 is one semitone. Since we are two semitones short, the result is ♭7. Instead of conducting the addition operation between 1–8, we worked within 1–TT here.

Add a ♭7ᵗʰ and a 7ᵗʰ (X = ♭7, Y = 7).
Again, these are large intervals. We are more comfortable dealing with small intervals. Instead of adding the two intervals, we'll add their inversion. ♭7's inversion is 2 and 7's inversion is ♭2. We add 2 and ♭2, that's ♭3. We invert that again, and the result is 6 (M6). Add compound back: 13 (M13). Alternatively, you can just think of ♭7 being two semitones short of an octave and 7 being one semitone short of an octave. That's a total of three semitones smaller than an octave, which is a ♭3 (be careful to get the right interval quantity).

Add a 3ʳᵈ and a 6ᵗʰ (X = 3, Y = 6).
We know that 6 + ♭3 = 8 (interval + its inversion = octave) so we are almost there. The result is one semitone larger than the octave because instead of ♭3, we are adding 3. That is ♯8.

This is just a glimpse of how such shortcuts can help us avoid the tedious mechanical addition. There are several ways to get to the result and it is up to you how you go about it. A fringe benefit from this intuitive approach is that you gain more awareness of actual intervals and distances involved. Let's summarise what these shortcuts do. The tritone gives you a familiar midpoint between two zeros in interval addition (the zeros are the unison 1 and the octave 8). So you can now add between 1 and #4 (between zero and that midpoint) instead of between 1 and 8. You just reduced the playing field. The inversion makes large intervals much smaller, and you might be more familiar handling 2nds and 3rds than 5ths or 7ths. That is because you know the major scale formula inside out, in particular the whole step / half step relationships between scale degrees. Other shortcuts use various properties listed in Table 3.1.

■■■■ *Interval addition in the physical world*

A side note on what interval addition means and what it's doing to physical quantities like frequency (pitch). We said in the previous chapter that an interval is the difference in pitch between two notes. Yet, an interval is represented as the ratio of the frequencies of the two notes. This may sound like two different definitions! No, it's not. That ratio of frequencies on a linear scale (no unit) becomes the difference of two frequencies on a logarithmic scale (cents). Dusting off some high school maths: $\log(a/b) = \log(a) - \log(b)$.

Let's add two intervals X and Y to form interval Z. We choose a reference frequency f_{ref} corresponding to the pitch of note N_{ref} and define each of these intervals with respect to that reference frequency: the ratio f_X/f_{ref} defines the interval X with f_X being the pitch of note N_X, f_Y/f_{ref} defines Y with f_Y the pitch of note N_Y, and f_Z/f_{ref} defines Z with f_Z the pitch of note N_Z. When we add X and Y, the frequency for note N_Z is defined as:

$$\frac{f_Z}{f_X} = \frac{f_Y}{f_{ref}}; \quad \text{therefore} \quad \underbrace{\frac{f_Z}{f_{ref}}}_{Z} = \frac{f_Z}{f_X} \times \frac{f_X}{f_{ref}} = \underbrace{\frac{f_Y}{f_{ref}}}_{Y} \times \underbrace{\frac{f_X}{f_{ref}}}_{X} \tag{3.1}$$

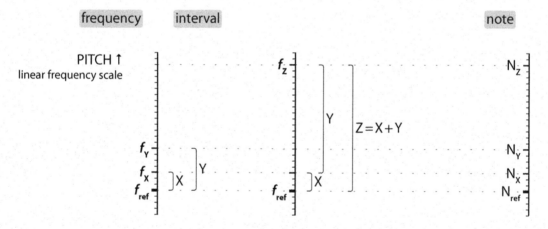

Figure 3.2 *Adding intervals multiplies frequencies*

This shows that **adding two intervals is the multiplication of two frequencies** with respect to a reference frequency. You will notice in Figure 3.2 that on a linear frequency scale, the interval Y built on note N_X is larger than interval Y built on note N_{ref}. On a logarithmic scale (such as a scale measured in cents, or in half steps), they would be of the same size.

Let's take a real-life example (numbers come from Table 11.1 in the Harmonics chapter). We choose the pitch of the open A (A2) on string 5 as our reference frequency $f_{ref} = 110$ Hz. Next, we pick out the note C (C3) on the same string, fret 3, which is an interval of a $\flat 3^{rd}$ above A, with a frequency of $f_C = 130.81$ Hz. Last, we pick out the note E (E3) on the same string, fret 7, which is an interval of a 5th above A, with a frequency of $f_E = 164.81$ Hz. If we add these two intervals $\flat 3 + 5$, we get a $\flat 7^{th}$ interval above A, corresponding to the note G. Based on what we just observed, the pitch for G should be: $f_E \times f_C / f_A = 164.81 \times 130.81 / 110 \approx 196$ Hz. This is exactly what we can read in the table for the note G3. In practice, it is more convenient to talk in cents, which uses a logarithmic scale where instead of multiplying pitch, we simply add.

3.2 Interval subtraction

▬▬ Definition

All you are likely to need is interval addition. Nevertheless, you may wonder how interval subtraction works. First, let's introduce the "–" sign (minus sign). How do we define a negative interval –X? Well, remember we said it would be nice for intervals to have a direction, so that we could differentiate an interval ascending in pitch and an interval descending in pitch? That's all it is: the "–" sign placed in front of the interval means it is descending in pitch. As an example, for an interval of a 5th, whether it is a melodic or harmonic interval, it doesn't matter, 5 means it is ascending in pitch, but –5 means it is descending in pitch. Note that $X - X = 1$ (unison or P1).

Now, how do we go about "interval X minus interval Y"? The operation $X - Y$ can be defined as:

> **SUBTRACTION:** Subtract interval Y from interval X and find interval $Z = X - Y$.
>
> 1. Compare X and Y: if $qn(X) \geq qn(Y)$, then $Z = X + \overline{Y}$, else $Z = -(\overline{X} + Y)$.
> 2. Find Z using the addition procedure. Reduce to simple interval if Z is compound.

Interval subtraction is simply interval addition with a signed interval: $X - Y = X + (-Y)$. Also, $X - Y = -(Y - X)$.

A few examples:
Subtract a 6th from a 2nd (X = 2, Y = 6), or $2 - 6 = ?$
1. $qn(2) = 2$ and $qn(6) = 6$, $2 < 6$ so $Z = -(\overline{2} + 6) = -(\flat 7 + 6)$.
2. Plug in the addition procedure (carry addition method) for $\flat 7 + 6$.
   Add a $\flat 7^{th}$ and a 6th (X = $\flat 7$, Y = 6), or $\flat 7 + 6 = ?$
   step 1: $qn(\flat 7 + 6) = qn(\flat 7) + qn(6) - 1 = 7 + 6 - 1 = 12$.
   step 2: $4 \leq 7$, so carry $\flat$. $4 \leq 6$, so carry $\flat$. Total carry $\flat\flat$.
   step 3: $qn(\flat 7 + 6) = 12$ and $11 \leq 12$ so carry ###.
   step 4: $ql(\flat 7 + 6) = ql(\flat 7) + ql(6) + \flat\flat$ (carry step 2) + ### (carry step 3) = $\flat + 0 + \flat\flat + \# \# \# = 0$.
   step 5: $Z = ql(\flat 7 + 6)qn(\flat 7 + 6) = 12$. Compound reduced to 5.
Therefore, we end up with $Z = -(\flat 7 + 6) = -5$, a descending 5th.

Subtract a 4th from a 5th (X = 5, Y = 4), or $5 - 4 = ?$
1. $5 \geq 4$ so $Z = 5 + \overline{4} = 5 + 5$.
2. Plug in the addition procedure for $5 + 5$.
We get $Z = 5 + 5 = 2$.

Subtract a 3rd from a 7th (X = 7, Y = 3), or 7 – 3 = ?

1. 7 ≥ 3 so Z = 7 + $\overline{3}$ = 7 + ♭6.
2. Plug in the addition procedure for 7 + ♭6. We just went through that in the first example. We can reuse the result because 7 + ♭6 = ♭7 + 6.

Therefore, we end up with Z = 7 + ♭6 = 5.

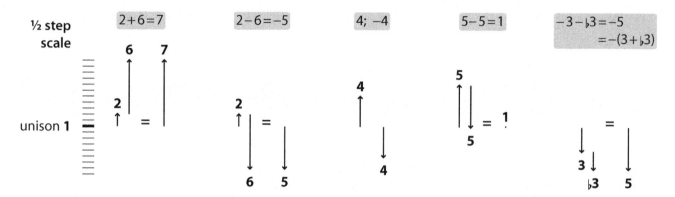

Figure 3.3 *Interval addition/subtraction recap*

▄▄▄ *A question of notation*

The minus sign introduced for the purpose of interval subtraction and to give the notion of direction to the interval (pitch rises or falls) is a non-standard notation. It begs another question: **how do we notate scale degrees below the tonic, i.e., below scale degree 1?** Intervals and scale degrees are closely related and their notation should be consistent. Remember that an interval is simple when it is smaller than an octave and compound when it is larger. Following this definition, scale degrees above the octave are routinely spelt 9, 13, etc., which is in line with the name of compound intervals (ninth, thirteenth, etc.). So how should we notate a scale degree once it drops below the tonic? Let's take an example (Figure 3.4).

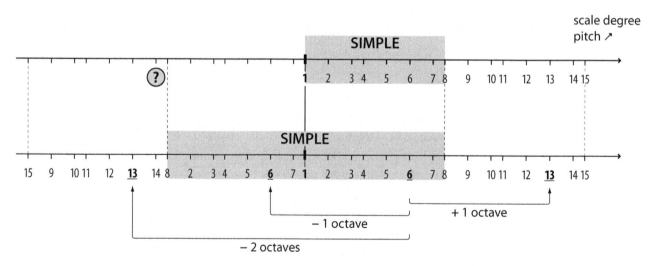

Figure 3.4 *Notation of scale degrees below tonic 1*

The scale degree we are looking at is the 6th. When it's between 1–8, the interval formed between 1–6 is smaller than an octave, the interval is a 6th (simple) and it is the 6th degree when counting from 1. If we add an octave to that, it forms a 13th interval with the tonic (compound) and becomes the 13th degree in the scale. Now, from the 6th degree, let's drop one octave below. This is an inversion and the corresponding interval between the bottom note and the top note (tonic) is ♭3. What is the scale degree of the bottom note? It's the 6th degree of the scale, an octave lower. The interval between that scale degree and the tonic is ♭3 (inversion of 6), which is smaller than an octave, so it makes sense to still call the scale degree a 6th. If the initial 6th is dropped by two octaves, the interval formed between that scale degree and the tonic 1 is a 13th (compound because larger than an octave), so it makes sense to call the scale degree a 13th.

If we stick to the definition of a simple interval, any scale degree up to one octave above or one octave below the tonic forms a simple interval with the tonic. This defines the greyed-out area on the diagram. It would be helpful to add a distinctive symbol to scale degrees below the tonic like a prefix or suffix (e.g., "." or "*") to set them apart from scale degrees above the tonic; the minus sign "−" would be a misleading choice as the maths won't work!

In spite of all we just said, this notation is a little odd because as you move along the axis in Figure 3.4, scale degrees suddenly jump (14 to 8, 8 to 2, or 7 to 1). This is one reason why frequently, scale degrees 1 through 7 only are used, regardless of the octave they're in—be it above or below the tonic—at the expense of clarity.

3.3 The Intervals Wheel

The Intervals Wheel is a tool that quickly performs the operation of interval addition for you. It takes away (most of) the mental effort required to add intervals and replaces it with a mechanical effort. The wheel implements the semitone method of adding intervals. If you are training yourself to add intervals together through the methods described in Section 3.1, you can check your answers against the results from the wheel.

▬▬ *DIY: build the wheel*

Before we look at how the wheel works, you must build your own. It's very easy and requires a little craftsmanship on your part. Photocopy the large and small wheel cutouts in Appendix B, and from this point onwards, work off the photocopy. **Don't tear or cut the page out of the book!** *Alternatively, you may download a copy to print from the website www.pelemeleworks.com.* On the photocopy, cut out the wheels along the dotted lines, or simply cut out the small wheel and mount it onto the large wheel. Hold them together at the centre with a pin (like a split pin paper fastener). There is a little handle on the small wheel you can also cut out for easy handling. For extra durability, stick the paper wheels onto corrugated cardboard.

▬▬ *How it works*

The Intervals Wheel functions like a lookup table, mapping intervals to the decimal system. It comprises a set of two wheels that give you the result of adding any two intervals. Each wheel is sliced into 12 equal wedges, dividing the wheel into 12 semitones and covering an entire octave, from 1 through to 8 (in terms of scale degree). Only perfect and major intervals are written around the wheels. For example, P5 is 5 on the wheel; m3 is ♭3 so starting on 3, you move back one semitone to get ♭3; A5 is ♯5 so starting on 5, you move forward one semitone to get ♯5; d7 is ♭♭7 so starting on 7, you move back two semitones to get ♭♭7, an enharmonic of 6. The wheels are numbered clockwise (large wheel) and counterclockwise (small wheel) but you needn't worry about that. To add two intervals X and Y with the wheel, follow these steps:

INTERVALS WHEEL ADDITION: Add intervals X and Y and find interval $Z = X + Y$.

1. Rotate the small wheel so that Y on the small wheel is aligned with X on the large wheel. If the arch from Y to 1 on the small wheel gets past "1" on the large wheel, keep a carry (7 for an octave).

2. The arrow on the small wheel points to the interval Z on the large wheel. The readout Z contains the correct number of semitones but its name remains to be determined.

3. Check for enharmonics. On the large wheel starting on Z, for each semitone separating interval Z and the interval "$qn(X) + qn(Y) - 1$," add $\sharp$ (clockwise) or $\flat$ (counterclockwise).

4. If there was a carry in step 1, add 7 to the result.

Figure 3.5 presents four examples of interval addition using the wheel. The first example adds intervals of a 2nd and a 5th. To find the result, we go through these steps:

1. Rotate the small wheel so that "5" (P5) on the small wheel is aligned with "2" (M2) on the large wheel. The arch from 5 to 1 around the small wheel does not cross 1 on the large wheel so no carry. The arch is drawn near the centre of the disc.

2. The arrow on the small wheel points to the wedge for 6 on the large wheel.

3. $qn(X) + qn(Y) - 1 = 2 + 5 - 1 = 6$. No adjustment for enharmonics is necessary.

4. No carry. The final result is $2 + 5 = 6$.

A second example shows the use of the wheel to add a 5th to a $\flat7^{th}$. Go through the same drill:

1. Rotate the small wheel so that "$\flat7$" (m7) on the small wheel is aligned with "5" (P5) on the large wheel. To get from $\flat7$ to 1 on the small wheel (clockwise), the arch crosses "1" on the large wheel so keep 7 as a carry (one octave).

2. The arrow on the small wheel points to the wedge for 4 (11) on the large wheel.

3. $qn(X) + qn(Y) - 1 = 5 + 7 - 1 = 11$. No adjustment for enharmonics is necessary.

4. A carry of 7 from step 1 brings the result to: $5 + \flat7 = 4 + 7 = 11$ (P11 compound).

The next example shows adding $\sharp4$ to $\sharp4$.

1. Rotate the small wheel so that "$\sharp4$" (A4) on the small wheel is aligned with "$\sharp4$" on the large wheel.

2. The arrow on the small wheel points to the wedge for 8 on the large wheel.

3. $qn(X) + qn(Y) - 1 = 4 + 4 - 1 = 7$. Need to add $\sharp$ to get from 7 to $\sharp7$, an enharmonic of 8.

4. No carry. The final result is $\sharp4 + \sharp4 = \sharp7$. Be careful, the result is $\sharp7$, not 8.

The last example shows adding $\flat\flat7$ to 3.

1. Rotate the small wheel so that "3" (M3) on the small wheel is aligned with "$\flat\flat7$" (d7) on the large wheel. $\flat\flat7$ is located where 6 is (enharmonic). To get from 3 to 1 on the small wheel (clockwise), "1" on the large wheel is crossed by the arch so keep 7 as a carry (one octave).

2. The arrow on the small wheel points to the wedge before 2 on the large wheel.

3. $qn(X) + qn(Y) - 1 = 7 + 3 - 1 = 9$. Need to add $\flat$ to get from 2 to $\flat2$.

4. Carry from step 1. The final result is $\flat\flat7 + 3 = \flat9$.

Next page:
Figure 3.5 *Examples using the Intervals Wheel*

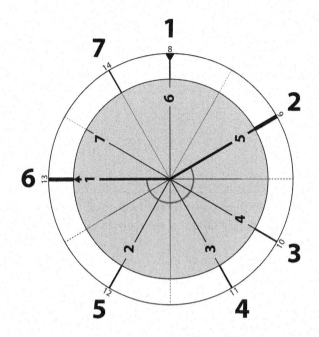

$$2^{nd} + 5^{th} = 6^{th}$$

$$qn(2) + qn(5) - 1 = 6$$

$$5^{th} + \flat 7^{th} = 11^{th} \ (4)$$

$$qn(5) + qn(\flat 7) - 1 = 11$$

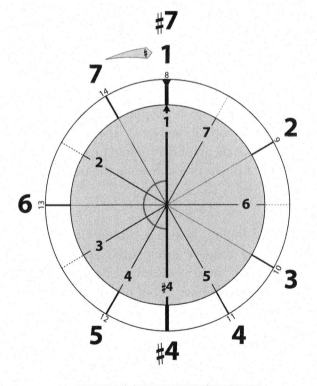

$$\sharp 4^{th} + \sharp 4^{th} = \sharp 7^{th}$$

$$qn(\sharp 4) + qn(\sharp 4) - 1 = 7$$

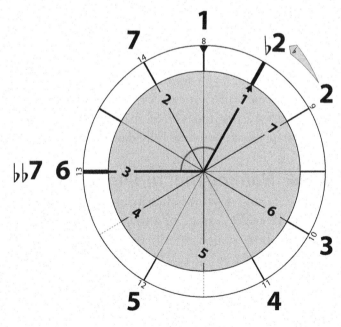

$$\flat\flat 7^{th} + 3^{rd} = \flat 9^{th} \ (\flat 2)$$

$$qn(\flat\flat 7) + qn(3) - 1 = 9$$

4 TUNING

The guitar's tuning lays out the canvas we play on. We usually tune our guitar and get on with it. But understanding the reason behind the tuning and the trade-offs involved will help understand the fretboard, use other tunings, or come up with your own. In this chapter, we stop to examine this overlooked aspect of the instrument.

4.1 Guitar tuning

What is a guitar tuning?

As we will see in a later chapter, the **horizontal layout** of the guitar is predefined: each fret along the string is spaced in half a step.[1] This cannot be changed, by design. What can be changed is which consecutive notes reside on each fret. Therefore, once the pitch of one fret is set, the pitch of the remaining frets on that string is defined. For convenience, rather than tune to a pitch at any fret (e.g., tune for A on string 6, fret 5), we tune to a desired pitch at the open string (fret 0); that way, the left hand can turn the tuning gear while the right hand is plucking the string to check its pitch. By virtue of changing the pitch of an open string, we are also changing the tonal distance between that string and the other strings. In other words, tuning also defines the **vertical layout** of the guitar!

To tune the guitar, you adjust each open string to a particular pitch. That pitch corresponds to a note in the music alphabet (all 12 notes: A B C D E F G and the five sharp or flat notes in between). The combination of these open string notes on all six strings is the *guitar tuning*: it's the makeup of the tuning. Once you have tuned your guitar, you have fully defined the layout of the notes (and pitch) everywhere on the fretboard.

Naming that tuning

A guitar tuning is named after its usage or its origin (e.g., standard tuning, Nashville tuning), its makeup (e.g., DADGAD tuning), or a characteristic aspect of the tuning (e.g., drop-D tuning, tuning in 4[ths]). But the name isn't enough to fully define the tuning because even though note names may be provided, the correct pitches aren't (e.g., DADGAD tells you strings 6, 4, and 1 are the note D but doesn't tell you the pitch of each note D). Hence, more information than its name is often necessary if you encounter a tuning for the first time.

Why tune the guitar?

A tuning's goal is twofold: 1- to provide the guitarist a reasonable pool of notes within reach of his fingers (**pitch location**), 2- to lock the sound produced by the instrument to the music alphabet (**pitch accuracy**).

---

1. Despite drawing the fretboard vertically sometimes, by "horizontal," I mean "along the string" and by "vertical," I mean "across strings."

Another way of saying this is that the guitar strings must be in harmony with each other (guitar in tune with itself: *relative tuning*) and the guitar has a position to fill in a larger music ensemble. Other goals of a tuning may be to match the range of another instrument or a singer, to enhance the guitar's sonic properties (like sound projection), etc.

A good tuning is a sensible trade-off between the number of different notes it makes available and the hand/finger movements necessary to reach them. The more notes available and the smaller displacements necessary, the better the tuning. Alternatively, a tuning may be designed to ease access to certain sounds difficult or impossible to finger with standard tuning.

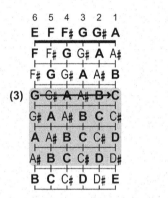 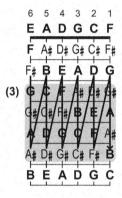

Figure 4.1 *"Good" and "bad" tuning: 1- tuning in half steps (bad); 2- tuning in 4^{ths} (good)*

Figure 4.1-1 shows a tuning where strings 6–1 are tuned to consecutive notes E F F♯ G G♯ A (all within the same octave); the distance between each string is only one semitone. If you position your hand on the fretboard, unless you shift your hand along the neck, there are only a few notes your fingers have access to in that position (position 3 is greyed out). Another way to look at this is to play the chromatic scale across strings (arrow): it can be played within only one fret! This tuning makes a lot of notes redundant, the same note appears on multiple strings within the position. The range covered on the same fret across strings 6 to 1 is a mere 5 semitones (perfect 4th) from E to A. This is a bad tuning and a poor use of the range six strings can offer. You can take it further and tune every string to the same pitch, say E E E E E E, a seemingly absurd tuning. It yields a range of zero semitone across strings 6 to 1!

Figure 4.1-2 shows another tuning. The strings are separated by a perfect ascending 4th: E A D G C F. The range covered on the same fret across strings 6 to 1 is 25 semitones (two octaves and a minor 2nd) from E to F. That's a lot more ground than the previous example. It's a good tuning but requires some finger stretching from one string to the next to get a hold of a semitone in the chromatic scale (arrow).

▬▬▬ *Tuning metrics*

We talked about the goals of a tuning and qualitatively defined a good tuning. Now, is there a way to measure how "good" or "bad" a tuning is? Some practical metrics for assessing the effectiveness of a tuning are:

- **How much of the chromatic scale you can play in one position.** The more notes repeat or the more incomplete the chromatic scale is in one position, the poorer the tuning. This in turn is a measure of fret hand stretching that may be involed on the instrument (position extension). We want continuity, no skips in the chromatic scale.
- **How easy it is to grip common chords.** If you find that fingering a major chord requires severe finger stretches or results in unpleasant voicings, the tuning is probably more exotic than you would like (e.g., tune all strings to the same note, you will find that a simple major chord requires an impossible stretch).

- **How comfortable it is to play.** String tension must be moderate and homogenous amongst strings. Gauge must be consistent. The tuning should promote good playability and feel (ergonomics).
- **What open string notes are made available.** Even though the tuning affects the entire fingerboard, some tunings are judged by their open strings. This is the case for legions of alternate tunings on acoustic guitar or tunings used on the electric guitar in country styles. The ringing quality of open strings and open chords make open strings a metric for the tuning.[2]

Order of pitch in a tuning

Most guitar tunings are ascending in pitch, each string is tuned at a higher pitch than the previous string (in standard tuning, from low to high pitch: E↗A↗D↗G↗B↗e), but that doesn't need to be so. For example, Nashville tuning is the same as standard tuning but with the low four strings raised a whole octave (string gauge is lighter too). This puts the G string at a higher pitch than the B string. If you play the ukulele, the standard soprano ukulele tuning is G↘C↗E↗A (strings 4 to 1), with the G string being a perfect 5th above the C string—sometimes spelt g C E A. This is known as a *re-entrant tuning*, where adjacent strings in a tuning do not all ascend (or descend) in pitch. The tenor ukulele's tuning is still G C E A, but the G is an octave lower, and the tuning is once again ascending in pitch (*linear tuning*).

4.2 Standard tuning

EADGBE

Strings on the guitar are numbered 6 to 1, from lower pitch to higher pitch strings. The guitar is tuned E A D G B E,[3] which is known as *standard tuning*. The high E string is sometimes written e in lower case, to differentiate it from the low E string with an upper case (E A D G B e). Each of these open string notes corresponds to a specific pitch on the notation staff. Standard tuning raises in pitch from string 6 to 1 and spans two octaves. The five notes of standard tuning E---G--A--B---D spell out an E minor pentatonic scale 1---♭3--4--5---♭7, or G major pentatonic. This is a singular property.

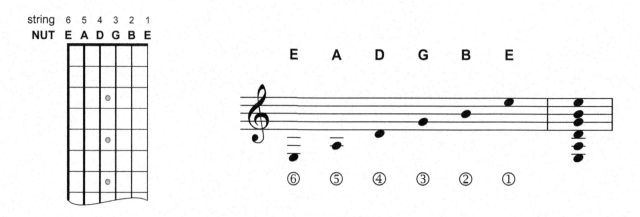

Figure 4.2 *Standard tuning: 1- fretboard; 2- notation staff*

---

2. We tend to associate open chords with the open position, but chords with open strings can be located anywhere on the fretboard. The terms *open-position chord* and *open-string chord* can help distinguish open chords in the open position and others.
3. I find it quickest to directly memorise the letters E A D G B E by verbalising them EAD-G-BE as "eed-guh-buh"!

Transposing instrument

The guitar is a *transposing instrument*. This means that the notation on the music staff does not match the actual/real pitch of the note, referred to as *concert pitch*. For guitar, notation shows a pitch that is **an octave above** actual pitch (Figure 4.3).[4] A transposing instrument is therefore confusing terminology because it has nothing to do with the instrument itself but has everything to do with music notation for that instrument!

String	6	5	4	3	2	1
Note	E	A	D	G	B	E
Pitch	E2	A2	D3	G3	B3	E4
Actual pitch (Hz)	82.41	110.00	146.83	196.00	246.94	329.63
Notation pitch (Hz)	164.81	220.00	293.66	392.00	493.88	659.26

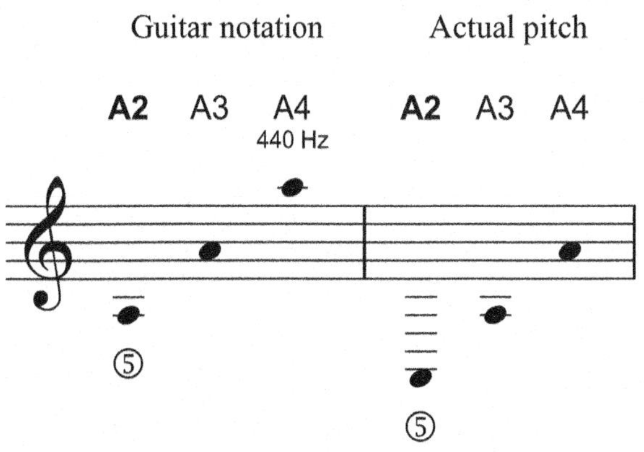

Figure 4.3 *Standard tuning pitch: 1- open string frequencies; 2- guitar notation vs. actual*

Why transpose? The bulk of music written for guitar can be played somewhere within the first twelve frets of the guitar. That's a range of three octaves from the low E open string to E on string 1, fret 12. If notation was at actual pitch, you would have to constantly add ledger lines below the staff or even introduce the bass clef $\mathbf{9}$. Instead, you could raise (transpose) the pitch of the notes on the staff by an octave and indicate this with the octave sign $\textbf{\textit{8}}^{vb}$ (*ottava bassa* for one octave below notation). For guitar, this is done permanently and is implied by the notation so the octave sign is not necessary.

> **NOTE**   Do not mix up a *transposing instrument* with *transposing* a piece of music. A transposing instrument is an instrument for which there is a difference in pitch between the sound it makes and the notation of that sound on the music staff. Transposing music is the action of taking that piece of music and shifting it to another key, without changing the tonal distance between the notes. We'll get to transposition on guitar in a later chapter.

Why standard tuning?

A question you may ask yourself is: "Why is the guitar tuned this way?" Figure 4.2 shows that all strings on the guitar are separated by a perfect 4th except for strings 3 and 2 that are separated by a major 3rd, resulting in a tuning of 4-4-4-3-4. This is two questions in one:

1. Why is the guitar tuned in 4-4-4-3-4 intervals (relative pitch: interval)?
2. Why is the guitar tuned to pitches E2 A2 D3 G3 B3 E4 (absolute pitch: register)?

WHY 4-4-4-3-4?

Two of the prominent predecessors of the guitar are the vihuela, a 6-course[5] instrument, and the 6-course renaissance lute. The former was often tuned to E A D F♯ B E (4-4-3-4-4) and the latter to G C F A D G (4-4-3-4-4). Both are almost like standard tuning. Another ancestor is the Renaissance guitar, a 4-course

---

4. A0, A1, A2, A3, A4, etc., denote the pitch of note A at octaves. A2 is the concert pitch of the 5th string of the guitar. A4 is two octaves higher and is the usual reference pitch found on tuning devices: A4 = 440 Hz. The guitar is tuned E2 A2 D3 G3 B3 E4.

5. A course on an instrument is a set of two or more closely spaced strings (usually tuned at octaves), played as one string. The 12-string guitar is another example of a 6-course instrument.

instrument tuned to D G B E or G C E A (4-3-4), and its 5-course version tuned to A D G B E (4-4-3-4).

Figure 4.4 shows the fretboard coverage required for the chromatic scale, for standard tuning and a few others (remember tuning metrics). An immediate question is why not tune all strings in 4ths: 4-4-4-4-4 (E A D G C F)? This tuning makes sense as it does away with the odd major 3rd interval between strings 3 and 2 and yields a logical and linear layout of the fretboard. It makes so much sense that some players have adopted this tuning. From a single line perspective (scale), it is very convenient, but from a harmonic perspective (chord, arpeggio), some fingerings become awkward. It isn't unsurmountable. Another tuning to consider is all 3rds: 3-3-3-3-3 (E G♯ C E G♯ C).[6,7] This tuning yields the best fingering for the chromatic scale, no contest: 4 notes per string, squarely fitting in one position.

Another legitimate question is why not use other tunings like all major 2nds, all major 6ths, combinations (e.g., 4-4-4-3-3), and so forth? The answer is that a 2nd or a 6th would yield either too close an interval or too wide an interval between strings, making for inconvenient fingerings. Figure 4.4 demonstrates that a ♭2nd tuning is clearly a waste of fingering coverage while a 5th tuning requires too wide a stretch. 3rds and 4ths appear to be a reasonable trade-off between musicality (adequate-sounding voicing) and playability (convenient fingerings and good coverage with some stretching). The historical aspect led to settle on the 4-4-4-3-4 combination of standard tuning.

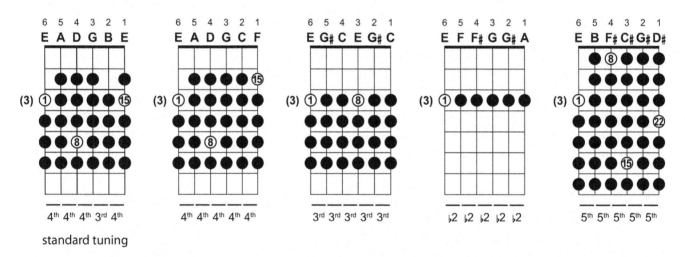

Figure 4.4 *The chromatic scale for various tunings (notes do not repeat)*

WHY E-A-D-G-B-E?

Assuming we're okay with 4-4-4-3-4, why tune to those pitches E A D G B E and not another set of pitches while keeping the same intervals between strings? We could tune down two whole steps to C F B♭ E♭ G C. It would slightly change the range of the instrument. Try it. What happens? String buzz and really slack strings! Tension can be restored by using thicker, less flexible strings, at the expense of playability. Why not tune up a 4th to A D G C E A (that's the same as fret 5 in standard tuning)? String tension would rise a lot or, thinner strings would have to be used to get some tension relief [see Equation (11.1)]. What really set E A D G B E in stone is therefore the historical aspects (earlier instruments), the role of the guitar (a midrange instrument, initially for accompaniment), and the physical constraints of the instrument.

---

6. G♯–C is technically a ♭4th interval, not a 3rd (enharmonic intervals). I write it G♯–C here to avoid the B♯ in G♯–B♯.

7. You may encounter another starting note than E for a tuning in 3rds, like G♯ C E G♯ C E.

ONCE A STANDARD, ALWAYS A STANDARD

Finally, usage is also what makes standard tuning a stronghold. Once a tuning gains traction, it is difficult to dislodge. Generations of guitar players have trained with this tuning, the majority of guitar literature is written for this tuning, same goes for guitar tuition material on tape, film, or paper. And it isn't simply a matter of retranscribing, some music is simply not practical to play if the tuning were changed (likewise, how do you get to low D if you aren't tuned in drop-D tuning?). Changing the slightest element of tuning renders most of this material difficult to use if not obsolete, and guitarists would need to relearn the fretboard.[8] Besides, guitarists need a common language to communicate with each other, especially the guitar being such a visual instrument where much is taught as shapes (e.g., chord shapes / scale patterns in all-4[ths] tuning don't apply to standard tuning). So by and large, standard tuning has become the tuning of choice.

There are other practical considerations too. You want fairly even tension for all strings to keep a consistent feel when depressing or bending the string. Equation (11.1) tells us this can be mitigated by the gauge of the string. You want flexibility more than stiffness in strings. You also want a ringing quality with long decay and rich overtones. In acoustic guitars, sound volume is also a desirable feature. Table 4.1 shows that a set of strings maintains progressive string gauge and string tension within a few pounds (for example, Super Light electric guitar string tension is within 11–16 lb).

Table 4.1 *Sample of string gauge/tension for electric and acoustic guitar*

String gauge/tension (in/lb)*	6	5	4	3	2	1	Total tension (lb)†
ELECTRIC							
Super light	.042 / 15	.032 / 16	.024 / 16	.016 / 15	.011 / 11	.009 / 13	85
Light	.046 / 17	.036 / 20	.026 / 18	.017 / 17	.013 / 15	.010 / 16	103
ACOUSTIC							
Light	.053 / 25	.042 / 28	.032 / 30	.024 / 29	.016 / 23	.012 / 23	158
Medium	.056 / 28	.045 / 33	.035 / 35	.026 / 34	.017 / 26	.013 / 27	183

Source: Data from manufacturer for Electric Nickel Plated Steel Nanoweb and Acoustic 80/20 Bronze Nanoweb Elixir strings.
* String tension is an approximation based on a 25.5" scale and standard tuning.
† Total tension may not add up due to rounding.

So is standard tuning the holy grail, an ideal combination transcending the laws of nature, or simply put, the best tuning there is? The answer is no. It does the job, and so do other tunings.[9] What's important to take away from this section is that standard tuning was not a random choice but the result of historical and practical considerations.

■■■ *Fretboard layout*

Now that the tuning is defined, the tonal distance between each fret and each string is known and so are the notes. The horizontal distance (along string) is always a half step between frets, regardless of tuning. The only parameter we can play with is the vertical distance (across strings). In standard tuning, that is 4-4-4-3-4. The guitar fretboard is all organised as an "almost-regular" grid made of strings and fretwire.

---

8. A new standard tuning would be similar to switching driving from right to left. It isn't impossible, but the logistics of such undertaking are dissuasive. Sweden switched from left- to right-hand traffic overnight in 1967.

9. If standard tuning could speak for itself, it would probably say: "I just work here!"

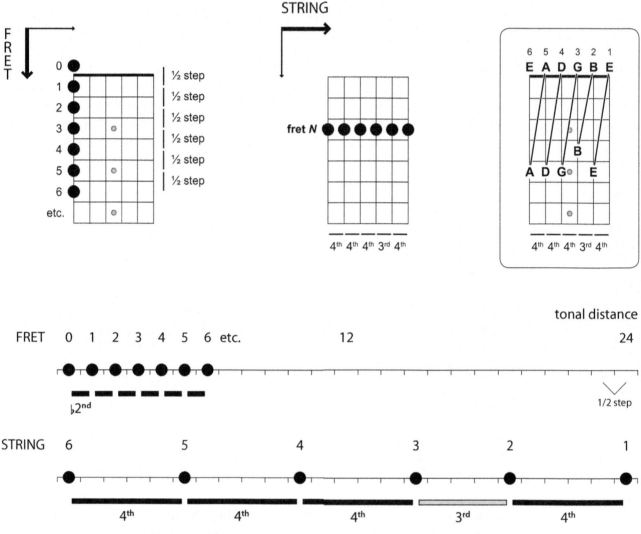

Figure 4.5 *Horizontal (across frets) and vertical (across strings) tonal distance*

It is clear from Figure 4.5 that for a given finger displacement, a horizontal movement covers little intervallic ground whereas a vertical movement offers large intervallic leaps. The two are complementary and the balance between them can serve as a tuning metric.[10]

DID YOU KNOW? On guitar, we tune one note on a string and all the notes on that string are automatically tuned in half-step increments. In contrast, the piano's layout is also a row of keys spaced in half steps, but every single one of them must be painstakingly tuned. Don't we have it easy with the guitar!

---

10. On a Fender Stratocaster (nut width = 1.685", scale length = 25.5"): distance between strings at the nut ≈ 1.685/6 ≈ 0.28", distance between frets 0–1 ≈ 1.43". 0.28" covers 4–5 semitones vertical, 1.43" covers 1 semitone horizontal: that's over 20:1 ratio interval covered vs. distance.

4.3 Other tunings

Other tunings are beyond the scope of this book but a few words on their existence is appropriate. *Alternative* or *alternate tunings* are frequently used on guitar. Common variants of standard tuning are the drop-D tuning (D A D G B E) and lowering the pitch of all strings by a half step (E♭ A♭ D♭ G♭ B♭ E♭). A prominent tuning in acoustic circles is D A D G A D, where the open strings are arranged to form a Dsus4 chord. Open tunings, where the tuning is designed to sound a chord (often a major chord), are another favourite. For instance, an open G tuning can be D G D G B D; the G major chord is made of 1–3–5 notes G B D. Open D tuning is spelt D A D F♯ A D and produces a D major triad.

Just like standard tuning, once an alternate tuning takes root, it helps it grow further. Some alternate tunings have stood the test of time and carved themselves a nice little niche.[11] Oddly enough, the acoustic steel string guitar—more so than the electric or the classical guitar—frequently explores alternate tunings.[12] Slide guitar is another consumer of alternate tunings (open tuning).

> **NOTE** Many instruments cannot change tunings, either because it is not practical (the piano) or not possible (the recorder). On guitar, we have this opportunity and it's quick and easy as pie!

Tunings of other instruments, remotely related to or resembling the guitar, can also enrich our analysis of the guitar's tuning. We can expect tunings for the bouzouki, the oud, the saz, the tar, the sitar, the samisen, etc.—instruments rooted in non-Western/European music—to be different from the guitar's tuning. Could tuning be a function of the kind of music being played on the instrument? Perhaps. Even on guitar, a tuning like DADGAD is often associated with celtic music.

4.4 The capo: a tuning transform

The *capo*[13] is a mechanical contraption that clamps onto the fretboard, positioned right behind the fret. Its most common embodiment is a device that frets all six strings. Some capos—*partial capos*—are designed to fret only select strings. Capos today look modern or futuristic but they have been around for centuries.

▬▬▬ *Full capo*

The main use of the 6-string capo is transposition, without altering the existing tuning. You can then play all the familiar shapes and fingerings (e.g., open chords) in a different key. The capoed fret is the new location of open strings. A capo does not affect the pitch of any note on the neck. The goal of transposing could be to raise the pitch a few semitones to match the range of a vocalist or, to play in a much higher register, perhaps in the hope of mimicking a brighter-sounding instrument like the mandolin.

---

11. A hurdle for other tunings to break through on guitar is quite simply the long-winded process of retuning to another tuning and tuning back to standard tuning. If it were instantaneous, at the push of a button, people would be more inclined to experiment with other tunings!

12. Why? I can only speculate. The repertoire for the acoustic guitar, with roots in a range of music (e.g., celtic, traditional Irish, American folk tunes, sometimes written for other instruments like the fiddle), explores such tunings. The electric guitar only appearing in the 20th century and the classical guitar being rooted in tradition, perhaps that explains why these two instruments did not venture much into other tunings beyond standard tuning. The unplugged nature of the acoustic guitar and fewer effects being available means that acoustic players have to do more with less to get the sounds they want.

13. From Italian *capotasto*, designating the head of the fretboard (the nut).

Often, even though the capo "changes" keys, guitarists still speak the language of standard tuning. For example, with the capo on fret 3, an open C chord shape with the root on string 5, fret 6, is effectively an open E♭ chord but it is understood if we still name it a C chord! Notation-wise, the use of a capo is indicated on the music sheet and all notation is as if there was no capo. You can think of the capo as a **moveable nut**.

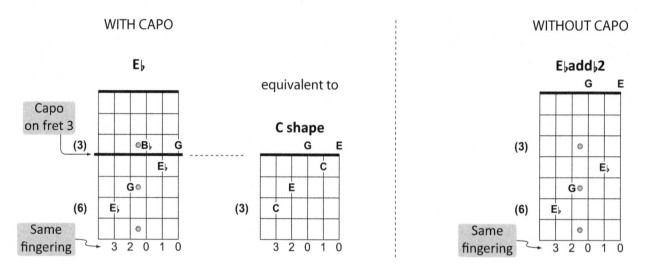

Figure 4.6 *Full capo: a moveable nut*

Partial capo

Another application of capos is the **emulation** of alternate tunings. You get a tuning that has the flavour of alternate tuning—as long as you don't fret uncapoed strings. For example, a partial capo placed on fret 2, clamping only strings 5–1, leaves the low E string unchanged and "shifts" the remaining strings up a whole step. This emulates drop-D tuning, shifted up two frets—but this isn't a drop-D tuning, nor a drop-E tuning, nor a raise–B E A C♯ F♯ tuning! What this is is a tuning that resembles drop-D in its makeup (the intervals between strings are the same as drop-D tuning) as long as you don't fret the uncapoed string 6. Instead of a partial capo, you can also use a regular capo for that and leave string 6 out. The example of Figure 4.7 emulates a DADGAD tuning (outlines an Esus chord), using a partial capo that clamps down only three strings. Again, this gives you a DADGAD look-alike tuning as long as you don't fret any open string. So partial capos have limitations as far as reusing your knowledge of the fretboard.

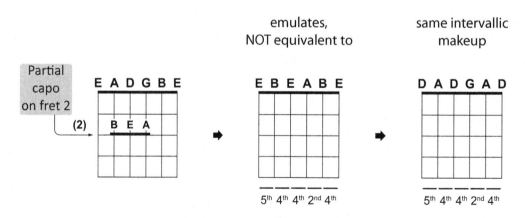

Figure 4.7 *Partial capo emulates DADGAD tuning*

DID YOU KNOW?   If one capo isn't enough, bring on multiple capos! A 6-string capo and a partial capo can combine to raise pitch and emulate alternate tuning, two partial capos can create complex open string layouts, capos can be used with alternate tunings, you name it. Guitarists can get very creative with capos!

Whatever the use of the capo, it presents the notable advantage of leaving string tension unchanged—the guitar's tuning at the nut stays the same and so do the notes on the fretboard. Changing string tension often wears the string and the guitar, beside being time-consuming.

Like alternate tunings, capos are more widespread amongst acoustic guitar players than electric guitar players. While there is no obvious reason for such preference, it may be due to the repertoire of the acoustic guitar, the playability and the sonic personality of the instrument, the matching of a vocalist's range the acoustic guitar is backing, as well as acoustic guitarists' tendency to experiment with different tunings.

4.5 Guitar-friendly keys

▬▬▬ *Open strings and keys*

You might have heard statements like: "G is a good key on guitar." or "The key of D is a staple of country guitar." What does that mean? What keys work well on guitar, i.e., are guitar friendly? All keys play the same role so why do some keys have more affinity with the guitar than others?[14] The tuning holds the answer. The tuning of the guitar makes certain notes available for play as open strings, therefore not requiring fingering. Let's take standard tuning and go through all 12 keys, listing open string notes within each key. The more open strings within a key, the more "friendly" that key.

Table 4.2 *Key and open string relationship*

KEY	Sharps/Flats	E	A	D	G	B
C		✓	✓	✓	✓	✓
G	F♯	✓	✓	✓	✓	✓
D	F♯ C♯	✓	✓	✓	✓	✓
A	F♯ C♯ G♯	✓	✓	✓		✓
E	F♯ C♯ G♯ D♯	✓	✓			✓
B / C♭	F♯ C♯ G♯ D♯ A♯ B♭ E♭ A♭ D♭ G♭ C♭ F♭	✓				✓
F♯ / G♭	F♯ C♯ G♯ D♯ A♯ E♯ B♭ E♭ A♭ D♭ G♭ C♭					✓
C♯ / D♭	F♯ C♯ G♯ D♯ A♯ E♯ B♯ B♭ E♭ A♭ D♭ G♭					
A♭	B♭ E♭ A♭ D♭				✓	
E♭	B♭ E♭ A♭			✓	✓	
B♭	B♭ E♭		✓	✓	✓	
F	B♭	✓	✓	✓	✓	

Table 4.2 lists which open string notes are in each key. As far as containing open strings:
- Best keys: C, G, D (contain all open string notes)
- Good keys: A and F, E (contain 5 and 4 open string notes respectively; E counts twice)

---

14. Even though Nigel Tufnel says so in the movie *This Is Spinal Tap* (1984), the key of D minor isn't the saddest of all keys! All minor keys are "equally sad."

- Worst key: C♯/D♭ (contains no open string note)

The affinity of those keys for guitar also relies on the availability of essential open chords (such as the I, IV, and V chords) and on the significance of the open string note within the key (scale degree). For example, the keys of E, A, and D, are strong contenders because the roots are open strings. The key of F however, even though it contains 5 open strings, is weaker because the root F is not available as an open string and the I (F) and IV (B♭) chords are not available as open chords.

By using a capo or altering the tuning, other keys become readily available. For example, drop-D tuning (D A D G B E) favours the key of D and facilitates the key of B♭. The note D is accessible twice in that tuning (once as the bass note).

Positions and keys

The keys discussed in Table 4.2 are only in the context of open strings. Wherever you are on the fretboard, so long as you are in one of those keys, you can rely on their open strings. Luckily, there are other good keys on guitar, only they might be more suitable to playing in positions, with less or no reliance on open strings. Inspecting the scale degrees of the major scale, there are two positions for each major key where the scale fingering/pattern fits completely (4 frets wide), all others require finger extensions. Two positions require only one extension. As a rule of thumb, those are "good" keys in those positions and can help you decide which part of the guitar you want to read a piece of music in.

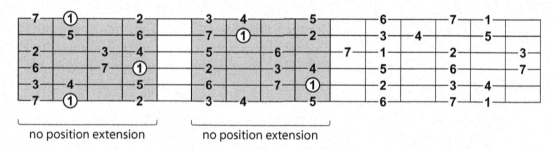

Figure 4.8 *Positions where major key fits with no finger extension*

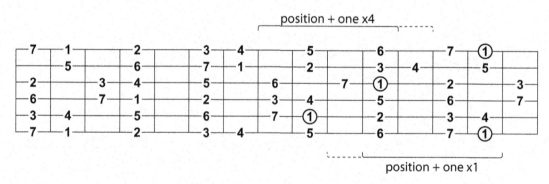

Figure 4.9 *Positions where major key fits with one finger extension only*

With these diagrams in mind, some good keys in the following positions are:
- Open position (position 1 + open strings): keys of F, E, G♭, D♭, B, A♭
- Position 2: keys of G, D, C, A

- Position 3: keys of A♭, E♭, D♭, B♭
- Position 4: keys of A, E, D, B
- Position 5: keys of B♭, F, E♭, C
- Etc.

Positions are sometimes labelled as sharp key or a flat key reading positions. For instance, position 2 lends itself well to sharp keys and position 3 to flat keys.

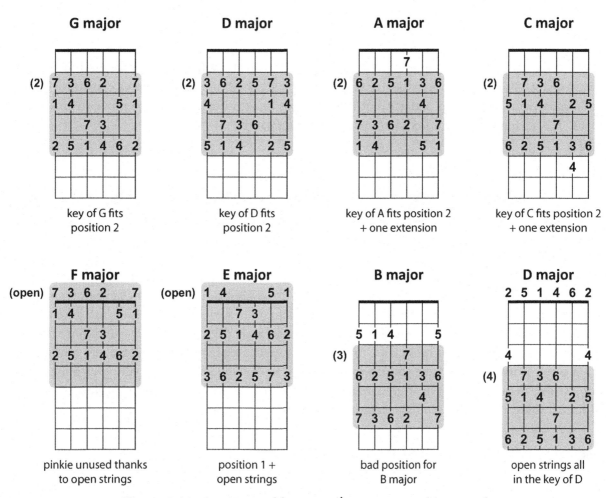

Figure 4.10 *1- some good keys in 2nd position; 2- other examples*

We are beginning to see that a lot on the guitar hinges on the choice of tuning. It doesn't hurt to experiment with tunings other than standard tuning: some require to completely relearn the fretboard, others need only minor adjustments to your fretboard knowledge. The guitar can accommodate a variety of tunings simply by turning the tuning gears (to adjust tension). But some tunings require hardware changes: changes to the string gauge (to change tessiture), changes to the guitar setup (bridge saddles for intonation or string action, nut slots, truss rod), additional hardware (capo), etc. For these reasons, most players stick to one tuning, not necessarily standard tuning.

5 NOTE NAMES

If you don't know the note names on the fretboard, you won't be able to use ANY method to navigate the fretboard: CAGED, intervals, dot markings, fingerings, position playing, notes (obviously), etc. You will know your shapes and patterns but not what to do with them or how to move them around the fretboard. This chapter gives you fretboard maps with note names.

5.1 Memorising the notes on the fretboard

■■■ *Why?*

You MUST learn the notes on the fretboard. This doesn't mean you need to sight-read or know where the notes are on the notation staff; of course, it would be best if you also learn to position these notes on the staff. The incentive to learn note names is to be able to take advantage of various tools to navigate the fretboard, to understand what you are playing (translate music theory like scale degrees or chord names onto the guitar), and to communicate with other musicians. Any approach to the fretboard calls upon a key, a fundamental, a root, in other words, a note name to map music theory to the fretboard. Eventually, you must be able to call out a string/fret location on the fretboard and instantly spell out its name and its position on the music staff. Quite frankly, there's no skipping memorising the notes on the fretboard!

■■■ *Strategies for learning note names*

- Learn notes in the tuning of your choice. In this book, that is **standard tuning**.
- Most of the learning can take place within the **first 12 frets**, as the fretboard layout repeats above fret 12.
- **Learn small chunks** of the fretboard, otherwise, it's just too much information.
- **Focus on natural notes.** Accidentals will take care of themselves and fill in the gaps!
- **Learn each note in isolation.** While using fretboard properties to find a note based on another note is helpful, it takes a fraction of a second too long. Go direct to the note!
- **Learn to recognise groups of notes too.** Groups help make connections and move around the fretboard. There are many ways to group notes. Here, they are grouped in: single strings, adjacent strings, fretboard sections, notes on frets 0–4 all over the fretboard (same pitch).
- **Time yourself.** As you become more familiar with note names, challenge yourself to be aware—in real time—of the names of each and every note you play.
- Learning to **map each note on the fretboard to a pitch on the music staff** is a separate but worthwhile effort. The two activities can be combined: memorising note names & placing each note on the staff.
- *Guitar Note Finder* divides up the fretboard into bite-size bits with a quiz to measure your progress and drill your knowledge of each note. Learning the notes on the fretboard and on the music staff, in a piecemeal and methodical manner, can be supplemented with that book (also by Pêle-Mêle Works).

5.2 Note names and pitch

Memorising natural notes is enough to gradually learn the fretboard. Take notice of the all-natural notes at fret 0 (the nut), fret 5, and fret 10. Fret 11 is all sharps/flats! In the beginning, you can lean on fret markers to locate yourself on the fretboard.

NOTE Within the first 12 frets, there are 48 natural notes but only 30 sharp/flat gap notes. Why not learn the gap notes instead? The short answer is that it would be more confusing and less practical.

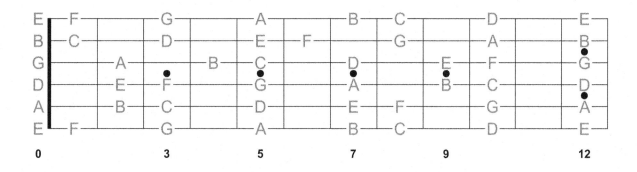

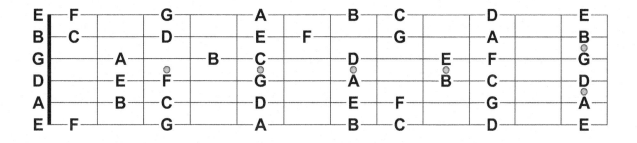

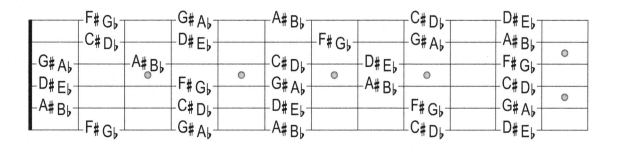

Figure 5.1 *Note names on the first 12 frets: 1- natural notes; 2- sharp/flat notes*

Natural notes are no other than the notes of the C major scale, shown in Figure 5.2 on the B string. Its formula, using whole steps / half steps, is 1–1–½–1–1–1–½ (C--D--E-F--G--A--B-C). Notes B & C and E & F always sit next to each other on the same string.

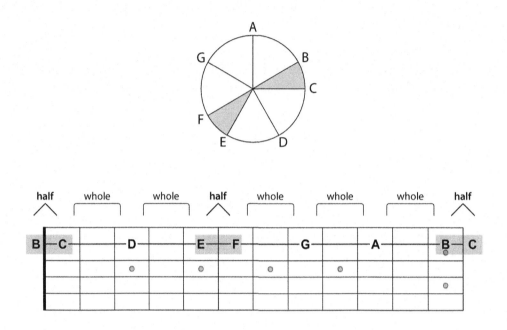

Figure 5.2 *Natural notes: the C major scale*

The fretboard repeats itself at fret 12. Learning can focus on frets 0–12 only but do venture onto higher frets with the guitar in hand because the real neck looks and feels different from the even neck diagrams on paper!

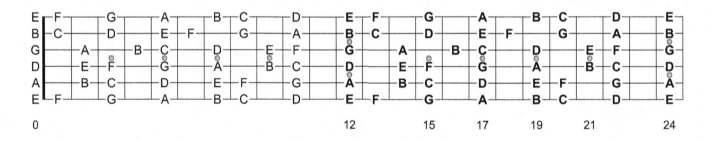

Figure 5.3 *Fretboard repeats every 12 frets (octave)*

The next set of figures reduces the learning process to notes on one string at a time. The pitch corresponding to each note is placed on the music staff beneath the fretboard diagram. Note names on strings 6 and 1 are the same. The order of notes on a string is always that of the music alphabet (A--B-C--D--E-F--G--A), repeating every 12th fret.

Next two pages:
Figure 5.4 *Notes on a string*

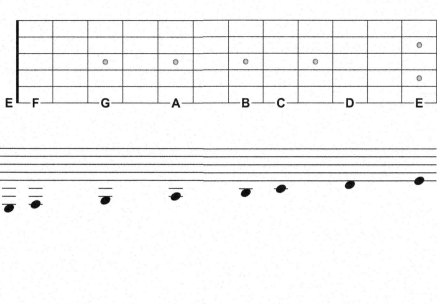

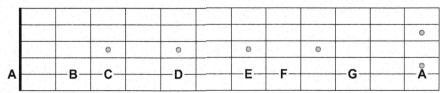

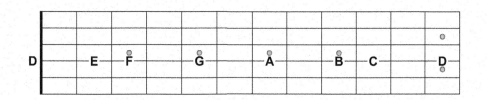

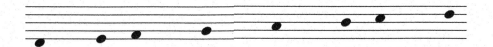

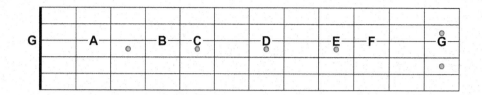

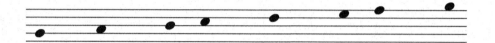

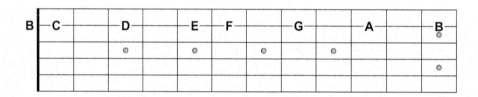

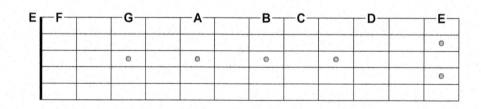

Figure 5.5 groups notes into pairs of strings. Compared to single strings alone, this view connects notes horizontally AND vertically by placing them in a larger context.

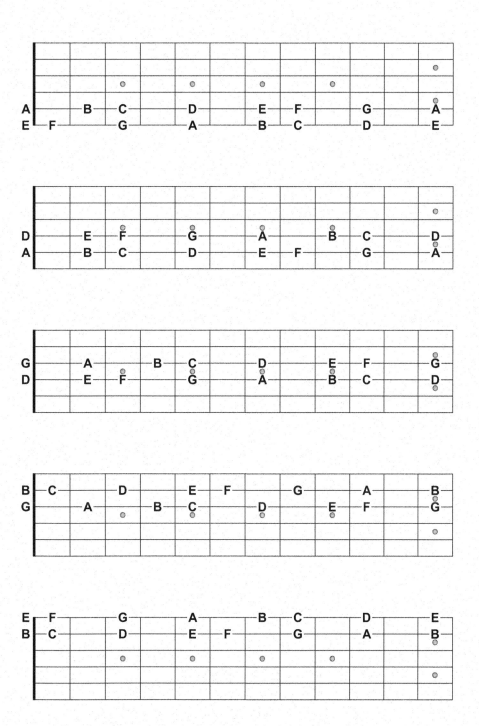

Figure 5.5 *Notes on adjacent strings*

Figure 5.6 splits the fretboard into three sections, each the size of a position. Learn one position at a time.

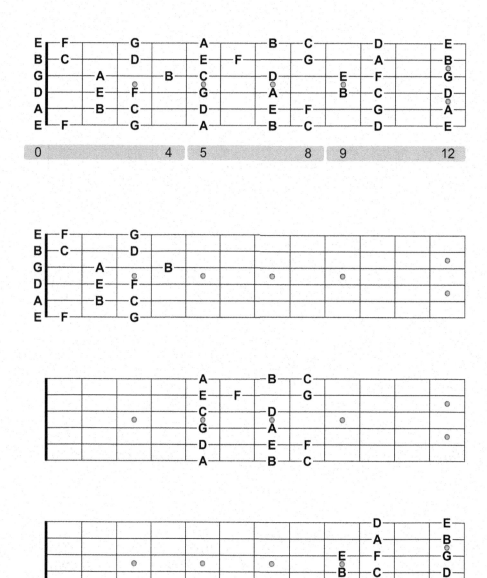

Figure 5.6 *Fretboard sections: frets 0–4, frets 5–8, frets 9–12*

The next set of diagrams takes the open position (frets 0–4) and goes through it one string at a time, displaying every occurrence of those same-pitch notes on the first 12 frets. Corresponding pitches on the music staff are pictured on the side. The last two diagrams complete the picture with the remaining notes on string 1.

Next page:
Figure 5.7 *Frets 0–4 notes within the first 12 frets: same-pitch notes*

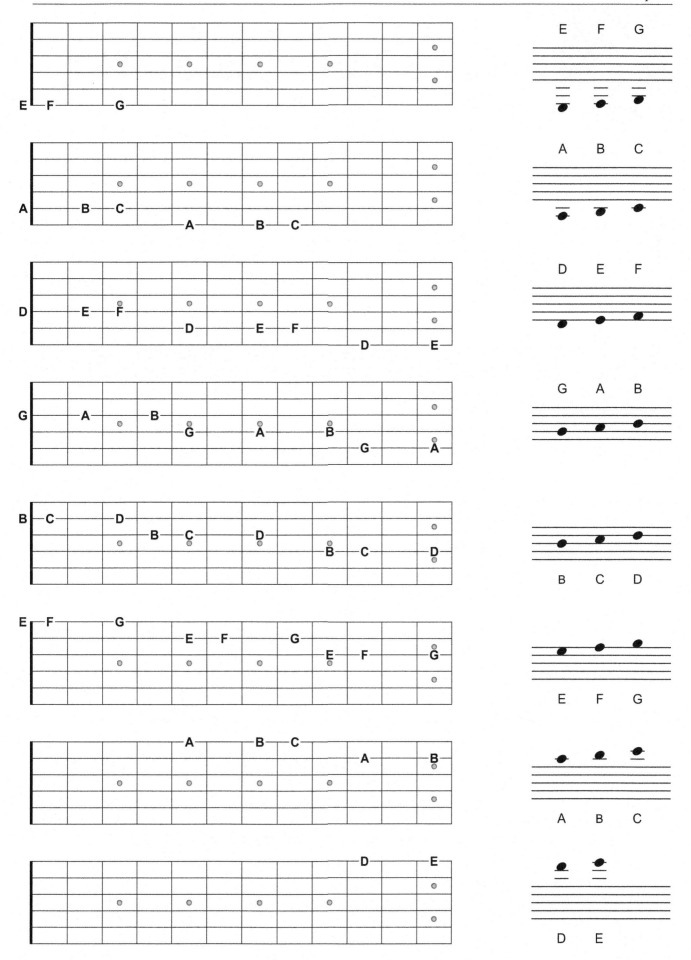

6 FRETBOARD GEOMETRY

In this chapter, we concentrate on the layout of the fretboard and its properties. Some of these properties originate in the construction of the fretboard and others in the tuning of the guitar. They will help you visualise the fretboard in multiple ways, make connections between all the 100+ notes on it, and prepare the ground for navigating it. This chapter is all about smart ways of looking at the fretboard.

6.1 String intervals

▬▬ *Almost-linear layout*

We saw in the Tuning chapter how the fretboard is laid out in standard tuning. The horizontal distance (interval between frets) is a half step and the vertical distance (interval between strings) is 4-4-4-3-4.

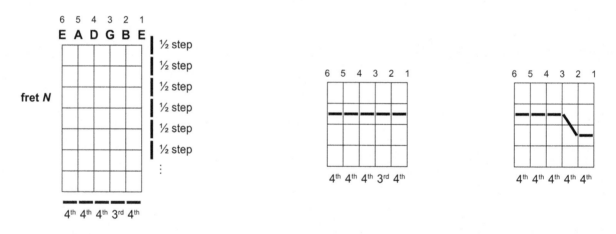

Figure 6.1 *Fretboard's intervallic layout and strings 3–2 half-step shift*

The fretboard's layout would be pretty linear (regularly spaced) if it weren't for the half-step shift between strings 3 & 2. This breaks up the fretboard into two groups: strings 6–3, evenly spaced in 4^{ths}, and strings 2–1, spaced by a 4th too. But the two groups of strings are spaced by a 3rd. Unfortunately, this shift makes learning the fretboard a little more difficult. One way to restore regular spacing is to shift the notes on strings 2–1 down a half step by tuning them up a half step to C and F, resulting in an all-4^{ths} tuning 4-4-4-4-4.

▬▬ *Vertical string intervals*

We are now going to turn our attention to the distance between strings: in other words, we travel from one string to another on the same fret. The tuning tells us the distance between every pair of neighbouring strings.

What about the distance between strings 6 and 4, strings 6 and 3, or strings 1 and 4? We are equipped with the tool to work this out: interval addition. We'll do the first couple of strings together and you can work out the other ones by yourself.

We want to find the interval between string 6 and string 4. From the tuning. we know the intervals separating strings 6–5 (4th) and 5–4 (4th). We also know that in standard tuning, we are ascending in pitch from low to high strings, so we simply add: $4^{th} + 4^{th} = \flat 7^{th}$. This is the interval separating strings 6–4 (i.e., the interval between a note on string 6 and another note on string 4, both on the same fret).

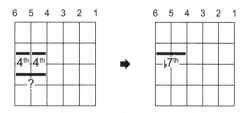

Figure 6.2 *Interval between strings 6 and 4*

Next, we want to find the interval between strings 6 and 3. We just figured out the interval between strings 6–4 and we know from the tuning the interval separating strings 4–3 (4th), so we just add them again: $\flat 7^{th} + 4^{th} = \flat 3^{rd}$. Proceeding the same way with the remaining strings, we figure out the distance between strings 6–2 (5th) and 6–1 (1). Effectively, we are making the note on string 6 the tonic (scale degree 1) and look at the position of each note on the same fret, next string up, with respect to that tonic's major scale.

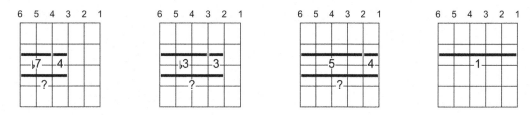

Figure 6.3 *Intervals between string 6 and other strings*

In terms of scale degrees, if the note on string 6 is the tonic 1, then the note on string 5, which is a 4th above it, is the 4th degree of the scale. Likewise, we can write the scale degrees on the other strings, for the tonic 1 located on string 6.

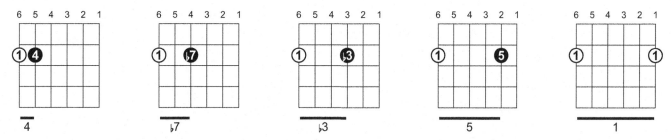

Figure 6.4 *Scale degrees between string 6 and other strings*

Let's pause for a minute and reflect on what we just did. The distance between string 6 and string 5/4 is a simple interval. However, in the additions for the intervals between string 6 and string 3/2/1, we discarded compound information. The real intervals between strings are as shown in Figure 6.5. While this is correct, it is not practical for memorisation, further manipulation, or for bringing out the relationship between scale degree and interval. In fact, to be consistent, even the scale degrees should be changed from ♭3, 5, 1 to ♭10, 12, 15. In musician talk, be it for scales or chords, we usually prefer to refer to the scale degrees between 1 and 7 (except for chord extensions).

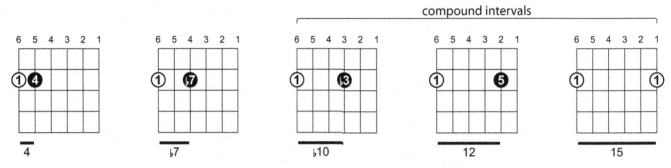

Figure 6.5 *Caution: discarding compound information*

Next, we follow the same procedure and determine string intervals separating string 5 and the other strings.

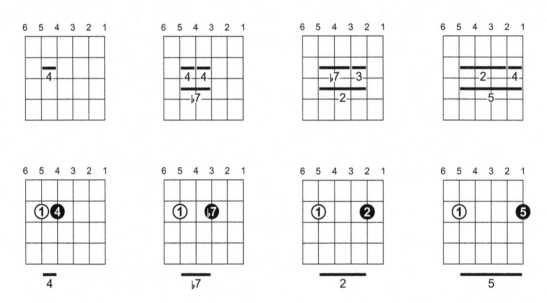

Figure 6.6 *String intervals between string 5 and strings 4–1 (ascending strings)*

For strings 5–6, we must be careful to take into account the fact that the 4th interval separating the two strings is descending—not ascending—because we are viewing the interval from the top note on string 5. From the inversion rule (Intervals chapter), we know that if the tonic is the top note of the interval, the bottom note's scale degree is the inversion of the interval. The inversion of a 4th is a 5th, the scale degree on string 6 is therefore 5. Remember this when you are descending strings!

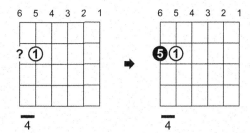

Figure 6.7 *String interval between strings 5 and 6 (descending strings)*

▬▬ *Horizontal string intervals*

The distance between neighbouring frets, on the same string, is a half step and is set by the guitar build. What we want to know is the distance between any two frets, on the same string. This is much easier than the distance between strings. There is no need here to work out intervals between frets or add intervals, we already know them: simply deploy the major scale, starting on the fret of interest (labelled as 1). Just be mindful that ascending, the interval's name is like the scale degree; descending, the interval's name is like the "inversion" of the scale degree (inversion rule). Figure 6.8 shows the scale degrees and the corresponding intervals on string 4; the diagram would be just the same for another string. For simplicity, I only show flat notes on the diagram but sharps (enharmonics) are equally valid.[1] In practice, you only need to know the scale degrees a few frets away from the tonic 1: 4 or 5 frets above and 4 or 5 frets below the reference fret 1 are enough—that's the size of a position on either side.

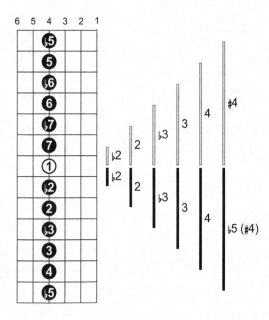

Figure 6.8 *Same-string intervals (and scale degrees)*

You should also become comfortable seeing a few frets above and below another scale degree (relative intervals). For example, can you draw a similar diagram with scale degree 5 at its centre, instead of 1?

---

1. To name intervals and scale degrees properly, the interval between 1 and the ♭5 scale degree above it is ♭5th, not #4th (enharmonic). However, the interval between 1 and the ♭5 scale degree below it is spelt as a #4th.

String intervals chart

Figure 6.9 charts out the fretboard in terms of string intervals and is a summary of the key diagrams you need to **commit to memory**. All these **diagrams are moveable** along the neck so don't worry about note names. Instead of learning all interval shapes on the neck, or going through the process of adding string intervals as we just did, you can memorise these diagrams and use them to work out other intervals (see next section). In context, you may resort to enharmonic notes in these diagrams (e.g., use ♯5 instead of ♭6). Remember that these diagrams are a unified representation of scale degrees and intervals; I colloquially refer to them as string intervals when they are in fact scale degrees (you know the relationship between scale degrees and intervals). Also, don't forget that any compound information is discarded.

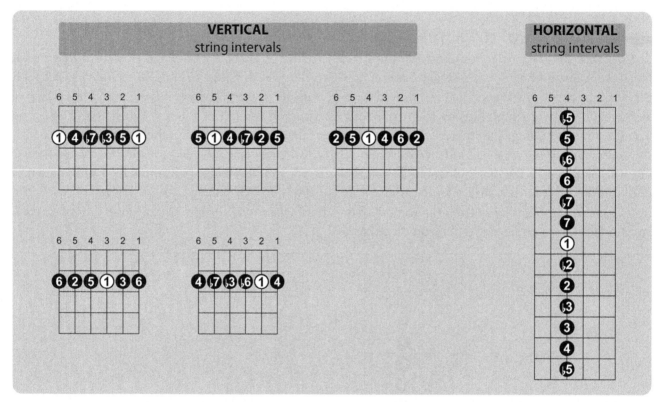

Figure 6.9 *String intervals (scale degrees)*

6.2 Oblique intervals

Oblique intervals (or diagonal intervals) are intervals between notes that are neither on the same string nor on the same fret. How do we find out the interval between two such notes? We use our knowledge of string intervals. Let's go through a few examples.

Figure 6.10 presents an interval with the bottom note on string 5 and the top note on string 1, two frets up. What is this interval? We start by breaking this down into two steps: 1- first going from the bottom note to a *corner note*, the note on the same fret but on string 1; 2- then going from the corner note to the top note on the same string. Knowing vertical string intervals, we immediately recognise the interval and scale degrees for the first step, namely 5th interval (ascending) and scale degrees 1 and 5. On string 1, horizontal string intervals give us the interval of a 2nd (ascending). We need to figure out the scale degree. To do this, we just add the two intervals: $5^{th} + 2^{nd} = 6^{th}$. We can do this methodically as we did in the interval addition chapter, but we could probably see immediately that two frets up from the 5th degree, there is the 6th degree. We now have the complete diagram with interval and scale degrees. **The corner note breaks down an oblique interval into a vertical string interval + a horizontal string interval.**

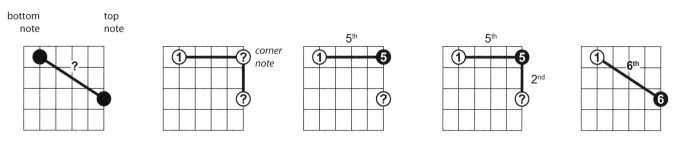

Figure 6.10 *Interval and scale degree derivation with corner note*

If you are not yet comfortable with string intervals but know your tuning well (4-4-4-3-4), you have to break down the first step into moving from one string to the next, adding intervals each time, as we did in Section 6.1. And in the second step, you move fret by fret, adding intervals. It takes longer but follows the same idea.

Another way to get to this result is to use another corner note. In Figure 6.11, starting with the bottom note of the interval and going to the corner note on the same string, we have an interval of a 2nd (ascending), with scale degrees 1 and 2. We then cross the strings on the same fret to the top note, which is a string interval of a 5th. To get to the resulting interval, we add the two intervals $2^{nd} + 5^{th} = 6^{th}$. The name of the top scale degree in an ascending interval is like the interval: 6. The corner note's scale degree 2 is easy to see but the top note's scale degree is harder to see immediately, at this point.

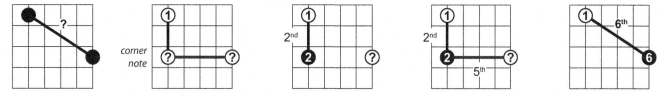

Figure 6.11 *Interval derivation with an alternate corner note*

For the example in Figure 6.12, we follow the same steps outlined in the first example. We pick our corner note and find the first vertical string interval of a 2nd (ascending). But from the corner note to the top note on the same string, the pitch is descending. We must be careful here: the horizontal string interval is a ♭3rd but since it's descending, we are going to append a minus sign to it $-\flat 3^{rd}$. We add (i.e., subtract) the two intervals to get the result: $2^{nd} - \flat 3^{rd} = -\flat 2^{nd}$, a descending ♭2nd. The inversion rule gives us the corresponding scale degree: 7th. In reality, the first leg of the path was not an ascending 2nd but an ascending 9th. This is because we discarded compound information. As a result, the final interval is not $2^{nd} - \flat 3^{rd} = -\flat 2^{nd}$ but $9^{th} - \flat 3^{rd} = 7^{th}$, an ascending 7th. It doesn't matter, for our purposes, we have the scale degree 7 we were looking for. Likewise, in the previous example of Figure 6.11, we actually had a 13th, not a 6th.

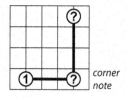 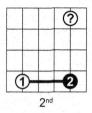 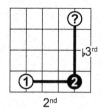 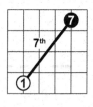

Figure 6.12 *Interval derivation with ascending & descending intermediate steps*

In this last example (Figure 6.13), we are going to approach the problem from a practical perspective. We can work out the interval just as we did before, starting from the bottom note, finding a corner note, and getting to the top note. But it turns out the top note on the high E string is the root of a chord we want to play, so we want to look at this note as 1 and we want to determine how this other note on the G string relates to our root. We "invert" our viewpoint and look at the interval while standing on the top note (becomes the root 1). First, we choose a corner note to go to, ours is on the same fret as the root 1. To get there, we have a descending 6th interval, corresponding to a $\flat$3 scale degree, so we append a minus sign to it (–6th). From that corner note, we move up a fret on the same string. That's a half step. We can choose to name this interval a $\flat$2nd but in our case, we choose to name it as an enharmonic $\sharp$1 (unison). You'll see why soon. To obtain the resulting interval and scale degree, we add the two intervals: $-6^{th} + \sharp1 = \sharp1 - 6^{th}$. Subtracting intervals, we have $1 < 6$, therefore $\sharp1 - 6^{th} = -(\overline{\sharp1} + 6) = -(\flat8 + 6) = -(\flat1 + 6) = -\flat6^{th}$, a descending interval of a $\flat$6th, so the top note is scale degree 3 (inversion rule). Or, we could just recognise on the fly that $\sharp$1 is like an accidental $\sharp$ so that $-6^{th} + \sharp1 = -6^{th} + \sharp = -\flat6^{th}$. Or, we just raise the $\flat$3 a half step and don't bother with formal calculations!

bottom   top
note   note

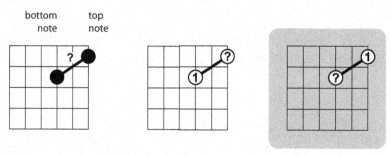

Figure 6.13 *Inverting viewpoints*

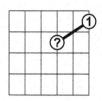 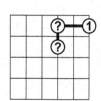 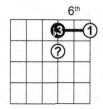 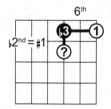 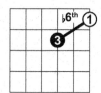

Figure 6.14 *Interval derivation from top to bottom note*

The reason I chose to name the second path a $\sharp$1 instead of its enharmonic a $\flat$2 is that if I had chosen $\flat$2, the final result would have been a descending $\sharp$5 and scale degree $\flat$4. In my chord with its root on the high E string, I prefer to call this chord tone a 3rd rather than a flat 4th!

Instead, we could have derived the result the usual way (middle diagram of Figure 6.13), from bottom to top note ($\flat$6th), and then taken the inversion of this interval to determine the scale degree of the bottom note (3).

INVERTING VIEWPOINTS...IN PRACTICE

We talked about inverting viewpoints and the inversion rule in the Intervals chapter. We just applied this rule a couple of times to determine intervals and scale degrees. It will show up again, sometimes in disguise (see "Stationary shift" in the Fretboard Transforms chapter). This isn't just a trick to work out scale degrees, it has practical value! As you learn to see an interval in terms of scale degrees and toggle viewpoints, it will further open up the fretboard for you. So before we move along, I want to hammer this in with the fretboard in sight. In its basic form, you need to see an interval not only at face value (here a ♭6th) but also as its inversion (switch position of 1 from bottom to top note). This really shines in the context of chords, where you can think up new voicings on the fly, beyond the common chord shapes everybody knows. To stay with our ♭6th interval on which we inverted viewpoints (inverted 3rd = ♭6th), add a 5th on top and you get a major triad in its first inversion. Of course, inverting intervals applies to any interval, whether notes are on the same string or not, on the same fret or not.

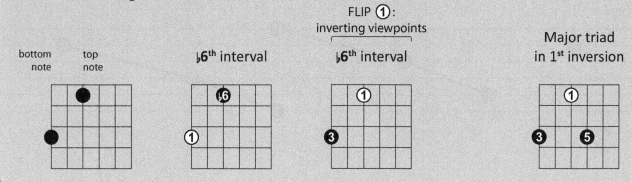

6.3 Basic fretboard properties

We have already come across the following properties but didn't explicitly name them. They can be obtained through various methods: string intervals, note names, tuning, etc.

12-fret repeats

Horizontal spacing being a half step per fret, an octave separates every 12 frets. This is how octaves are laid out on a string. For example, on string 4, D3 is at fret 0, D4 is at fret 12, and if your guitar has 24 frets, D5 will be at fret 24. Another way to say this is that within any 12 frets, a note occurs once and only once, on every string. For example, within frets 3–14, the note D occurs once on each of the six strings.

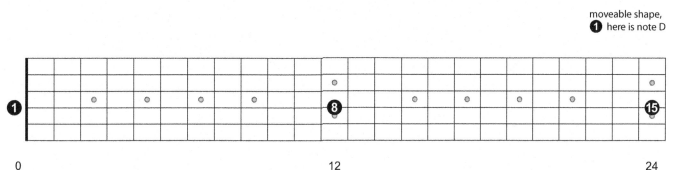

Figure 6.15 *Octaves on a string: note repeats every 12 frets*

Octaves

Octaves on a string are a subset of octaves across all strings. A note appears multiple times on the fretboard, either at the same pitch, or at octaves. The patterns formed by these notes are commonly referred to as *root shapes*.[2] They're like the backbone of the fretboard. Each shape spans 3–4 frets, and fits nicely within a position (i.e., the notes the left hand can cover without lifting the hand off the neck). Learn to see each shape individually. Then learn these shapes together on the neck. Each shape has at least one note in common with its neighbouring shapes. A popular application of these shapes is to find note names on the fretboard: as long as you know the location of one note name, you can find all occurrences of that note name on the fretboard. For example, if you know the note name on string 6, you can find the same note on string 4 (two frets up) and string 2 (another 3 frets up). Likewise, if you know the note name on string 5, you can find the same note on string 3 (two frets up) and string 1 (another 3 frets up). So by learning note names on strings 6 & 5, you can quickly find those notes on the other strings.

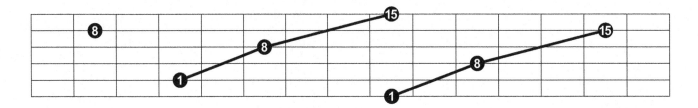

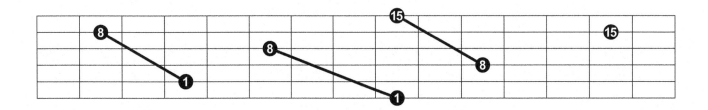

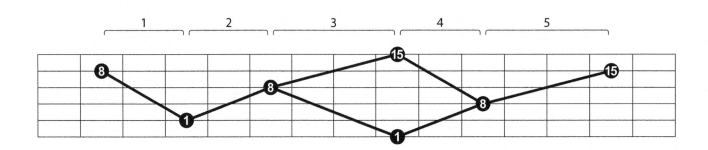

Figure 6.16 *Octaves*

---

2. A more accurate name is *octave shapes* because root implies chords and these shapes apply to anything (chords, scales, etc.), not just chords.

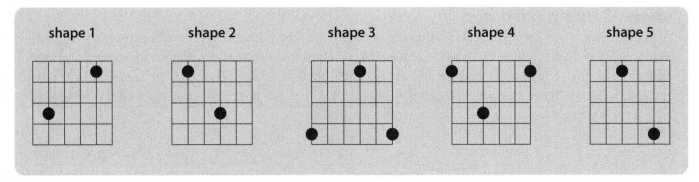

Figure 6.17 *Octaves grouped as root shapes (pictured vertically)*

1, 8, 15 are indicative of relative pitch and labelling depends on the placement of 1. I generally choose to ignore the sign of intervals in this book, to lessen clutter, but be aware of the relative pitch between notes.

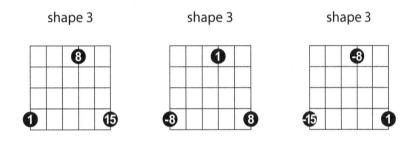

Figure 6.18 *Changing the relative order of pitch*

An equally important view of root shapes is the ability to visualise two neighbouring shapes together. Figure 6.19 shows the neighbouring octaves to a note labelled as 1, for every string. These octaves can be above (8, 15) or below (–8, –15) the root note 1 being considered. The two outer diagrams are the same except for the position of 1.

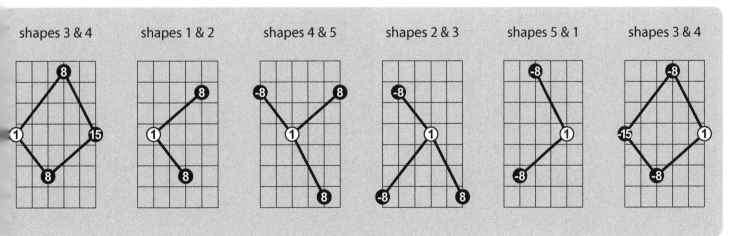

Figure 6.19 *Neighbouring root shapes*

Same-pitch notes

A characteristic property of the guitar is that the same pitch can be played at various places on the fretboard. While this gives you a choice for location and timbre, it also means you must make decisions on fingerings and where to play a note. For comparison, on the piano, there is no such choice: there is only one key for each pitch. In the figure, the note E4 is chosen because it is the only note that appears on all six strings (on a 24-fret guitar) but the entire pattern is moveable.

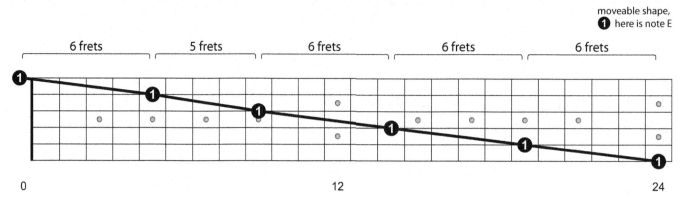

Figure 6.20 *Same-pitch notes*

Low/high E string: more of the "same"

The notes on the high E string (string 1) are the same as the notes on the low E string (string 6), only two octaves above. This is a simple but remarkable property. An all-4^{ths} tuning, for example, doesn't exhibit this characteristic. An immediate benefit is that when you learn the notes on string 6, you've also learnt the notes on string 1. But there's more than meets the eye—we'll explore this property shortly.

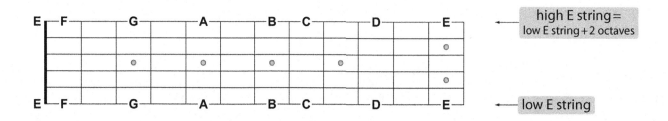

Figure 6.21 *Low & high E strings*

FRETBOARD TRANSFORMS

A fretboard transform takes a group of notes and subjects them to a transformation. One such transform is transposition. In this chapter, we look at ways to manipulate our knowledge of fretboard geometry—string intervals in particular—in order to reuse or repurpose the shapes we already know. Let's create new from old material, shall we?

7.1 Transposition

Definition

Transposition is the operation of rewriting or playing music in another key or tonality than it was originally written in. When transposing, pitch and note names change but relative intervals (and scale degrees) are preserved: every note is shifted up or down by the same interval. On guitar, we transpose all the time, but not necessarily with the goal of changing keys. We often transpose small fragments of music such as a chord, a scale, a lick, with the goal of reusing a shape or a fingering pattern we are familiar with (moveable shapes). So instead of changing keys of a tune from G major to A major, we might simply want to use the G major chord shape we know to play an A major chord with the same shape, no matter what key we're in. We can do this easily thanks to the layout of the instrument.

A special case of transposition is when all the notes shift in pitch by one or several octaves (*N* octaves higher or lower). The resulting key is still the original key. For example, shifting all the notes from the key of A one octave higher keeps the tune in the key of A. Another situation is where in a piece of music, some notes shift by an interval X while others shift by an interval X ± octave(s). This is not transposition per se. However, in the context of chords, it results in inversions, and leaves the chord progression intact. That can be viewed as transposing the harmony (with revoicing).

> **NOTE** On guitar, we tend to associate transposing with changing keys while keeping the same shapes. It is not necessarily so. While transposing assists in reusing shapes in all 12 keys, given the redundant/non-linear layout of the guitar, transposing can also completely reshuffle shapes or patterns (and consequently fingerings).

Notation shift

We discussed the guitar as a *transposing instrument* in the Tuning chapter. Guitar notation is written one octave above actual pitch (i.e., the guitar sounds one octave lower than notation). In that sense, transposition takes place on the notation staff rather than on the fretboard. In this section, we deal with transforms on the fretboard.

▬▬ *Horizontal shift*

This is the most common and straightforward way to transpose. If we take a shape and move it by any number of frets (*N* frets), we have transposed that shape by as many semitones (*N* semitones). We must be careful to move the entire shape, including any open string notes. In practice, when transposing, we hang all the notes in the shape off a particular note, usually the root of a chord or the tonic of a scale. We use that note as an *anchor*. In Figure 7.1, a stock G major barre chord is moved up a major 2nd to form an A major chord: same shape, just two frets up. In Figure 7.2, an open Dmin chord is moved up a minor 3rd (three frets up) to form an Fmin chord. The middle diagram is wrong because it has left behind the open D note on the D string. To transpose correctly, that open D note must also shift up three frets to F.

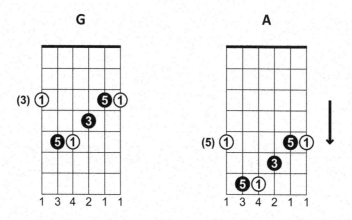

Figure 7.1 *Shifting a G major chord shape to A major, 2 frets up*

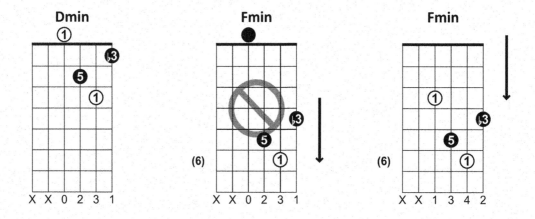

Figure 7.2 *Shifting a D minor open chord to F minor, 3 frets up*

A shape that can undergo a horizontal shift without any change in fingering is a *moveable shape*. Such shape contains no open strings. In Figure 7.1, the G chord is a moveable shape (fingering stays the same as the shape shifts along the fretboard). In Figure 7.2, the Dmin chord includes an open string and isn't a moveable shape, but the last Fmin shape is moveable (the same fingering can be reused).

Horizontal shift is the primary reason for a capo and sometimes for a change in tuning, but that's static transposition (it's done once and for all, until the capo is moved to a new position or the guitar is retuned). Here, we transpose dynamically with our fingers!

Vertical shift

A vertical shift is typically a shift in 4^{ths}. For every 4th, the shape simply shifts up or down by one string. The only catch is that any note crossing strings 3 to 2 (or 2 to 3) must also scoot up one fret (down one fret) according to the diagram in Figure 7.3-1. The example in the figure shows how an A major chord shifts up one string to become a D minor chord. All the notes in the chord undergo a 4th shift, except for the top note which is raised by a 3rd. To restore an even shift of a 4th for all the notes in the chord, the note crossing strings 3 to 2 must move up one fret to fret 7. This way, the chord becomes D major.

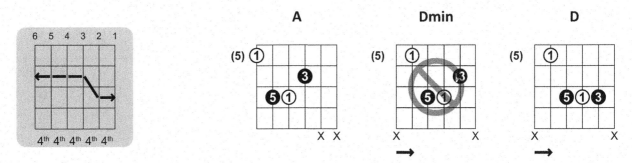

Figure 7.3 *1- vertical shift pattern in 4^{ths}; 2- shifting an A major chord up a 4th to D major*

Of course, navigating the fretboard isn't just made of horizontal shifts and vertical shifts, it's a combination. You can break down this combination into elementary horizontal and vertical shifts but more often than not, the thought process is different (see the chapter on anchoring).

7.2 Other transforms

Transposition shifts a group of notes, all by the same interval. In this section, we investigate other transforms that also change the location or the order of notes.

Stationary shift

The title sounds contradictory. How can you move while standing still? Transposition is about changing pitch and preserving scale degrees. What if instead, we preserved pitch but reassigned scale degrees? Can we emulate anything useful? Yes, by changing the reference point (tonic 1), we change our viewpoint/emphasis and see the same notes in a new light. We touched on this topic for intervals, in the context of inverting viewpoints. We can expand on this concept. In the following examples, changing our viewpoint brings about new meaning to the notes on the fretboard. Figure 7.4 starts with a minor triad with the root on string 3 and shows what becomes of the same notes if another note plays the role of the root 1.

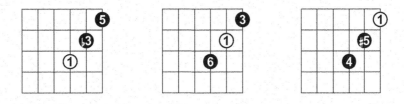

Figure 7.4 *Reassigning root position within triad*

Figure 7.5 shows two pairs of chord homonyms. The first chord is a C6 with its root on the low E string. If we keep the same notes but think of the note on the D string as the root, we have a whole new arrangement of scale degrees within the chord (pitch and interval remain unchanged). It turns out this new chord is Amin7 in its first inversion (♭3 in the bass). The second pair of chords puts a twist on this approach. The chord is a half-diminished E chord with the root on the A string. Now picture an imaginary root for this shape on the low E string, how would that affect the intervallic relationships between the other chord tones and the root? They would relabel as a C9 chord! So you can think of Emin7(♭5) as a C9 chord, omitting the root (which can be taken care of by another instrument like the bass guitar).

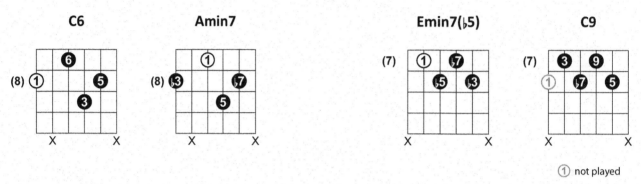

Figure 7.5 *Chord homonyms*

We can apply this type of thinking to scales too. Figure 7.6 presents a D Lydian scale 1--2--3--♯4-5--6--7-8 (the 7ᵗʰ degree is not shown), with its tonic D on the A string, fret 5. If we change our viewpoint and make the note A the tonic, the D Lydian scale is simply a fragment of the A major scale. This is the principle behind modes of a scale: a different viewpoint of the same notes brings about new colour! Even though the two scales are related (A major is the parent scale of D Lydian), we view them on the fretboard as two separate and unrelated entities, each with its tonic and characteristic scale degrees. To do this, we must be able to rewire our thinking and lay out the D Lydian scale degrees on the fretboard (e.g., recognise that D is on string 5, fret 5 and is scale degree 1, and not think of it as scale degree 4 of the pattern for A major).

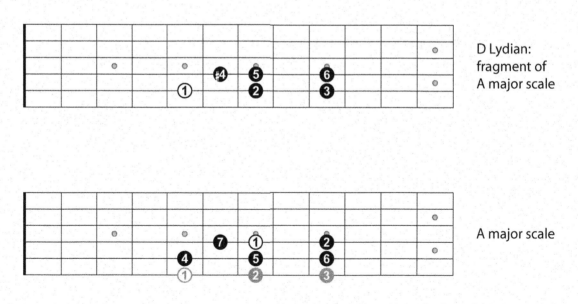

Figure 7.6 *Mode of a scale*

Stationary shift is a product of the mind's eye (notes are unchanged) and applies to any instrument, not just guitar. This kind of mental gymnastics—adapting to context—requires you to rewire your vision of the fretboard, based on your knowledge of intervals (e.g., know how a ♭3rd looks like between strings 3 and 2) and your knowledge of music theory (e.g., know the formula for the minor scale 1--2-♭3--4--5-♭6--♭7--8).

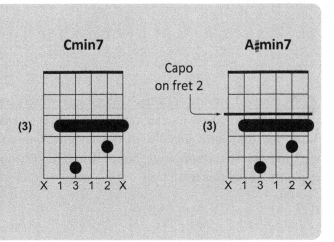

NOTE The capo is chiefly associated with tuning and key changes. In that sense, it implements horizontal shift (transposition). Even so, the capo does not affect notes, scale degrees, or pitch. The only change the capo brings is to transform our view of the notes. In the example to the right, our fingers form a Cmin7 chord grip in 3rd position. Then we place a full capo on fret 2 and we have an A♯min7 chord. Yet, nothing has changed, only our view of the notes and of the fretboard has changed. We now think of fret 2 as being the nut. So a capo can also be a vector for a different kind of stationary shift, where pitch and scale degrees are preserved but the notes are "changed"!

▬▬ *Hybrid shift*

Hybrid shift is a catchall term I am using for transforms that combine two or more uneven shifts. For example, some scale degrees would shift by a 3rd while others would shift by a 5th. Under this banner, I also include string shifts, something that is at the heart of tunings. For example, a drop-D tuning shifts all notes on string 6 up two frets but leaves other strings untouched (compared to standard tuning); a tuning in 4ths shifts the notes on the top two strings down one fret; DADGAD tuning shifts all notes on strings 6 & 2–1 up two frets.

One special type of hybrid shift is to shift one or more notes in octaves while other notes stand still. This includes the concepts of octave displacement, interval inversion, and *chord inversion*. A chord inversion is a chord where one or more chord tones are raised/dropped one or more octaves, resulting in the chord's root no longer being the lowest sounding note in the stack (i.e., root no longer in the bass).

The example in Figure 7.7 shows a major triad on the top three strings, in its second inversion (5th in the bass). By dropping the 3rd an octave, we get the same major triad on strings 4–2, in its first inversion (3rd in the bass). To do this, we can think octaves pattern applied to the 3rd (root shape 4). But it can be more fitting to think string intervals, referenced back to the root 1.

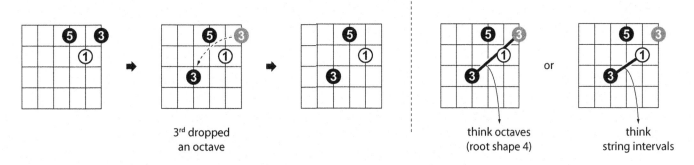

Figure 7.7 *3rd dropped an octave: 1- think octaves; 2- think string intervals*

8 FRETBOARD MIRROR

Standard tuning features a seemingly unremarkable property: the 6th string and the 1st string are both tuned to E. The mirroring concept exploits this property to extend the fretboard…beyond the fretboard, literally. In this chapter, we look at some applications of mirroring such as interval recognition and extensions of transposition. Mirroring is a simple concept but perhaps you had never looked at the fretboard this way!

8.1 Mirroring

Low E = high E

In the Fretboard Geometry chapter, we singled out a property resulting from the guitar's tuning, which is that the 6th string (low E) and the 1st string (high E) are both tuned to the note E. The low E is two octaves below the high E string. All the notes/frets on these strings share the same name. Most of us acknowledge this as a byproduct of standard tuning with convenient consequences: for instance, by memorising the notes on string 6, we automatically learn the notes on string 1, or, the high E string can double up the low E string in chords. And we leave it at that. But we can take it further!

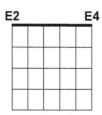

Figure 8.1 *Low E2 and high E4 strings*

NOTE   In standard tuning, the 6th string and the 1st string are tuned to the same note. Many a tuning (like a tuning in 4ths) doesn't share this property with standard tuning but some tunings do (like DADGAD).

You may recall from the Intervals chapter that we value the simple interval a little more than the compound interval. The reason being that the simple interval is enough to carry the harmonic function of a note. So let's put aside the two-octave difference that separates the low E string and the high E string and consider that they are virtually the "same" string (in a functional sense). For every note on string 1, I can find the "same" note on the same fret on string 6 (Figure 8.2). This goes both ways: for every note on string 6, I can find the "same" note on the same fret on string 1. These two strings *mirror* one another and the fretboard effectively folds onto itself.

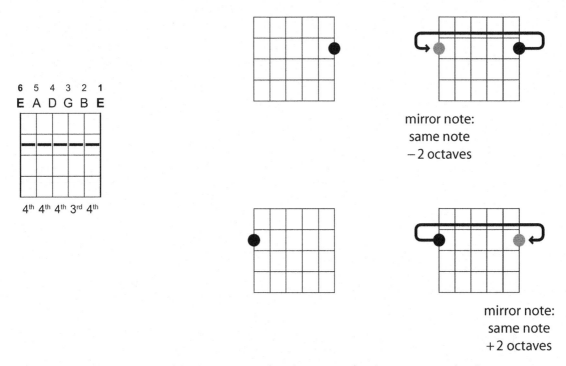

Figure 8.2 *Low E and high E strings play the same role: they mirror each other*

The tuning circle

Let's say we are walking across the strings, along the same fret, going up towards string 1. If we start our walk on the D string (4), then we go on to the G string (3), then the B string (2), and last we reach the high E string (1). Once we're on string 1, thanks to mirroring, we are virtually taken back to string 6, on that same fret, and we can resume our walk going up the strings: 5, 4, 3, etc. There is no stopping (picture a hamster tirelessly running in a wheel). We can therefore think of standard tuning as a revolving tuning, starting over at E, and defining a *tuning circle*. Remember: we ignore the two-octave gap between the low and the high E strings. Of course, we could have walked in the opposite direction too, towards the low E string.

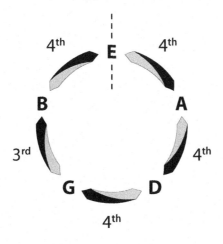

Figure 8.3 *The tuning circle (EADGBE or 4-4-4-3-4)*

Another way to look at this walk is that once we reach the high E string, we can add another (virtual) string to the guitar, an A string, then add yet another string, a D string, then a G string, etc. By carefully choosing a string to add, we pave our way to prolong the walk. Picture this idea as a virtual fretboard sitting right next to the high E string, and another right next to the low E string (for a walk towards the low E string). Mirroring replicates the fretboard: each mirror fretboard folds back onto the real fretboard, mapping string for string (high E maps to low E, added A string maps to string 5, added D string to string 4, etc.).

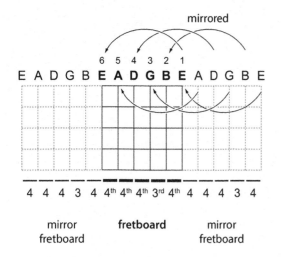
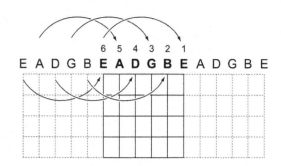

Figure 8.4 *Mirror fretboards*

8.2 Applications

What can you do with this mirroring concept? Mirroring can help you see things that might otherwise take longer to recognise or that you might miss altogether. Gradually incorporate this concept into your fretboard toolbox. It adds a dimension to your visualising of the fretboard and extends your ability to manoeuvre around the neck. Here are two practical use cases where mirroring can speed up your thinking.

▬▬▬ *Interval recognition*

Let's say you are faced with the interval separating the two notes on strings 5 and 1 (Figure 8.5) and that you don't recognise it immediately because you are still learning intervals on the fretboard. To find out what this interval is, we use interval addition, ascending the strings (as we did in the Fretboard Geometry chapter). Adding vertical string intervals together, we have: $4 + 4 + 3 + 4 = \flat7 + 3 + 4 = 2 + 4 = 5$ (adding two intervals at a time). This gives us the result: an interval of a 5th (simple interval, we discard compounds as usual) and the 5th degree of the scale on string 1. That was not difficult but required several additions. There is a shorter way: enter mirroring. Instead of walking up the strings, why not go the other way and descend from string 5 towards string 6? It's just one string interval and doesn't even require an addition! We know that the note on string 6 is the mirror of the note on string 1—the note we're looking for—so once we know the interval between 1 and the note on the same fret on string 6, we effectively know the interval with the note on string 1. We remember that this interval is a 4th (we know this from the tuning). But since we are descending strings in pitch, we must use the inversion rule to give us the scale degree: 5th on string 6. This is the same note on string 1; we have our result.

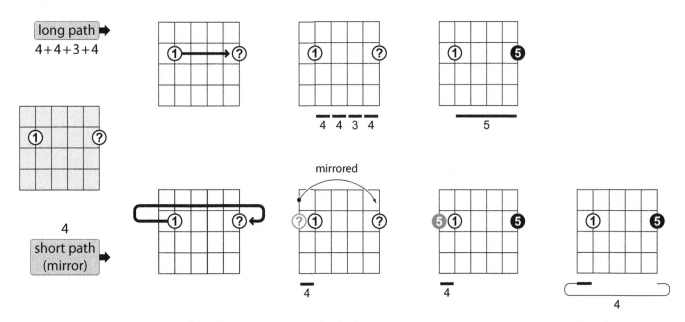

Figure 8.5 *Identifying intervals with mirroring: long path & short path*

Figure 8.6 shows another example where we want to identify the interval separating strings 5 and 2. The conventional way is to ascend strings, that's three intervals to add: $4 + 4 + 3 = \flat7 + 3 = 2$. A shorter way is again to descend strings. First, we walk down from string 5 to string 6 (4th). That note is mirrored on string 1. From string 1, we resume our walk and descend towards string 2 (4th). We only need to add two intervals: $4 + 4 = \flat7$. The inversion rule gives us the scale degree on string 2: 2. You don't need to work out the scale degree of the note on string 6, I just put it on the diagram as an indication.

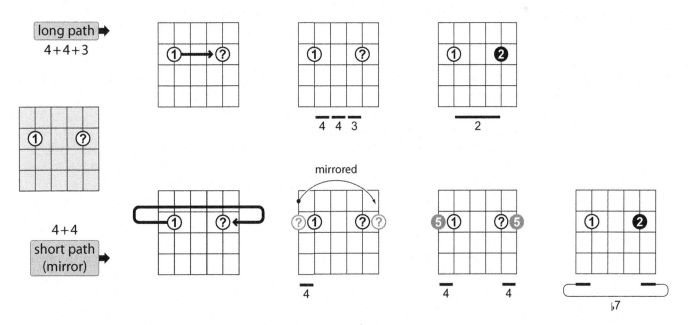

Figure 8.6 *Long & short paths*

Figure 8.7 is an example where mirroring is not the shortest way. Also, we are looking at the interval standing on the top note here. The conventional way is to descend strings and yields the shortest path to the result with two interval additions only: $3 + 4 = 6$. Because we descended strings, we must use the inversion rule to give us the scale degree on string 4: ♭3 (inversion of a 6th). The other way, using mirroring, ascends string 2 to 1. The note on string 1 is mirrored on string 6, and we resume our walk, ascending string 6 to 5, then 5 to 4. That's a total of three interval additions: $4 + 4 + 4 = ♭7 + 4 = ♭3$, and is longer than the conventional way.

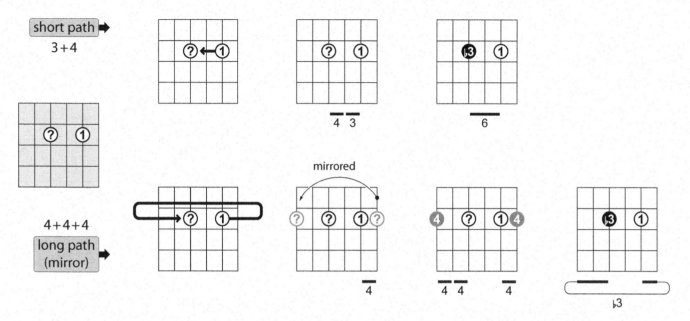

Figure 8.7 *Mirroring is not always the shortest path*

Of course, mirroring can be used with oblique intervals too: use it for the vertical component of the oblique interval. So to recap, when you are faced with an unknown interval, there is always a **short path** and a **long path** to identifying the interval. Use your judgement to decide which is the shortest: walking on the fretboard or wrapping around the neck with mirroring. For more practice, instead of the conventional method, use mirroring to find other vertical string intervals, for example with 1 on string 3 (answers in Figure 6.9).

> **NOTE**   You may wonder why in the previous examples, there is one interval value when ascending and another value (its inversion) when descending strings. Remember that the interval is always referenced back to the bottom note. The actual interval between the two notes is that given when we "walk up the strings" from bottom to top note and is a 5th. So when we "walk down the strings" in Figure 8.5, the short path interval of a 4th is purely for calculation purposes and we ignore the two-octave jump separating strings 6 and 1. Taking the two-octave jump of a 15th into account results in $-4^{th} + 15^{th} = 12^{th}$ which is a 5th simple interval, and we land on our feet. Having said that, what we are really after is the scale degree, not the interval.

▬▬▬ *Hybrid shift / transposition*

Transposing in 4^{ths} is a natural transform on the guitar since it can be conveniently performed through a vertical string shift. The only glitch to mind is the 3rd between strings 3–2. Unfortunately, this vertical shift can only go as far as the edge of the fretboard. But we kind of want it to go on! After all, the circle of 5^{ths} (or 4^{ths}) is a circle that goes on and on. With mirroring coming to the rescue, this shift can be extended beyond the fretboard. Figure 8.8 calls the mirror fretboards for duty and shows the path that a note would take across the strings as it shifts a 4th, up or down. But because each string of the mirror fretboards folds back onto the same string on the real fretboard, the transposition of a 4th becomes a hybrid shift: notes on the fretboard shift by a 4th while the mirrored notes, when folding back, shift by a $4^{th} \pm 2$ octaves.

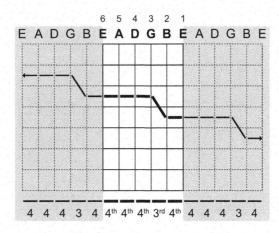

Figure 8.8 *Transposing in 4ᵗʰˢ: ascending or descending*

The trajectory described by shifting in 4ᵗʰˢ + mirroring can be thought of as a coil spring wrapping around the neck.

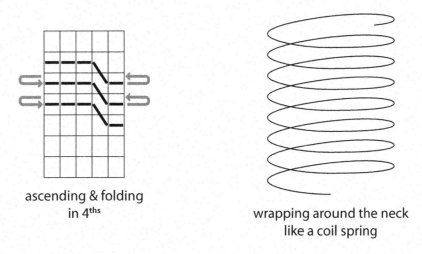

ascending & folding
in 4ᵗʰˢ

wrapping around the neck
like a coil spring

Figure 8.9 *Hybrid shift in 4ᵗʰˢ: wrapping around the neck*

This works great with chords and puts a lot of inversions at our fingertips, for free. Let's go through a couple of examples to see this process at work. In the first example, we take a closed-form[1] major triad and shift it up a 4ᵗʰ at every iteration. To understand what is going on, the left column displays the chord tones as they spill over onto the virtual fretboard above the high E string, the right column displays what this looks like on the real fretboard, with mirroring. The chord goes through several transpositions and inversions and after five iterations, the initial triad shape is obtained again, up a half step (up a fret). When the note is mirrored, either or both notes can be played. The second example is the same exercise with a minor triad, descending a 4ᵗʰ at every iteration.

To skip ahead to the CAGED chapter, do this exercise over again starting with one CAGED shape. What do you get? You'll find that you get all five CAGED shapes in the process.

---

1. Closed-form: the chord tones are on adjacent strings. Open-form: the chord tones skip some strings.

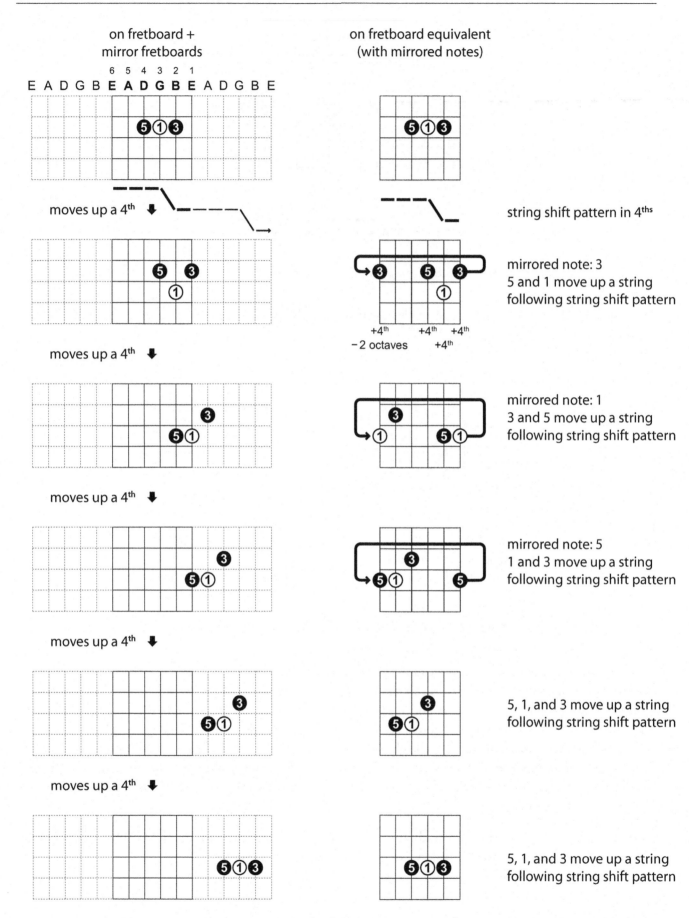

Figure 8.10 *Hybrid shift in ascending 4ᵗʰˢ*

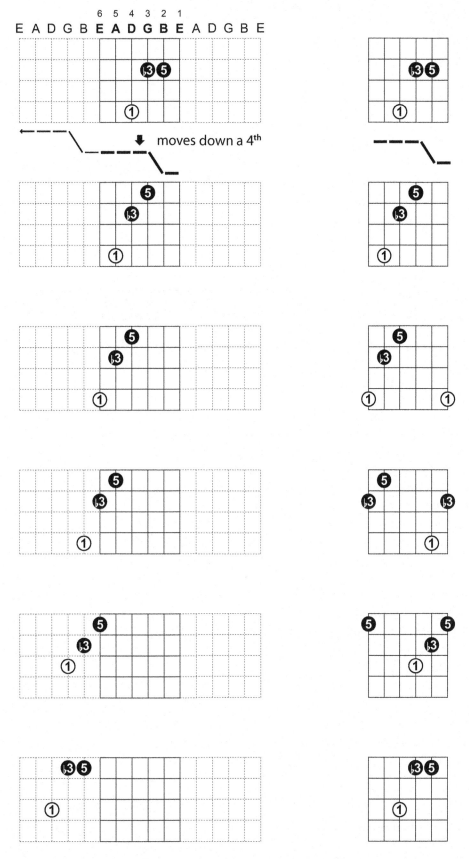

Figure 8.11 *Hybrid shift in descending 4ths*

9   ANCHORING

Why learn all this information about the fretboard and its layout? All this fretboard knowledge has one and only goal: fretboard navigation. This chapter introduces anchoring, a dynamic method of charting a small area of the fretboard to fit what you're about to play and to go from point A to point B, with as little memorisation and recollection effort as possible.

9.1   Fretboard map hallmarks

Before we begin, let's take inventory of what we expect from any method of mapping the fretboard. What would be the characteristics of an ideal system for partitioning the fretboard? We are looking for a map that will allow us to navigate the fretboard freely.

Most of the time, we only play in a small area of the fretboard for a period of time. This timeframe can range from a couple of beats, one bar, to several bars or an entire tune. Within that timeframe, we don't necessarily need to see the entire fretboard or even a full position. All we need to see is the playing area.

We want to understand what the fretboard map contains in this area. Ideally, there should be bridges between the information we see on the fretboard and music/theory. If the map only says where to put our fingers (paint-by-numbers guitar playing), then we know those frets are safe, even though we don't really know what they mean. We shall be damned if we ever venture onto all the other frets where we aren't allowed to put our fingers: mysterious, murky, and possibly dangerous places!

Our fretboard map must adapt to the situation, it must be reconfigurable! If we play in the key of A major, we want the notes of A major to light up. If we play D Mixolydian, we want to see the notes of that mode. If we play an Emin7 chord, we want those chord tones to pop out. We don't want to see much else. Also, when we play A Dorian, we want to think A Dorian and not relate it to something else like the fingerings for its parent scale G major.

We want to memorise less but memorise smarter. We don't want to memorise five G major scale patterns and fingerings over the entire neck, and then another five patterns for G minor scale. If we were given a few signposts on the fretboard, with our knowledge of music theory and fretboard geometry under our belt, we'd quickly connect the dots and figure out G minor from G major.

To summarise our shopping list, we want a map that is:	▪ SMALL/COMPACT ▪ MEANINGFUL ▪ RECONFIGURABLE/REUSABLE ▪ NIMBLE

9.2 The anchoring principle

Anchoring crystallises the requirements we set for our fretboard map. To be successful with this method, you must have a good knowledge of note names on the entire fretboard, string intervals, chord and scale formulas.

As an ongoing assignment to exercise your mind and become familiar with the anchoring principle, take chords and scales you already know and put them through the step-by-step process I am about to describe. Start small with simple chords and one-octave scales.

▬▬▬ *Viewing area*

First, we scope out our playing area and reduce our field of vision to what we need: the note pool we're about or likely to play from, within a certain period of time. That's not the entire fretboard! An area 3–4 strings tall × 5–6 frets wide is all we're likely to need within that timeframe, give or take (≈ the size of a position).

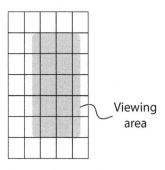

Figure 9.1 *Viewing area (shown is 3 strings × 5 frets)*

There is no cut-and-dry recipe for defining the *viewing area* (or playing area). It depends on the material that is about to be played: scale, chord, arpeggio, fragments thereof, etc. So this area can be made slightly bigger or smaller to fit the occasion. But if it's 10 frets long, you must think differently and break it up. The viewing area doesn't have to be rectangular, it can form-fit the notes to play, but it's easier to picture a rectangle.

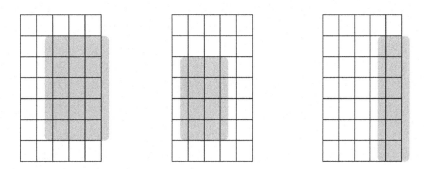

Figure 9.2 *Different sizes of viewing area*

Though we outline the viewing area on the diagrams to set some boundaries, it's something you don't need to think about or visualise on the fretboard. Its purpose is to help you focus your attention on the notes you are about to play and put blinders on the remainder of the neck.

▬▬ *Anchor*

In music, we think in terms of key centre, or tonic for a scale, or root for a chord/arpeggio. We always have a reference point to go by. This reference point can last an entire piece, a couple of bars, or change multiple times within a bar. For example, if we're in the key of A, we think A as our reference, if we want to play D Dorian, we think D as our reference, if we want to play a Gmin7(♭5) chord, we think G as our reference. This reference is our *anchor* (or primary anchor). That's home, at least until we move to a new home!

Our fretboard map requirements included "meaningful" and "reusable." Intervals or scale degrees are a perfect fit. They define the musical devices we use via formulas (e.g., 1–♭3–5 minor triad formula) and are reusable (the minor triad formula is the same for all 12 possible roots). They're quick to recall too.

So within our viewing area for the time being, let's plant our primary anchor, labelled 1. 1 is the scale degree of our reference.[1] All writings will be in terms of scale degrees referred back to our reference 1.

If you are thinking D Dorian, then you must know that behind 1 is the note D. Therefore, to place 1 on the fretboard, you must know the note names on the fretboard.

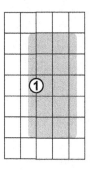

Figure 9.3 *Anchor 1 within the viewing area*

The placement of this anchor can be anywhere within the viewing area but shouldn't be too off-centre. If you consider root shapes, there is a replica of the anchor nearby—within 3 frets and 3 strings—and the replica may be a better choice. By "better," I mean more central to the note pool, more suitable for fingering, or more in connection with the notes that precede or follow. For example, assume I select anchor 1 on string 2, fret 10 and my hand position (defined by the index finger) happens to be on fret 6 or 7. That means anchor 1 is played by the pinkie. It might be okay or I might look for another instance of 1 nearer fret 7 (root shape: there is a replica on string 4, fret 7).

That being said, the anchor is not necessarily played and can serve as a visual aid only. For instance, you can play D Dorian, anchor to D, but never play the note D.

---

1. Nothing prevents you from anchoring to another note than scale degree 1, if you wish. But scale degree 1 makes the most sense for tying what you see on the fretboard with the music (or music theory). For example, you could choose your primary anchor as scale degree 6 in a major scale (perhaps of relevance if you modulate between relative major/minor keys). Still, that would be an odd choice!

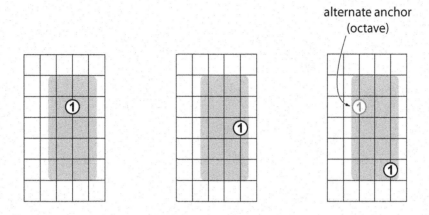

Figure 9.4 *Anchor placement to suit the occasion*

▬▬ *Vertical scope*

Within the viewing area, let's roll out vertical string intervals on the same fret as anchor 1. Those are secondary anchors (here, scale degrees 4 and 6). Note that an anchor is placed on every string of the viewing area.

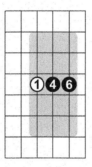

Figure 9.5 *Primary anchor (1) and secondary anchors (4 and 6)*

In our case, the anchor 1 is on string 4. Depending on which string 1 is on, string intervals will be different.

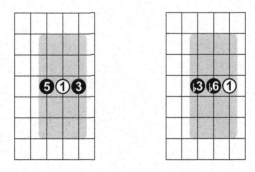

Figure 9.6 *Anchor 1 location and string intervals*

▄▄▄ *Horizontal scope*

It is fairly easy to roll out scale degrees on the same string as our primary anchor, on either side of it. Recall horizontal string intervals. We just need to see 4–5 frets on either side, at most.

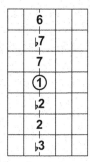

Figure 9.7 *Horizontal string intervals around anchor 1*

From now on, we assume we'll be playing anchors 1 4 6 so we roll out notes around these anchors in the viewing area. We can simplify this diagram and remove some of the clutter by only visualising natural notes. In fact, we can only visualise what we need: if we are thinking minor, we only visualise 1--2-♭3--4--5-♭6--♭7--8. If we want to play a major triad arpeggio 1–3–5, we can narrow down our view to those notes only. In both cases, the anchor 6 is not part of the note pool so we can push it to the background of what we see.[2]

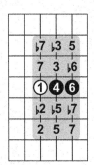 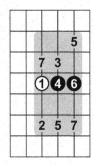 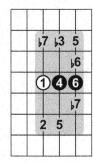

Figure 9.8 *Simplifying and adapting string intervals to context*

This is the working picture we need in front of us during this timeframe. We don't need to see beyond that on other frets or strings. We didn't use any memorised scale pattern or fingering shape (e.g., form 3 of 3-note-per-string minor scale pattern), just string intervals, the knowledge of the note name behind 1, and a formula (here it's a scale but it could be a chord formula). Then, we build our map, on the fly. Quite nimble, isn't it?

An anchor is placed on every string, this pretty much scopes out the viewing area. From there, we roll out horizontal string intervals as needed. In other words, we place a signpost on every string and that is enough to chart out the entire viewing area. The philosophy behind anchoring is to light up only the notes that are needed and to put the lights out when they're no longer needed, as we go!

---

2. The note pool is driven by what will be played and a formula. The primary anchor 1 is the fundamental in the formula. But the choice of secondary anchors is not necessarily part of the note pool. Here, the note pool is the minor scale: anchor 4 is within the minor scale but anchor 6 is not. Anchors are landmarks to help us know where we are, they don't have to be part of our itinerary.

▬▬ *Choosing anchors: clusters*

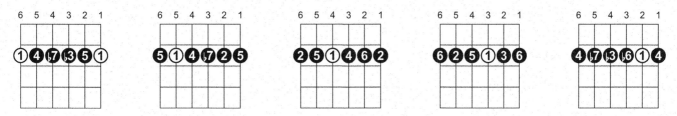

Figure 9.9 *Default anchors (vertical string intervals)*

The default anchors for anchoring are vertical string intervals. They are a convenient and logical choice because they are all lined up on one fret, putting the anchor on each string on an equal footing with the next one. But the choice of anchors is personal and over time, you may find that you gravitate more towards different sets or *clusters of anchors*. For chords, vertical string intervals are usually a great choice of anchors. Chords have one note at most on each string and don't spread much horizontally so a vertical anchor is a close signpost. Scales and arpeggios can spread further out, even within a position, so ad hoc anchors can sometimes be more helpful.

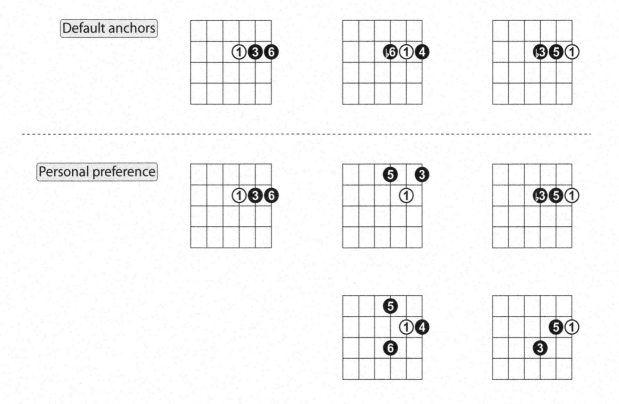

Figure 9.10 *Default and personal choices of anchors for 1 on strings 3–1*

I'll give you a couple of personal examples of how I see areas of the fretboard. Most of the time, I tend to picture three adjacent strings at once (my viewing area), occasionally four strings. Let's take the top three strings for instance. First of all, I make a point of being able to place 1 on any of the three strings and see secondary anchors on the remaining strings with equal ease. When 1 is on string 3, I like to see 1–3–6 (the default view). When 1 is on string 2, I can see ♭6–1–4 but prefer 5–1–3 or 5–6–1–4! Because I like to grab the ♭7 on string 3, I felt the need for an extra signpost (6) on that string. When 1 is on string 1, I see anchors ♭3–5–1 (default view) or 3–5–1. These are practical because they outline a minor or major triad, something that comes into play often. On the other strings, I tend to follow the default view. At all times, I try to keep in the back of my head the location of the octave within the position (e.g., 1 on string 5 two frets up for 1 on string 2) because it is quite possible that my playing area gradually shifts to lower strings within the position.

Figure 9.11 presents an arpeggio and a chord example. The notes to be played are shown on the left and two options for anchor selection are shown on the right. You'll notice that they include replicas of the anchor 1 and cover a large number of strings (5 and 6 strings).

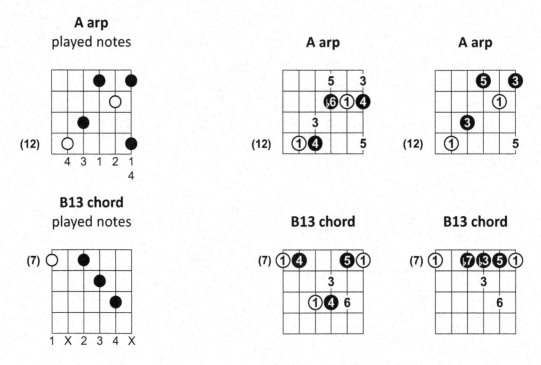

Figure 9.11 *Possible anchor choices for an arpeggio and a chord*

The beauty of anchoring is that the kernel you need (the anchors) is so small that there is little to change or memorise as the kernel is plugged into different parts of the neck. Also, except for anchor 1 for which you must know the note name, you don't think note names anymore but intervals (scale degrees). Once a change occurs in any of the components of anchoring (viewing area, anchor, formula), you forget the old state—you wipe if off your memory—and focus on the new state. Since the fretboard map is built as you go, you are less likely to get bogged down by shapes or boxed patterns. The mantra is to travel light with only the relevant information and snapshot of the fretboard.

ANCHORING, STEP BY STEP:

1. Determine what is to be played: reference note (anchor 1) + formula = note pool.

2. Eyeball the viewing area.

3. Place instance(s) of anchor 1.

4. Place anchors on every string of the viewing area (default: vertical string intervals).

5. Expand horizontally around each anchor within the viewing area (preferably only place the note pool).

9.3 Fretboard navigation with anchors

We've defined our viewing/playing area within a given period of time, and we've built the note pool we are to choose from. So we're all set for now. But once that period of time has lapsed, the viewing area might change (change in size or move to a new area of the fretboard), the note pool might change (go from G major to G minor), the viewpoint might change (go from G major to A Dorian). How do we adapt the anchoring principle to these changing factors, over the entire fretboard? We'll go through several examples.

Before jumping in, I'll make a mundane observation about how compact musical devices are when laid out on the fretboard, in real playing situations.[3] A chord is one position wide at most; we sometimes say a *chord grip*, because it fits in the palm of our hand! A chord has zero or one note per string. An arpeggio or *broken chord* frequently fits in one position but can spread beyond. It includes up to two notes per string. A scale can spread out well beyond one position, incorporating several notes on a string (three to four notes per string). This is something to take into account to gauge the size of the viewing area and to realise that one anchor may not be enough.

Table 9.1 *Typical viewing area (from most to least compact)*

Horizontal spread on the fretboard		
Chord ➡	Arpeggio ➡	Scale

▬▬▬ *Playing in one position*

A crucial aspect in using anchoring—or any method of partitioning the fretboard—is to be able to **play anything and everything in one position**. A symptom of a guitar player who is uncomfortable playing in one position is that he changes positions every time the key, chord, or scale changes, frequently hopping from one area of the fretboard to another. Playing in one position requires that you instantly rewire your vision of that area of the fretboard (e.g., in terms of scale degrees) and reconfigure anchors or notes.

A number of things can change here, and we'll look at each change separately, all other parameters being the same. These changes can also take place concurrently but the recipe for handling them is the same. Changes are for: viewing area, anchor, formula. As a reminder of signposts in one position, root shapes are shown again in Figure 9.12.

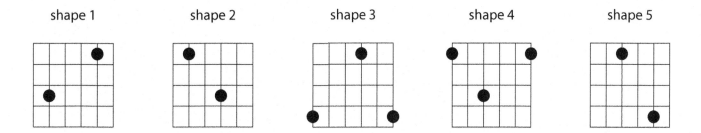

Figure 9.12 *Reminder: root shapes*

---

3. Of course, we often play fragments of these devices so that reduces the field of view, thankfully. And special cases, like single-string playing, can stretch arpeggios and scales well beyond a few notes per string. Therefore, this analysis is only for the average playing situation.

CHANGE IN VIEWING AREA

The viewing area can extend to include more strings, or, we might need to shift from top strings to lower strings, all within the same position. Let's look at a couple of examples. In Figure 9.13, the viewing area increases in size from strings 4–2 to strings 5–2. All we need is to place an anchor on string 4. That can be the default: 5. Another scenario is where the playing area shifts from strings 4–2 to a new area of the fretboard: strings 6–4. We don't want to extend the viewing area to include strings 6–2 or to all six strings when we no longer need to play on strings 3–2. We would have to keep track of five strings instead of three, that's too much effort.[4] At this point, we change viewing areas and focus our attention on strings 6–4 only. That's easier and less memory intensive. Luckily, there's a copy of anchor 1 in this new area or nearby (root shape). Here, it's on string 6. Now there are two instances of anchor 1 in view. Whether you think note names or root shapes to locate the copy of anchor 1 nearby, it's your choice; you've got to know your note names anyway!

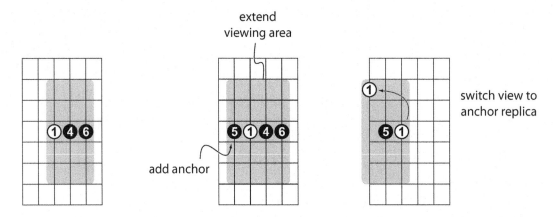

Figure 9.13 *Change in viewing area: 1- initial area; 2- extending area; 3- shifting area*

CHANGE OF ANCHORS

When the anchor 1 changes (not simply in location but to a new anchor altogether), the note name of the new anchor is different. For example, we want to shift from playing A major to G major, near the 5th position. The old anchor was note A and the new anchor is note G. We must locate an instance of G near the 5th position that is in our viewing area. From there, we apply anchoring (string intervals, deploy horizontally), rewiring our view of the fretboard around the new anchor G.

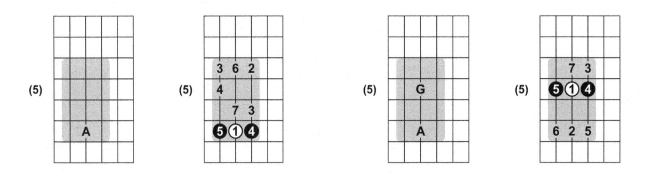

Figure 9.14 *Change of anchors: from A major to G major*

---

4. By analogy with computers, you would need more RAM to view six strings in one position than two strings only.

Not for a single moment do we think fingering patterns (switch between forms 4 and 5 of the 5-form major scale)[5] or note names (switch from A--B--C♯-D--E--F♯--G♯-A to G--A--B-C--D--E--F♯-G).

CHANGE OF FORMULAS

Let's say we are playing a two-string line that switches from A major to A Dorian, near the 5th position. The formula changes from 1--2--3-4--5--6--7-8 (major scale formula) to 1--2-♭3--4--5--6-♭7--8 (Dorian mode formula). The viewing area remains the same, the anchor 1 (note A) remains the same, only the formula changes. In fact, only two notes are different: 3 becomes ♭3 and 7 becomes ♭7. So here, we keep our vertical anchors and lower the 3rd and 7th degrees on the strings. That's all. It sounds simple but had we not known the scale degree of each note (and only knew black dots), this exercise would have been much more difficult.

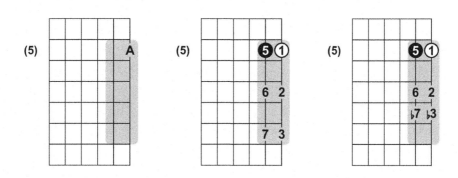

Figure 9.15 *Change of formulas: from A major to A Dorian*

The thought of overlaying on those strings an entirely new pattern for A Dorian or bringing in the G major scale pattern (A Dorian's parent scale) doesn't even cross our mind. Instead, we are able to hand-pick the notes to change and the notes to play. That's powerful!

Connecting positions

There is more to the neck than one position…there is the entire neck! The same changes (viewing area, anchor, formula) we just discussed apply when changing positions but in this section, we're only concerned with moving to a new position on the fretboard while keeping the same anchor 1 and the same formula. This new position overlaps or is adjacent to the initial position. If the position is far away, apply anchoring from scratch.

On guitar, we tend to learn information position by position, because it fits the range our hand can cover and the load our brain can process. Rewiring is a challenge when playing in one position. Interconnecting/extending the wires is the challenge when connecting positions. To make these connections, we can expand our viewing area to include a large area of the neck but that is too much information to process. Besides, making this connection is a **transient state**: we don't need to play or view two neighbouring positions for a long period of time, just long enough to make the connection. So instead, we are going to break down the large viewing area into several small viewing areas over time. In the process of switching viewing areas, we are inevitably going to shift to a new anchor several frets away. To accomplish this task, we must call upon neighbouring root shapes (Figure 9.16). Moments before transitioning to the new area, we view replicas of our anchor 1 via neighbouring root shapes, and use the appropriate replica anchor as a *pivot* or bridge to successfully transition to the new area of the fretboard. This is *staging* the transition.

---

5. The 5-form major scale patterns are built around the five root shapes. Forms 4 and 5 are the patterns built around root shapes 4 and 5.

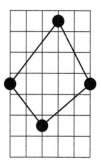 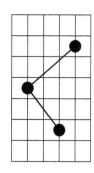 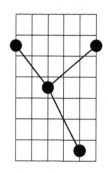 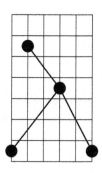 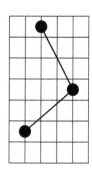

Figure 9.16 *Reminder: neighbouring root shapes*

In the example that follows, we want to play notes of C harmonic minor (1--2-♭3--4--5-♭6---7-8) amongst the note pool that is outlined in Figure 9.17. The line starts near position 3 and gradually ascends the strings and the fretboard. If we picture all the notes we need at once, we end up with a very large viewing area: 5 strings × 8 frets! A little less in reality because we ignore notes in the top right and bottom left corner of the greyed-out area. We don't want to view that much of the fretboard at one time. Instead, we'll think and progress step by step and break down the large area into smaller areas, each the size of a position or so. We will be playing in each position for a short period of time, before moving to a new position.

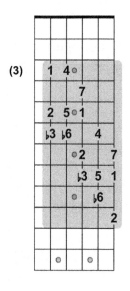 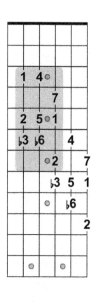 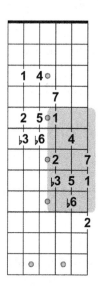 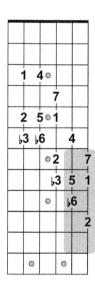

Figure 9.17 *Breaking down a large viewing area into smaller areas*

To make this move painless, we need to put the blindfolds on and visualise only the notes we need in the position we're in for the short period of time, with anchors. However, because we know we are moving to a neighbouring position imminently, we need to bring a neighbouring anchor 1 into our field of view, ahead of the move (staging). We do this thanks to neighbouring root shapes. Each viewing area has its usual anchors and a connecting anchor or pivot, that will also be part of the next viewing area. This way, like a well-rehearsed relay team, we safely pass the baton onto the next team to carry on.

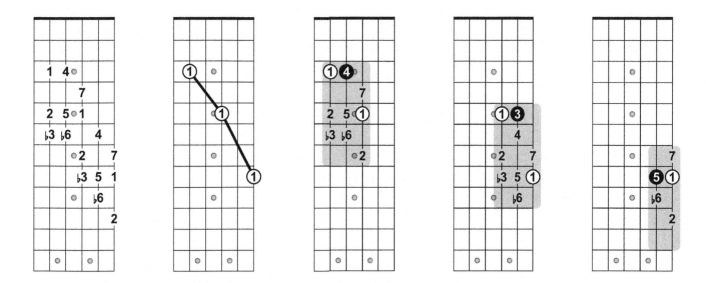

Figure 9.18 *Staging: visualising neighbouring anchors (octaves) as the viewing area shifts*

▬▬▬ *Fast-tracking: hanging shapes off anchors*

I claim that all guitarists have, are, and will continue to anchor all the time, perhaps without realising it. But they are using a fraction of the possibilities offered by the anchoring principle. When you plug in a G major scale pattern or a C major chord you know in an area of the neck, you are anchoring to note G or note C. That anchor is almost always the tonic of the scale or the root of the chord (often in the bass). What you don't do is worry about rolling out all the other notes you use; instead, you have learnt a shape or a fingering pattern, found the anchor / note name you need, and hang everything else off that anchor. This is fast but there is little you can change to those "other notes" if you have learnt the shape as a tonic/root and a collection of black dots and you don't know what lies behind the black dots. Alternatively, you may know the notes by their note name or scale degree, but with no structured method of relating them to each other and reusing them. As a result, if you must change from a C to a Cmin7 chord, you would recall an entirely new shape for Cmin7, even though it can be easily linked to the C shape. It's a shame because you have put in the energy learning the chord shape but have not pursued the most efficient learning curve.

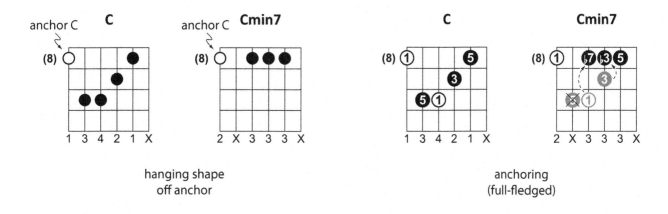

Figure 9.19 *Hanging shapes vs. full-fledged anchoring*

Fast-track anchoring (hanging shapes off an anchor) requires more memorisation and less on-the-spot thinking whereas full-fledged anchoring, in comparison, requires less memorisation and more on-the-spot thinking. When you need to play fast or run through a lengthy passage or you want to give your head a rest, you can go on autopilot and let your fingers take over, regurgitating licks or shapes you've practised. There is little time to think in those situations and often, fast-track anchoring is all you need to plug those rehearsed notes in the right key.

Strangely enough, with experience, full-fledged anchoring also leads to fast-track anchoring. Because we often use the same chords or scales, we end up memorising them and don't need to work them out on the fly anymore. We find an anchor on the neck and hang the remainder of the shape off that anchor. However, we know exactly what every one of those notes in the shape is, as far as scale degrees—they're not black dots. So we can use the full potential of anchoring to modify the shape at will.

To anchor, or not to anchor, that is not the question.[6] We do anchor, one way or another. The question is: what anchor(s)? Are we going to anchor to one note, like the root? This is anchoring in its most naked form, but it is also the most difficult to "domesticate" because we literally have to pave the way for every note. Are we going to anchor to a group of notes, like a cluster of anchors of our choosing? Or are we going to anchor with something bigger, already thought out and built out, some kind of a system? This is the topic of the next chapter. Your goal is to be comfortable with all flavours of anchoring. For you might find yourself using several flavours within a single piece of music (root, closed-form cluster, CAGED shape, scale pattern, etc.). As your thought process with anchoring matures, the choices for viewing area, anchors, and so forth, will become second nature and you will make anchoring your own.

Let me emphasise this again so that your expectations don't quickly lead to frustration. Anchoring is not exclusive to any other tool or method you can learn to visualise the fretboard with, it's a complementary approach. In fact, it's as complementary as you want it to be: it can be dessert or it can be the main course. So keep learning the patterns, the boxes, the CAGEDs of this world (or don't throw them out the window if you know them already). They have their purpose, speed is one. But don't expect yourself to learn anchoring overnight or as quickly as you can learn patterns. You're investing into anchoring and an intervallic approach to the guitar for the long haul. The benefits will come gradually.

NOTE   The anchoring principle works in any tuning, not just standard tuning. Merely adapt the default anchors (vertical string intervals of Figure 9.9) to the new tuning.

---

6. There are more pressing questions in life!

THE CAGED SYSTEM

10

As a guitarist, you have certainly come across or used CAGED already. This system organises the fretboard by dividing it up into "hand-sized" sections, based on five major chord shapes. In this chapter, we introduce CAGED through our intervallic lenses and see that it is an application of the anchoring principle. The system will serve as a laboratory to explore how anchoring, at a macro level, can develop into a powerful system for fretboard navigation.

10.1 CAGED

Anchoring with 1, 3, 5

With our knowledge of anchoring, let's choose 1 as the primary anchor with the 3rd and the 5th as the secondary anchors, and set out to deploy them over the entire fretboard (we limit ourselves to one octave only, about 12 frets). 1–3–5 forms a major triad, so we are looking for every location on the fretboard where we can find such a triad. We do this for C major (1–3–5 is C–E–G) and build the diagrams in Figure 10.1.

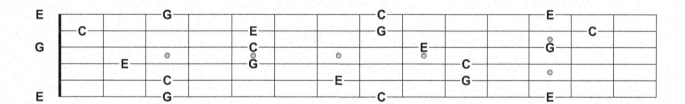

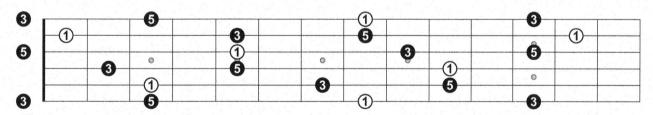

Figure 10.1 *C major triad (C–E–G or 1–3–5) over the fretboard*

At first sight, the neck looks crowded, doesn't it? There are notes everywhere and we wonder how we can learn this. But do you recognise anything familiar? Yes, the roots form the octaves pattern that we talked about in the Fretboard Geometry chapter. Remember we further broke down this octaves pattern into five individual shapes (root shapes or kernels). Figure 10.2 superimposes the octaves pattern on the previous diagram. For each root shape we identify, we'll also attach its secondary anchors 3 and 5 (E and G). We get five different shapes of the C major triad. With these five shapes, we covered the entire fretboard (12 frets or so).

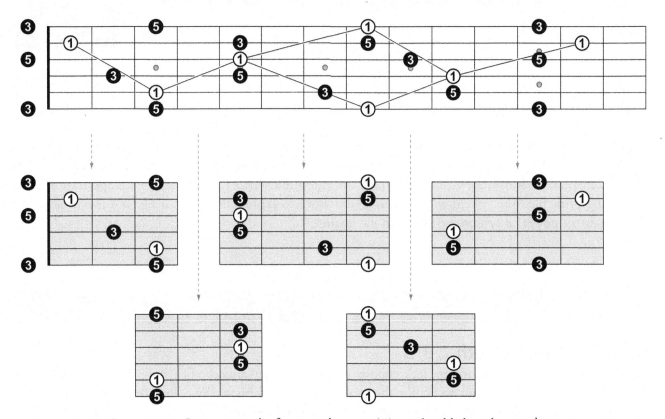

Figure 10.2 *Recognising the five root shapes 1 (C), with added anchors 3 & 5*

To be sure that what we laid out for C is repeatable, let's start over with A as the root 1, and see if we can reproduce this. This time, C♯ and E are 3 and 5 (Figure 10.3). The octaves pattern is the same but offset compared to C. The root shapes are also identical. The only difference is that 1–3–5 is now an A major triad.

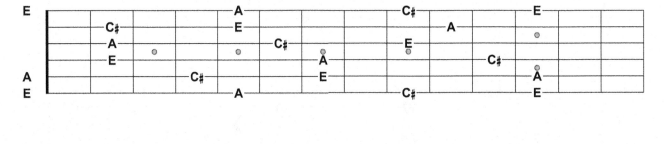

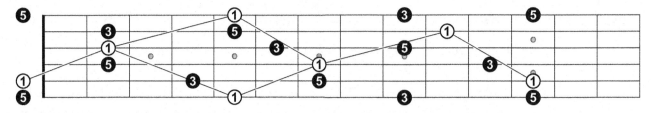

Figure 10.3 *A major triad (A–C♯–E or 1–3–5) over the fretboard*

NOTE The octaves pattern applies to any note, including the 3rd and the 5th, not just 1! Only it is shifted horizontally compared to the pattern for 1. We focus on visualising the octaves pattern for 1 because 1 is the primary and foremost anchor used for positioning (we hang everything off 1).

Open chords spell C-A-G-E-D

We looked at the entire neck, now let's turn our attention to the open position. In the example we just studied for C, there is one root shape that happens to form a C major triad as an open chord. The example for A also has one root shape forming an open chord—I didn't pick these notes randomly! Can we choose any other note as the root 1 in the hope of obtaining the three other root shapes as open chords? Yes, we can. G, E, and D are contenders: we have the diagrams of Figure 10.4.[1] From now on, we'll call the shape formed by the C major triad the C-shape, the shape formed by the A major triad the A-shape, and so forth.[2] These familiar chords in open position form the acronym C-A-G-E-D and give its name to the CAGED system. **These shapes are no other than the five root shapes with the added 3 and 5 chord tones.**

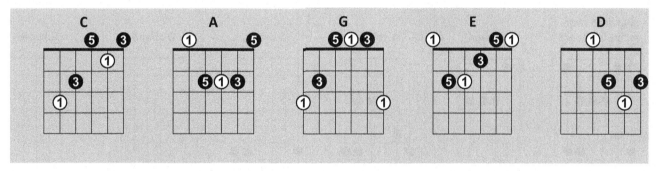

Figure 10.4 *Open chords C A G E D (based on the five root shapes)*

It is crucial to learn the chord tones (1, 3, 5) within the CAGED shapes in order to get the most out of the system. Don't just learn shapes (dot markings) or fingerings.

DID YOU KNOW? Open chords C A G E D have always been there but articulating a coherent system around them has not. The origin of the CAGED system is unclear. Researching the topic, some reports credit Bill Edwards' book *Fretboard Logic* (1983). Teaching material by Santa Barbara guitar instructor Bill Thrasher, dated 1963–1976, accounts for comprehensive notes on CAGED. Others point to Jack Marshall, a guitarist active in the 1950s and 1960s with ties to Capitol Records and the University of Southern California. The system is even linked back to classical guitar. Perhaps you can help me identify the pedigree of CAGED. For now, it is mystery unsolved!

10.2 Transposing CAGED

The CAGED system comes into its own when it's moved over the entire fretboard and not just confined to the open position. A prerequisite to transposing is a good knowledge of note names on the fretboard so that root notes can be swiftly located.

---

1. Do the same exercise we did for C and A but for G, E, and D. These will prove to be the only "moveable" options.
2. C-A-G-E-D are root shapes 1–5 from Figure 6.17. I refrain from using numbers to designate each shape because people use different numbers and it leads to confusion. It's best to remember each shape by its open chord name C, A, G, E, D.

Moveable shapes

As we saw with C and A, by (re)locating each of the five CAGED shapes to a root location on the fretboard, five embodiments of the same chord are obtained, covering the entire fretboard.

We'll go through an example and highlight various attributes of deploying the system around the neck. The example demonstrates the process for the B♭ major chord (1–3–5 or B♭–D–F). As we did in the introduction, we want to place the B♭ major chord wherever it can be found on the fretboard but we'll think differently: instead of looking for notes B♭, D, and F, everywhere on the neck, we'll use the CAGED system. For every occurrence of the note B♭ on the fretboard, we plug in the corresponding CAGED shape. We don't have to visualise all two or three B♭ notes within the shape, or even the whole shape, but can concentrate on one root B♭ only (either the bottom note or the top note). So for the first shape, we go to B♭ on string 5, fret 1, and hang the A-shape, which has a root on string 5, off B♭. We could have picked the C-shape, which also has a root on string 5, but the remainder of the C-shape would lie behind fret 1. Next, we choose B♭ on string 2, fret 11, and plug the D-shape (root is the top note). Another choice is the C-shape but that extends past fret 13. And so forth. Once we have all the shapes and put them side by side, we get the diagrams in Figure 10.5.

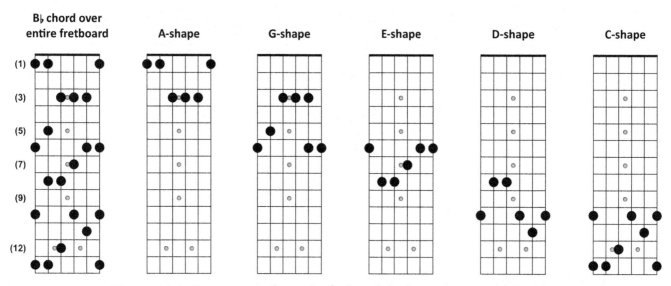

Figure 10.5 *B♭ major triad over the fretboard, broken up into CAGED shapes*

This takes us from the CAGED open chord shapes to the moveable shapes. The entire open chord—with its open string notes—is shifted as is, in one block, along the neck.

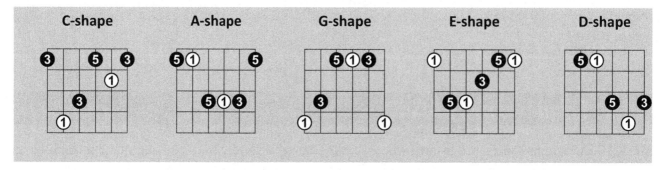

Figure 10.6 *Moveable CAGED shapes*

Don't let the name fool you. A G-shape chord isn't necessarily a G major chord. It can be any major chord (like B♭ major in the last example), depending on where it's played on the fretboard. The only place the

G-shape chord is indeed a G chord is in open position and 12 frets higher. Say we want to find a B♭ major triad near the 7ᵗʰ position. A B♭ note is located on string 6, fret 6. There are two CAGED shapes with the root on string 6: G-shape and E-shape. If we hang the G-shape off B♭, it would span frets 3–6, right behind the desired 7ᵗʰ position. The E-shape stuck on B♭ would span frets 6–8: this is closer to the 7ᵗʰ position. Figure 10.7 shows the E-shape that we simply moved from open position to fret 6. We could have also hung the same shape off the B♭ note on string 4, fret 8, or string 1, fret 6.

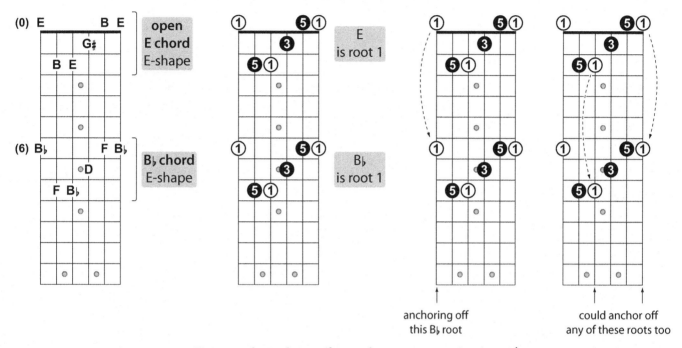

Figure 10.7 *Hanging the E-shape off B♭ to form B♭ major chord in 6ᵗʰ position*

> **NOTE** Students are sometimes confused by *deploying CAGED in one position* vs. *deploying CAGED over the neck*. This is similar to the confusion surrounding modes vs. parent scale. A same chord can take on any of the five CAGED shapes (e.g., B♭ major triad takes on all five forms when played over the neck). A same mode can take on any of the scale patterns of its parent scale (e.g., C Dorian mode can be played within any of the B♭ major scale patterns over the neck—same notes, different emphasis).

Left-out notes

You may have noticed that the open chord shapes slightly differ from the moveable shapes, which in turn differ from the shapes drawn over the fretboard (see previous neck diagrams)! In teaching CAGED, a number of notes are typically left out. CAGED is referenced back to the open chords that give its name, all in root position. This dictates what notes are played and what notes are left out. They are highlighted here in grey.

It makes sense to leave out these notes for practical reasons: 1- Chord shapes are always in root position (non-inversion form: root in the bass); 2- There is only one chord tone per string; 3- Chords are "fingerable" (e.g., try playing the top four notes in the moveable D-shape and add the 3ʳᵈ on the low E string: it's impossible). However, the omitted notes are within the bounds/frets of a shape and because CAGED is not only used for basic triads but also for all sorts of chords, scales, arpeggios, etc., these left-out notes are equally as significant as the other notes. Generally, I leave these notes in so you don't forget them. There is plenty of use for them!

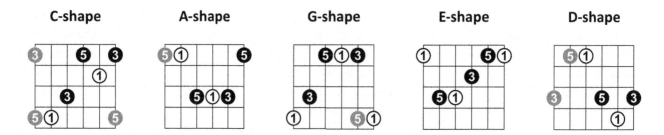

Figure 10.8 *Left-out notes (grey)*

> **NOTE**   In the C-shape, the omitted 5s are mirrors of each other; the omitted 3 is the mirror of the 3 on the high E string. In the A-shape, the omitted 5 is the mirror of the 5 on the high E string. In the D-shape, the omitted 3 is the mirror of the 3 on the high E string. The point is that a note you have on either E string is available on the other E string too.

▬▬ *Fingerings*

Fingerings shown here for CAGED shapes in the context of chords are only a starter kit because in practice, you may not play the full CAGED chords but only partial chords, or arpeggios, in which case fingerings will be different. The diagrams for the moveable shapes are shown with a full barre but barring with the index finger can be a half-barre or ad hoc (or think of it as an imaginary barre). Some notes can be played or left out, either fingered/muted or not fingered at all. Be careful when barring the D-shape: the note on string 6 of the barre is the 2nd degree of the scale and isn't part of the major triad.

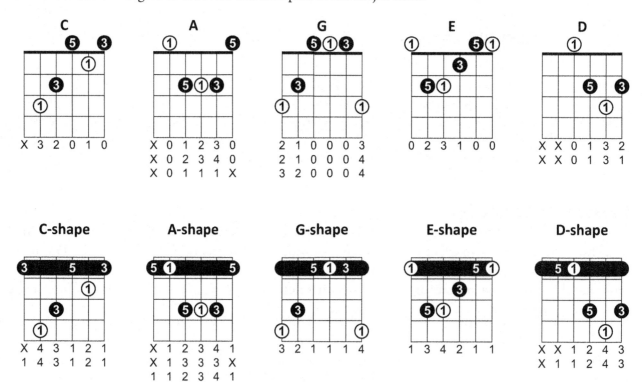

Figure 10.9 *Suggested fingerings: 1- open position shapes; 2- moveable shapes*

You can think of the open chord shapes as the moveable shapes in position 0 (open position), with the index finger barring right behind the nut, as it were.

It is preferable not to learn CAGED or any shape/pattern as fingerings. Fingerings are an accessory and a personal choice. If they become too front and centre, they will further contribute to box you into a position and overshadow what matters most (e.g., intervals, note names).[3]

> **DID YOU KNOW?** Three moveable CAGED shapes are enough to get almost all the notes of the major triad 1–3–5 over the fretboard. For example, C-A-E covers everything except the 3rd on string 5, or C-G-E covers everything (if you include the left-out 5^{ths} on strings 6 and 1). Likewise, three root shapes are enough to populate the entire fretboard with that root note. For example, root shapes 1, 3, 5, or 2, 4, 5. See for yourself on a neck diagram.

10.3 Fretboard navigation with CAGED

Moving a CAGED shape over the fretboard is one thing. Moving the CAGED system over the fretboard is another. To do this well, staying in one position and connecting positions are key.

▬▬ *Playing in one position*

Being able to play in one position is an important aspect of using CAGED. Just as it does with anchoring, playing in one position requires that you instantly rewire your vision of that area of the fretboard (e.g., in terms of scale degrees) and re-engineer CAGED shapes for what you're about to play (chord, melody, etc.). In chords/arpeggios, this may imply revoicing; in scales, it may imply playing an octave away. In most cases, it requires refingering. It takes longer to achieve this level of proficiency than simply shifting the same shape up and down the neck.

The most effective assignment to improve playing in position is simply to do it: apply it to scales, chords, arpeggios, progressions, improvisation, any compartment of your playing really. You can force yourself to play and think in one position with just about any piece of music or music exercise. For starters, you must be able to apply all five CAGED shapes within the confines of one position (4–6 fret wide area of the fretboard). That is, whether you change keys, chords, scales, you must be able to hang the appropriate moveable CAGED shape onto an anchor within the position.

To play in one position, we transpose the CAGED shapes. But rather than think in terms of transposition, we think in terms of anchoring, and typically, we anchor off the root 1 (primary anchor). So, locate the root/tonic of what you want to play, and hang off that root the CAGED shape that is the best fit within the position. Then, derive the chord or scale you need from that CAGED shape (we talk about that in the next section).

In Figure 10.10, we do this in 4th position for three chords: A, B, C♯. The CAGED or playing-in-one-position novice would simply shift the most familiar barre chord shape (E-shape) up and down the neck. Unfortunately, this doesn't fit in 4th position. To make all three chords fit in one position, we must apply a different CAGED shape for each of the three chords.

---

3. Another reason why CAGED is such a good acronym: it tells you what happens if you misuse it! On guitar, our playing would benefit if we were a tad claustrophobic.

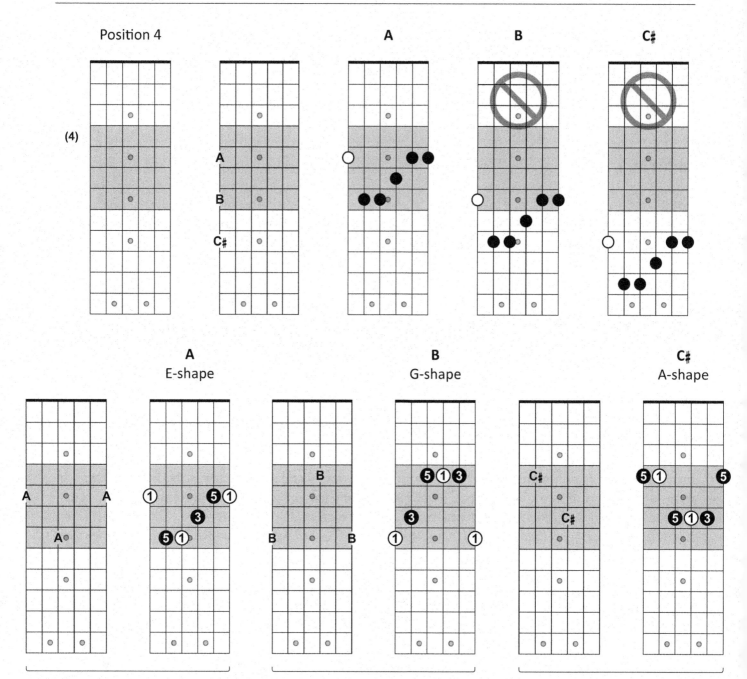

Figure 10.10 *Rewiring CAGED shapes in one position*

NOTE Position playing is playing *something* in one position. In the top row, we play in positions 5, 7, 9. Playing in one position is playing *everything* in one position. In the bottom row, we play only inside position 4.

▬▬▬ *Connecting positions:* unCAGED*!*

Once we break up the fretboard into smaller sections, there is a danger of losing sight of the big picture and being boxed in within each individual CAGED shape. So after taking the fretboard apart, we must be able to put it back together and connect CAGED shapes to each other. This is an important step in using CAGED to its full potential. Many students have a hard time stringing CAGED shapes together and viewing them as one big unit. Here, we take one major triad 1–3–5 and move that same triad along the fretboard.

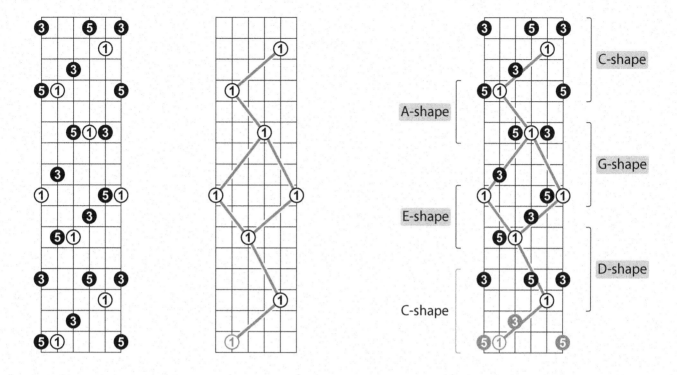

Figure 10.11 *CAGED and the octaves pattern*

Let's begin with a few observations. The diagram in Figure 10.11 shows all the CAGED shapes on the fretboard (1, 3, 5). The octaves pattern serves as a guiding thread running through all five shapes.

- Each root note is **associated with two** of the five CAGED shapes. Therefore, each CAGED shape has one shape preceding it and another shape following it on the neck.

- The **sequence** of the CAGED shapes is invariably the same, regardless of which shape you start with. As you move up the neck, this recursive sequence is:

$$\rightarrow C \rightarrow A \rightarrow G \rightarrow E \rightarrow D \rightarrow$$

So when you're on the G-shape, the A-shape is right behind it and the E-shape is right after it…always.

- Notes from one shape **overlap** with notes from the following shape, over a fret or two (the overlap always includes 1). For example, the root 1 on string 3, along with the 3rd and the 5th on that fret, are shared between the A-shape and the neighbouring G-shape.

- The roots within a shape roughly determine the **playing position**. Say we take a root on string 5, fret *N*, the corresponding C-shape has the bulk of its notes behind fret *N* and the corresponding A-shape has the bulk of its notes after fret *N*.

- Shared notes between neighbouring shapes—the root in particular—can serve as **pivots** to connect one shape to the next.

Juggling panoramic and close-up views of the fretboard must be a seamless and fluent process, just as working within a shape or position is. To do this, it's essential to visualise two neighbouring shapes at once.

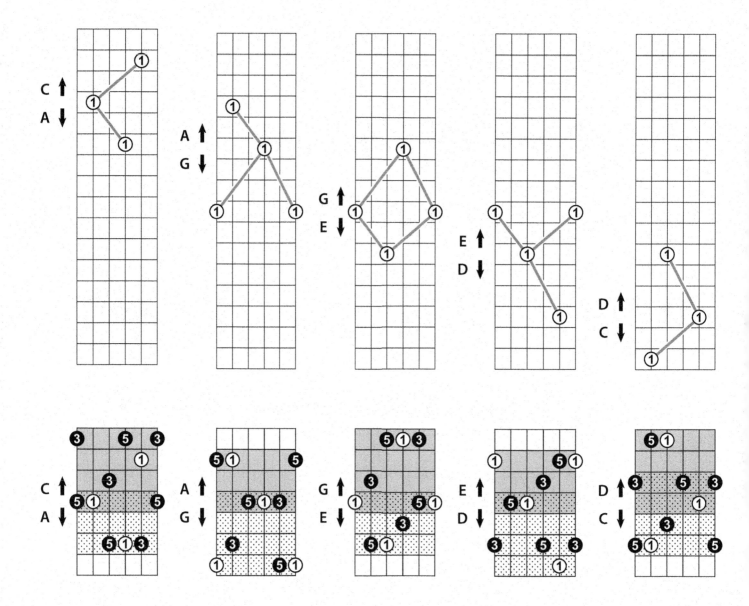

Figure 10.12 *Neighbouring CAGED shapes*

10.4 Building with CAGED: chords, scales, and more

The purpose of CAGED is not to give us five major triad shapes we can play all over the neck. It's more than that. The purpose of CAGED is to help us find our way around the fretboard. To do this, it breaks up the fretboard into five smaller areas, each based on a major triad shape. Within each shape, it maps out the 1, 3, 5 scale degrees. It also puts these shapes back together (think Lego), connecting them via the notes they share, so that we can cruise from one shape to another. CAGED is an application of the anchoring principle, where the anchors are 1, 3, 5 and grouped into clusters of two or three roots. This gives a more detailed snapshot of the fretboard than a single anchor does. The choice of 1, 3, 5 as anchors lays out the skeleton for building chords, and eventually arpeggios, scales, and more.

So, to fully benefit from CAGED and use the system to BUILD—not REGURGITATE—you need to learn it based on the knowledge of:

- Note names on the fretboard: so you can locate a primary anchor (root 1).
- Scale degrees 1, 3, 5 within each shape: so you can refer back to them for positioning and also alter them.
- Neighbouring shapes: so you can connect two positions or play in between positions.

In other words, you need to develop quite a toolbox to take full advantage of CAGED. If you only learn CAGED as shapes (black dots), shapes + root, or fingerings, you miss out on most of the benefits.

It is important to realise that you don't need to visualise an entire shape or two neighbouring shapes all the time. Most of the time, you are working (playing) in a small area of the fretboard—maybe up to 4 strings × 6 frets—and only the relevant fragment of a shape is necessary. For instance, you might be playing triads on the top three strings in which case you only need to see the top three notes of CAGED shapes. This idea is at the heart of the anchoring principle. In Figure 10.13, we take the fragment of the CAGED shapes on strings 4–2 and run with it (notice the disconnect between neighbouring shapes: partial shapes may no longer share any common note). You should learn to handle CAGED shapes whole, in pieces, on adjacent strings, on skipped strings, patched together, etc.

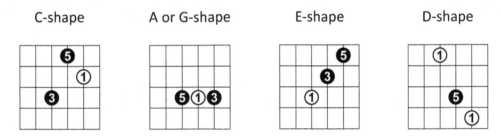

Figure 10.13 *Partial CAGED shapes (on strings 4–2)*

By simultaneously transposing, altering, adding or removing notes within the five CAGED shapes, any musical device such as chords, arpeggios, scales, runs, riffs, or licks, can be derived. The examples in Figure 10.14 illustrate how full or partial chords, arpeggios, and scales, can be obtained from the five original CAGED shapes. To build a chord or a scale from a CAGED shape, you simply use the shape's anchors (1, 3, 5) and shift them horizontally (i.e., on the same string) to get to the desired note. In the Gmin7 chord example, the root 1 is moved back two frets to get ♭7 and the 3rd is moved back one fret to get ♭3. With a note on every string, CAGED shapes facilitate horizontal note manipulation. The examples are just a glimpse of what can be achieved with CAGED and how to put it to work. They are a far cry from the simple open chord or the moveable chord forms that serve as the basis for the system.

NOTE When building a chord or a scale from a CAGED shape, some notes can be closer to a neighbouring CAGED shape. You may wonder whether using that neighbouring CAGED shape as a basis for building your chord or scale is not a better choice. Either choice might be suitable. It also depends on the position / fretboard area you're in. For example, in the F9 chord, the 3rd fits right in with the C-shape but all the other notes (♭7, 9, 5) are a better fit with the neighbouring A-shape.

Next page:
Figure 10.14 *Building chords, arps, scales with CAGED*

How to build from CAGED

D-shape ➡ **Gmin7 chord**   A-shape ➡ **D minor scale**

Chords

A-shape   E-shape   C-shape   E-shape

Cmin   **E7**   **F9**   **D♭Maj9**

Arpeggios

C-shape   E-shape   A-shape   A-shape

E   **Fmin7**   **Dmin11(♭13)**   **Emin**

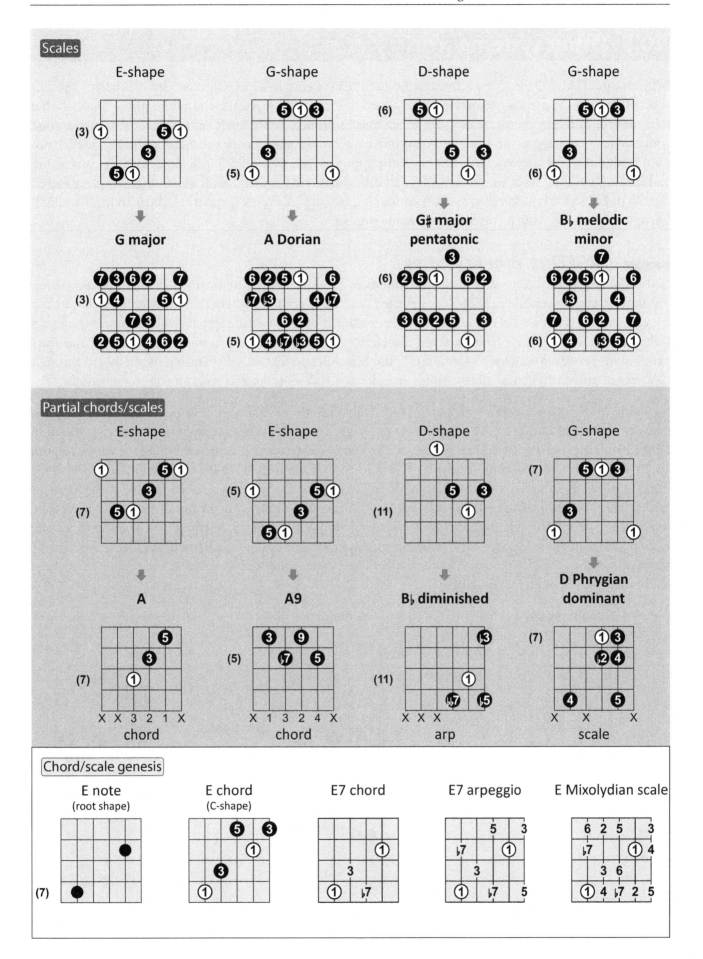

10.5 Other systems

Before we put CAGED into perspective and look at other systems, let's just reflect on CAGED itself. CAGED is no more than the five root shapes with the added 3^{rds} and 5^{ths}. Nevertheless, adding those notes is a big step towards building chords, scales, and other musical devices, from such system. Root shapes are quite convenient for moving around the fretboard but have a lot of gaps (strings without a note) so they're not ideal for building from them. CAGED fills those gaps with the 3rd and 5th, placing a note on every string and making building what we want to play (chords, scales, etc.) easier. This is anchoring at a macro level: each CAGED shape is a cluster of anchors containing two or three roots (primary anchor) and 3^{rds} and 5^{ths} (secondary anchors). Guitar "orienteering" made simpler.

▄▄▄ *CAGED vs. other systems*

CAGED is frequently compared to other methods of breaking up the fretboard such as 3-note-per-string scales, Segovia scales, or other chord- or scale-based systems. Every approach to the fretboard has its merits but the comparison is not always meaningful. For example, a 3-note-per-string system is geared towards playing scales, not chords so much. These systems are often typecast as exclusive to one another (e.g., "You can't play 3-note-per-string scales with CAGED."). But it needn't be that way. Visualising the fretboard through CAGED or anchors (octaves) allows you to include such scales—as long as you can connect positions!

Fingering for 3-note-per-string scale patterns spans two positions. That can be handled by CAGED but it requires two neighbouring CAGED shapes for coverage. To do this with ease and without clutter, you only need to visualise partial CAGED shapes (which brings you a step closer to the anchoring principle). Figure 10.15 shows a 3-note-per-string scale pattern for G major. It spans the E-shape and the D-shape. To play it using CAGED as a framework (how you think or visualise the fretboard), you need to have both shapes in the back of your head: think E-shape while you're on strings 6–5, then bring the bottom part of the D-shape into the picture and think both shapes while on strings 4–3. Once you reach strings 2–1, you can forget the E-shape and think only D-shape. This will help you find the notes of the scale in each area, using the relevant fragments of the CAGED shapes. Also, in the E-shape, there is no need to visualise the top notes (5, 1) at all. Remind you of anything? Staging.

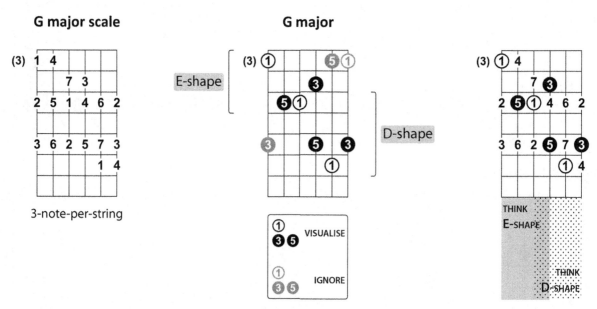

Figure 10.15 *Building 3-note-per-string scale pattern with CAGED*

This last example teaches you that to be effective, you need to mould CAGED to the circumstances. CAGED or anchors are means for going from point A to point B on the fretboard, the way you want and without strings attached (e.g., not restricted to playing in one position only). Something else that the example demonstrates is that if you learn these systems as fingerings, you will have a very, very hard time relating one shape to another or connecting them, especially if you have no knowledge of the underlying scale degrees.

CAGED-inspired systems

The idea behind CAGED is to divide the fretboard into a few small shapes and use them to organise the entire fretboard (divide and conquer, if you will). Can't we apply this idea to build other systems? Well, CAGED is based on 1, 3, 5 anchors. These anchors form the basis for building chords in tertian harmony (stacking up 3^{rds}) and mesh nicely with the guitar's tuning (lay out on the fretboard in "fingerable" shapes and with few left-out notes). What if we picked other anchors, or a different number of anchors? We can try 1, 3, 5, 7 (or ♭7), which would come in handy in chords. But there are too many chord tones, resulting in several left-out notes, because non-fingerable. And 1 and 7 are too close to each other; once we know where 1 is, we pretty much know where 7 is (right next to it, a fret down) so having both 1 and 7 as anchors is not more helpful than 1 alone. We can try 1, ♭3. This would take care of the proximity issue between anchors but there are now too many gaps (too few signposts). Another combination is 1, 4, 5, or 1, 3, 6. A system could omit 1 altogether (like 3, 5, 7) but it is convenient to have 1 as the primary anchor. You can cook up combinations of your own and see what they amount to on the fretboard.

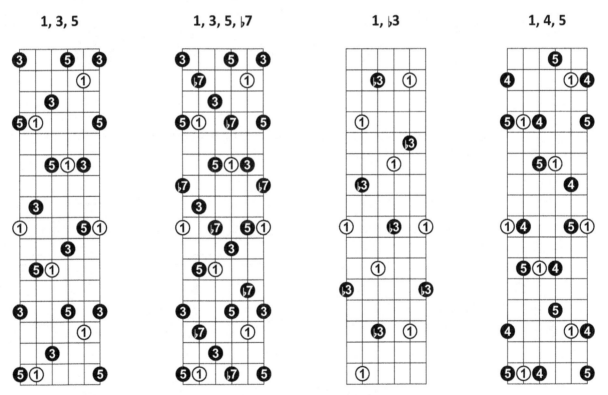

Figure 10.16 *Some CAGED-inspired systems*

Two combinations stand out with some interesting characteristics: 1, 3, ♯5 (augmented triad) and 1, ♭3, ♭5, ♭♭7 (diminished 7th chord). Let's examine them more closely. In the augmented triad, there is one shape and three rotations. In the diminished 7th chord, there is one shape and four rotations. The notes cycle within the shape.[4] Both systems were chosen so that neighbouring shapes don't overlap but it doesn't have to be that way, you can choose larger overlapping shapes.[5]

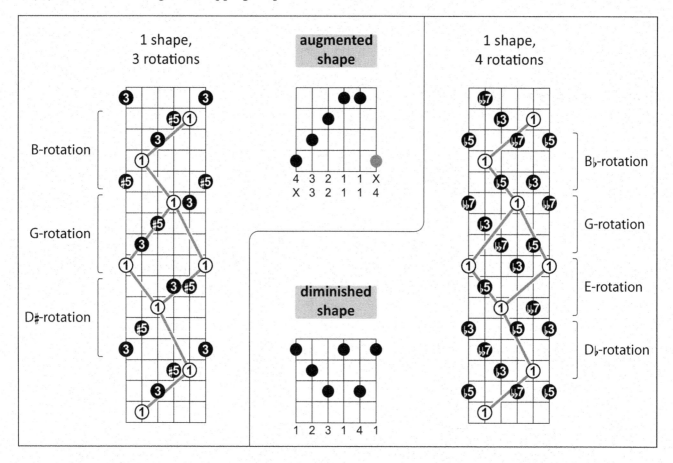

Figure 10.17 *One-shape systems: A-system and d-system*

Another approach is to view A and d as two-shape systems, underlining their resemblance. Each shape in one system is then the mirror image of a similar shape in the other system (reflection around the vertical axis).

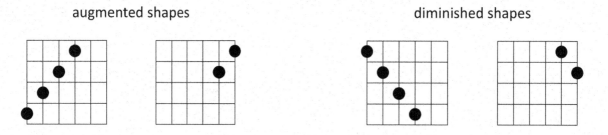

Figure 10.18 *Alternate two-shape A & d systems underlining symmetries*

The symmetrical nature of these scales explains their unique characteristics. With very little information—one shape repeating every four or three frets—you can cover the fretboard. However, the layout of the shapes on the fretboard (gaps in coverage) and the selected scale degrees reduce the practical value of these systems. A major triad is more readily adaptable to usage in popular music than a diminished 7th tetrad.

---

4. In the augmented triad, each note can play the role of 1, 3, or ♯5. In the diminished chord, each note can play the role of 1, ♭3, ♭5, or ♭♭7.
5. On the diagrams, the rotations are named after their open chord forms. You can ignore those names.

So far, we've looked at a system based on chords (CAGED), and others based on chord tones. Systems do not necessarily have to be based around chords. We can divide up the fretboard simply with the five root shapes (that's just one note), or other methods. One such method is to rely on a scale. A perfect candidate is the major pentatonic scale 1--2--3---5--6---8 which also breaks up the fretboard into five positions or pentatonic boxes. Just as the open chords in CAGED are amongst the first chords a guitarist learns, the pentatonic scale is amongst the first scales a guitarist learns. You will recognise that, organised in 2-note-per-string patterns (the most frequent way pentatonic boxes are presented), the pentatonic system incorporates the five root shapes, or the five CAGED shapes. Minor pentatonic works too (same shapes): 1---♭3--4--5---♭7--8.

Major pentatonic system
1--2--3---5--6---8

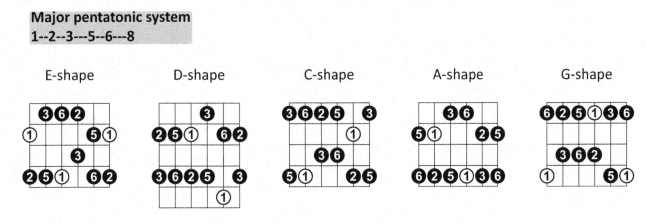

Figure 10.19 *Scale-based system: pentatonic system*

Any system is a view of the same thing: the fretboard, which is a constant. So it comes as no surprise that a system can usually be related to CAGED, or to the root shapes.

NOTE As seen in the examples with A & d systems, the same scale degrees (or chord tones) can result in systems with different shapes. In a system based on 1, 3, 5, can you think of shapes other than C A G E D?

▬▬ *Did you say BAGED?*

Now that we've had a 360 tour of the CAGED system, let's go back full circle to where it all began: the open chords. Something is odd about CAGED: there is an open chord named after every open string except one, the B string. Had there been a B open chord, the system would have possibly become BAGED, a straight collection of open chords for every open string. But C, which isn't an open string, took the spot, the system became CAGED and the rest is history. What caused B to be ousted? Can we build an open B chord? Is it fingerable? What about a moveable B-shape? We can't close this chapter without answering these questions!

The B major triad is B–D♯–F♯. The only chord tone that is an open string is B. This makes things difficult. Assuming the open B would be part of the B-shape chord (like A, G, E, D, in the AGED open chords) and knowing that CAGED chords are built on one root shape (not two), we conclude that a B open chord would either be based on root shape 1 (what became the C-shape) or on its neighbour root shape 5 (what became the D-shape). Given that open B is on fret 0, root shape 5 would be positioned before fret 0 and that is not possible. So the only root shape our open B chord can be based on is root shape 1 (C-shape) which is in open position. The B open chord would take on the role filled by the C open chord in CAGED. The resulting B chord spans three frets with a muted G string. A few fingering options are provided in Figure 10.20. If we were to make this a moveable shape, it would be near impossible to finger (G string must be muted too).

So the B major open chord is a non-starter. That's why BAGED did not work out. If you build an elegant system of your own, let me in on it!

NOTE In CAGED open chords, not all open strings are played. In particular, for the D chord, the 6th string is not even part of the major triad (2nd degree). So in our quest to find a suitable B open chord, not all open strings need to be included, but the more the merrier.

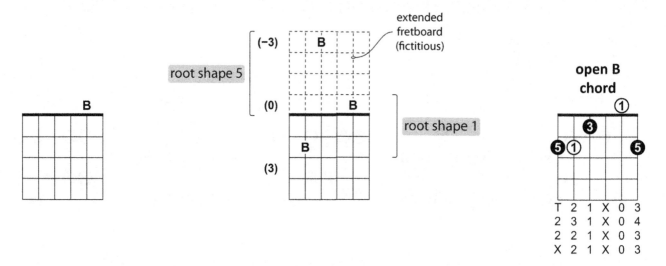

Figure 10.20 *The open B chord, in an unlikely BAGED system*

To wrap up this chapter, I shall leave you with a shapes-only representation of CAGED. Candy for your mind's eye, or just a visual to get acquainted to!

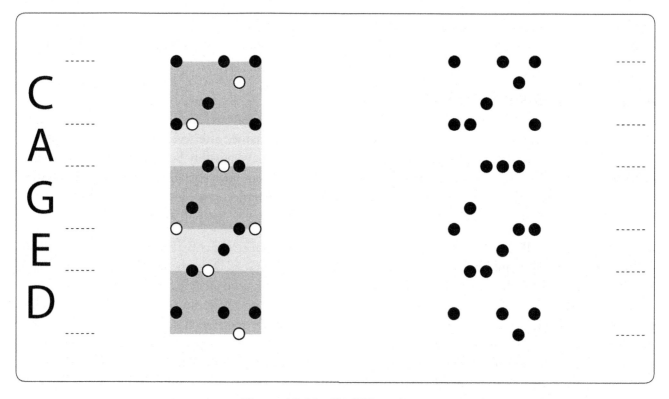

Figure 10.21 *CAGED...shapes*

HARMONICS

H armonics are as mysterious a topic as the chiming sound they make. In this chapter, we are going to peek at the physics behind harmonics, map out harmonics on the fretboard, and examine some properties and applications of harmonics. Fear not the numbers—if there is anything you should remember as a guitarist, it is the location of the principal harmonics on the fretboard. But by understanding the why and how of harmonics, you learn a wealth of information about various aspects of music and guitar.

11.1 String theory

Unlike "standard" playing, which relies on frets to indicate where to position our fingers on the strings, harmonics provide no such cues. They seem to randomly pop out at various spots along the string, sounding nothing like fretted notes, and unpredictable in every way. In this section, we wear our scientist's hat (it's a hard hat, don't you worry!) and investigate the physics behind harmonics. We want to understand where harmonics come from in an intuitive fashion, going through the physical phenomena that take place but without formalising them into equations. So you will have to take some results for granted. **You can read on or skip this section and simply retain that:** *the sound of a guitar's open string can be modelled as **a sum of sine waves (harmonics)**, with each sine wave's frequency (or pitch) being a multiple of the open string's frequency.*

▬▬▬ *Waveform parameters*

Before we start, we need to become familiar with some characteristics of signals.

A *waveform* represents a quantity as a function of another quantity. In our case, this waveform can be sound (e.g., voltage or current if captured by a transducer, air pressure if produced by a speaker) against time, distance against time if measuring the displacement of a point on the guitar string over time, or distance against distance if measuring the displacement of the guitar string as a function of position along the string.

Let's take the waveform of Figure 11.1, representing a sine wave (sinusoid), as a basis for this section. This waveform repeats, it is said to be *periodic*. The part that keeps repeating is a *cycle*. When the waveform is measured against time, the *period T* is the time for one cycle to complete before it repeats again. The unit for T is the second (s). For example, a heart at rest can beat once every 0.75 second or so (look at an ECG); that heartbeat is a periodic signal of period $T = 0.75$ s.

How often this cycle repeats over time is called the *frequency f* and is directly related to the period: $f = 1/T$. The unit for f is Hertz (Hz) or 1/s. A heart at rest, when beating every 0.75 s, repeats at $1/0.75 \approx 1.33$ Hz; in other words, it beats 1.33 times per second, that's 80 beats per minute. The most common tuning fork has a fundamental frequency of 440 Hz (A4, better known as A440), it "beats" or oscillates 440 times per second. Human hearing typically ranges from 20 Hz–20 kHz, so 440 Hz is a low frequency.

This waveform reaches high and low peaks. The high peak is a *crest* and the low peak is a *trough*. The difference between the two is double the *amplitude 2A* (peak-to-peak). If we slightly shift the signal in time, all other parameters being the same, we introduce the concept of *phase* φ.[1]

Figure 11.1 *Waveform parameters: period, amplitude, phase*

A waveform can be represented in the time domain or in the frequency domain (spectrum).

Travelling wave

Take a jump rope lying around on the floor. Grab one end of the rope and make one swift whipping movement (up and down). You create a disturbance that appears to travel along the rope (Figure 11.2 shows this wave at instants t_0, t_1, t_2). Once it reaches the end of the rope, it sort of expels itself and the rope goes back to lying still on the floor. If the string was longer, the wave would keep on going, gradually becoming smaller, and eventually fading away. We call this wave a *travelling wave*. When the wave travels through the rope, that part of the rope moves up then down in time, but does not move horizontally. Overall though, the wave—not the rope—appears to be moving from left to right.

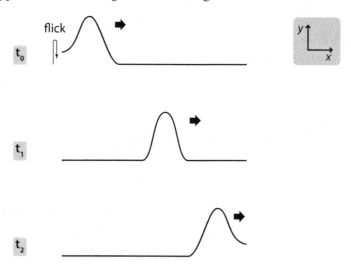

Figure 11.2 *Travelling wave through a rope*

Instead of making a single whipping movement, keep doing it regularly every T seconds. The rope would propagate a train of pulses/waves (Figure 11.3). The waveform is periodic of period T and amplitude A. The distance separating two consecutive crests is the *wavelength* λ. The wave propagates at a speed v corresponding to the time it takes for one wavelength to fully get past one point on the string, that's: $v = \lambda / T$. As a function of frequency, that is: $v = \lambda f$. This velocity depends on the medium the wave travels in (e.g., air, water, steel). Therefore, in a given medium, wavelength is inversely proportional to frequency.

---

1. When the waveform is a sine wave, all these parameters can be expressed in an equation like so: $y(t) = A\sin(2\pi / T \times t + \varphi) = A\sin(2\pi f \times t + \varphi)$.

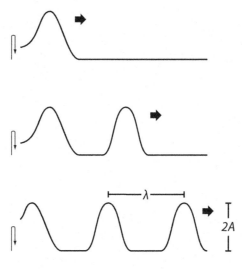

Figure 11.3 *Periodic wave*

> **NOTE**   In our rope, the wavelength is the distance along the rope between two repeating waves on the *x*-axis. The period is the time between two repeating peaks on the *y*-axis. The figure is a snapshot at three different times, so you can clearly see the wavelength but not the period. **For the waves in our rope, wavelength is the period of movement in space, period is the period of movement in time.** Don't mix up the two quantities.

Now nail one end of the rope to the wall at 30" from the floor. Grab the loose end of the rope and while holding it tautly, make the same single whipping movement then keep your end of the rope still. A wave forms and travels towards the wall. Once it reaches the wall, it comes back towards you. Interestingly, the wave comes back upside down (Figure 11.4). Why is that? When the wave reaches the wall, energy must be conserved. The wave has nowhere to go but the rope, so it is reflected back. Because the fixed end of the rope does not move, the reflected wave and the incident (incoming) wave must cancel out at the fixed end, so the reflected wave is a flipped version of the incident wave.

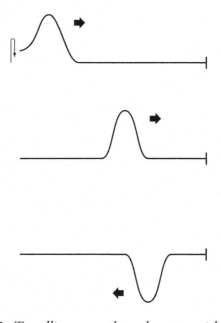

Figure 11.4 *Travelling wave through a rope with a fixed end*

NOTE   The rope's motion occurs along an (*x*, *y*) plane. Later in this chapter, the guitar string's motion is pictured in such a plane, appearing to be perpendicular to the fretboard. In reality, this plane's orientation depends on the picking angle and can be near parallel to the fretboard.

━━ *Standing wave*

Ask a friend to hold one end of a long rope; you hold the other end. Pull on the rope a little to tighten it. Have your friend make that single whipping movement and a fraction of a second later, you do the same. What happens? Figure 11.5 shows a wave travelling from left to right (generated by you) and a wave travelling from right to left (generated by your friend), on the same rope. As these two cross, they add up where they meet, and then carry on with their journey. They pass right through one another! This is the principle of *superposition*: waves propagating in a medium add up. When two waves are superimposed, they reinforce each other (constructive interference, as shown here), or they weaken or cancel each other out (destructive interference). This demonstrates that waves interact.

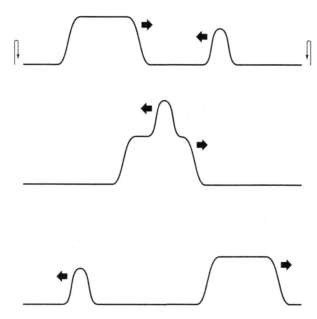

Figure 11.5 *Superposition of waves moving in opposite directions*

Now, you and your friend really get into the swing of things and keep flicking the rope repeatedly and steadily, each producing perfect sine waves W1 and W2, with the same amplitude and wavelength, travelling at the same speed along the rope, in opposite directions. At time *t* = 0, you have barely started and the waves have not reached one another yet. Then the waves blend into one another, and we take snapshots of the rope at times t_1, t_2, and t_3. The rope's shape is that of W1 + W2 but we can imagine the individual contributions of W1 and W2. If we compare these three snapshots, we observe that some points along the rope do not move at all while others move up and down. Though overall, the waveform on the rope appears to stand still and no longer travel from left to right or right to left. At the points where the rope is still, the waves W1 and W2 always cancel out (destructive interference).

This example shows that if the waves keep coming at each other in a certain fashion and interfere, the resulting wave can be made to look as though it is not moving: the rope stays still at some points and oscillates up and down elsewhere, but there is no apparent motion towards the left or the right. We call this wave a *standing wave*.

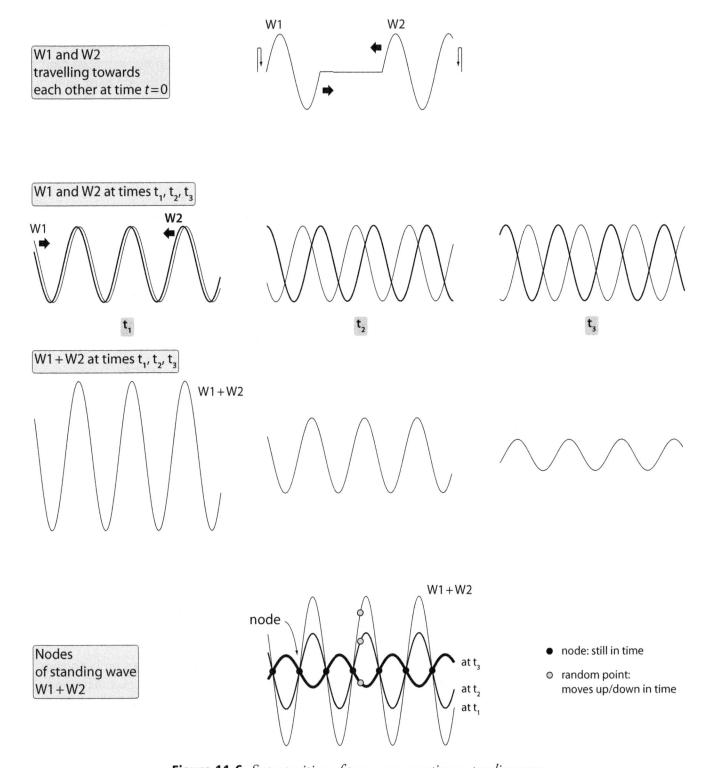

Figure 11.6 *Superposition of two waves creating a standing wave*

Figure 11.7 shows four scenarios of standing waves. The points where the wave is always still over time are called *nodes* and the points of maximum amplitude are called *antinodes*. The rope vibrates at its resonance frequencies (or natural frequencies). The waveform with the largest wavelength $\lambda_1 = 2L$ has a frequency $f_1 = v/\lambda_1 = v/(2L)$ (v is a constant for the rope). Other waveforms are of wavelength $\lambda_k = 1/k \times \lambda_1$ resulting in a frequency $f_k = k \times f_1$. The waveform with the lowest frequency is called the first *harmonic* and the others are the kth harmonic (or harmonic of order k). Other names you will come across to designate harmonics are the *fundamental* for the lowest frequency harmonic and *overtones* for other harmonics. You may also encounter the term *partial* instead of harmonic, because oftentimes, the full waveform is the sum of several harmonics and each harmonic is a "part" of the waveform. Each harmonic is a standing wave, with nodes spaced every $\lambda_k/2$. I will be using shorthand notation to designate harmonics: ×4, h4, #4 all refer to the 4th harmonic.

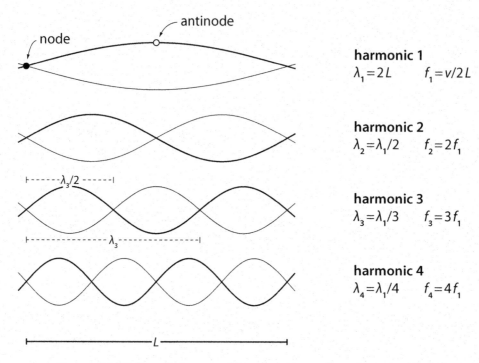

Figure 11.7 *Standing waves (shown at times of maximum swing)*

In the example, the two ends of the rope were put in motion manually, held at each end by you and your friend who continuously fuelled this motion. But standing waves can also happen if one end of the rope is fixed or if both ends of the rope are fixed (each fixed end is a node). In this latter case, a wave travels to one end, is reflected back towards the other end where it bounces back again, and so on. The rope's motion is initiated and sustained at a location along the rope other than at its ends (e.g., for a guitar string, it's initiated by the pick near the pickguard).

▬▬ *Application to guitar*

We can now shift our attention to the guitar string. Unlike the rope, the string is tied down on both ends tautly: one end at the nut N and the other at the bridge B. We want to find out how the coordinate y of a point on the string varies over time and along the neck of the guitar. Given the symmetry of the system—it behaves in the same way looking at it from N or from B—and the principle of superposition, we surmise that the solution is a standing wave. Figure 11.8 shows how the string looks like, at time $t=0$, when we are about to pick the string. The string is stretched, forming a triangle with N and B.

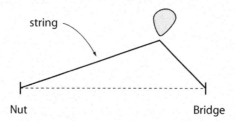

Figure 11.8 *String about to be picked (modelled with sharp corners)*

The guitar string is first set in motion, not by you and your friend flicking both ends (the ends are fixed), but by the pick striking the string somewhere in between. Since this energy is provided only once to the string, the string's vibration will not sustain for long and will decay, eventually dying out. But for our purposes, we'll assume the vibration is even and steady long enough.

This sets our initial conditions for our waveform (the shape of the string) at time $t = t_0 = 0$. We can think of this waveform W as the sum of two waveforms W1 and W2 moving along the string, at the same velocity (same medium), in opposite directions (W1 from left to right and W2 from right to left). Figure 11.9 shows these waveforms. We don't know what W1 and W2 look like yet so I just drew two placeholder waveforms we will be working with. These waveforms must always add up in such a way that at point N, $y_{W1}(N) = -y_{W2}(N)$ and at point B, $y_{W1}(B) = -y_{W2}(B)$, so that the sum is zero because $y_W(N) = 0$ and $y_W(B) = 0$. At time $t = t_1$, the waveforms have moved the same distance in opposite directions. Thanks to the condition of zero sum at points N and B, we can draw the shape of the waveforms as they move. It turns out waveform W1 outlines W2 and waveform W2 outlines W1, as they were earlier. At time $t = t_2$, the waveforms have travelled distance L (scale length), the distance separating the nut and the bridge.

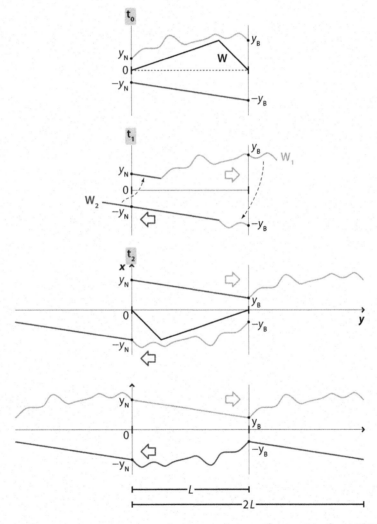

Figure 11.9 *String movement, at $t = 0$, t_1, t_2, as sum of two waveforms W1 and W2, moving in opposite directions, and forming a standing wave W*

Looking at the entire waveforms W1 and W2, we see that they are in fact the same waveforms! Both are periodic waveforms of period $2L$. At all times, $W = W1 + W2$, which is made of the shape of the string at time t to which a flipped copy of that shape is appended. The resulting waveform is a continuous and periodic waveform of period $2L$.

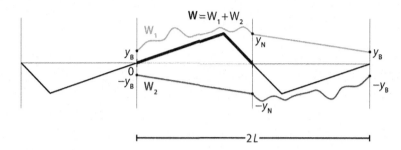

Figure 11.10 *String movement as standing wave W of wavelength 2L*

We need an important result before we can move on. The theorem, first stated by French mathematician Joseph Fourier in the 19th century, reads as follows:

> THEOREM. *A continuous and periodic waveform of period P can be written as an infinite sum of sines and cosines of period $1/k \times P$, where k is an integer.*

Since our waveform W satisfies the conditions of Fourier's theorem, it can be written as a Fourier series, which is a sum of carefully weighted sines and cosines of wavelength $\lambda_k = 1/k \times (2L)$, that is a sum of *harmonics* with the first harmonic of wavelength $\lambda_1 = 2L$. Thus, this first harmonic h1 has a frequency $f_1 = v/\lambda_1 = v/(2L)$. $\boldsymbol{f_1}$ **is the pitch of the ringing open string.** The higher order harmonics have a frequency $f_k = k \times v/(2L) = kf_1$. The period corresponding to the harmonic k is $T_k = 1/f_k = (2L)/(kv)$. At any time, the string's vibration is the sum of all these harmonics, that is, the superposition of the harmonic waveforms.

As an example, for a string being plucked at 3/4 of its length near the bridge—that's right above the 24th fret—Figure 11.11-1 shows the first five harmonics along the string, at time $t = 0$. The nodes are located at $y_{\text{harmonic}} = 0$. Figure 11.11-2 shows the resulting waveform produced by adding these first five harmonics: it's close but not quite the ideal shape of the string (pointy). The more harmonics are added, the closer the sum gets to the actual shape of the string (remember Fourier's theorem: an infinite number of harmonics make up the waveform). This is shown in Figure 11.12 where the waveform is a snapshot of the string at nine equally-spaced points in time. The first set of graphs takes only the first 8 harmonics into account while the other set of graphs takes 32 harmonics into account.

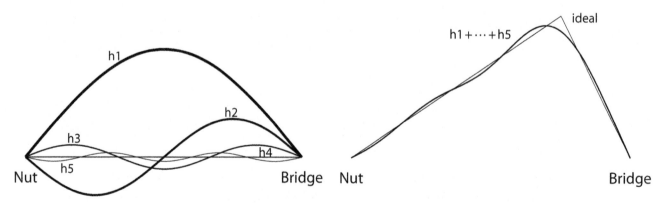

Figure 11.11 *1- harmonics 1–5 for plucked string at t = 0; 2- resulting string shape vs. ideal*

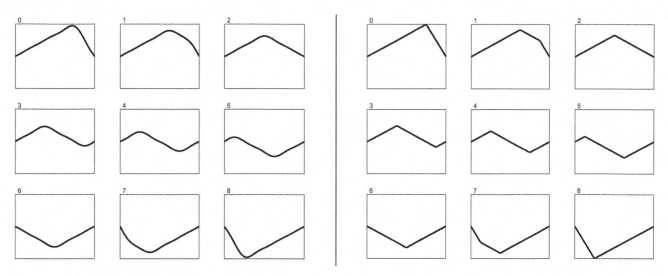

Figure 11.12 *Plucked string time lapse for sum of 8 harmonics and sum of 32 harmonics*

We can make a few observations from Figure 11.11-1. It turns out that when the string is picked at 3/4 of the length, the 4th harmonic h4 (as well as 8th, 12th, 16th, etc.) is zero. If the string is picked elsewhere, the 4th harmonic may be present.[2] We can also see that the 1st harmonic is the strongest—as a rule of thumb, harmonics weaken as their order gets higher. The bar charts in Figure 11.13 show the strength (amplitude) of the first 8 harmonics for the string picked at 3/4 of its length (0.75 L, that's right over fret 24), and for a string picked at 0.9375 L (that's three quarters of the way from fret 24 to the bridge). The string picked at 0.75 L doesn't have the 4th and 8th harmonics, the other does. It also has a stronger harmonic 1, making for a fuller sound. Note that the displacement produced by the pick is chosen so that the length of the string under tension is the same in both cases.

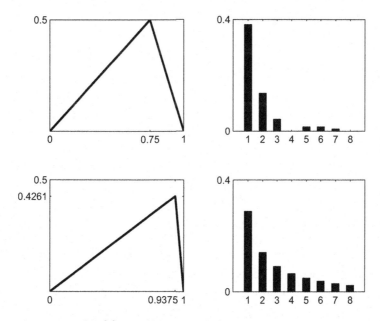

Figure 11.13 *Strength of first 8 harmonics of string picked at 0.75 L and at 0.9375 L*

---

2. In Figure 11.13-1, h4 and h8 (and all multiples of h4, if they were pictured) are zero. The string is plucked at $3/4 \times L$, which is a node of h4. Generally, when the string is plucked over a node, all harmonics sharing that node will be zero in the resulting waveform. For example, if the string were picked right above a node of h3, harmonics h3, h6, h9, h12, etc., would be zero. Although an interesting observation, this is of little use because in practice, the absence of these harmonics is not particularly audible.

The pitch of a string is defined by the lowest order harmonic (h1). Nonetheless, the sound made by the vibrating string is more complex than a single harmonic: it contains an infinite number of harmonics, in theory. The proportion (weighting factor) of each harmonic is what makes the same pitch sound different on different instruments. For example, the note A2 produced by a steel string guitar sounds different from that produced by a classical guitar, or by a piano. The harmonics determine the *timbre* of the instrument. Even on the instrument itself, the location and manner in which the same string is picked (initial conditions) will produce a different proportion of harmonics in the resulting sound. If you pluck the string away from the bridge, the sound will be fuller than if you pluck the string near the bridge where it will be thinner.

Keep in mind that all the waveforms shown in this chapter are wildly exaggerated. On guitar, the vibrating string is almost straight and the swing (peak-to-peak variation) is very subtle.

DID YOU KNOW? By carefully superimposing sine wave signals on top of each other, you can get all sorts of signals. Even the distorted signal produced by a guitar pedal or a saturated amplifier can be broken down into the sum of a fundamental sine wave and its harmonics.

Fretboard equations

To conclude this section, here are the basic equations resulting from the material we discussed. They describe pitch of the open string, frequency of a note at fret N, and fret spacing. These simple mathematical formulas are merely here to give you a sense of how a parameter depends on other parameters (e.g., if L increases, T increases with all other parameters the same). These equations are not necessary to understand the underlying concepts. Don't let them scare you!

PITCH

Pitch is determined by several factors: string length, string gauge, string material, string tension. The pitch or frequency of the open string is given by:

$$f = \frac{v}{2L} = \frac{1}{2L}\sqrt{\frac{T}{\mu}} \tag{11.1}$$

where f: fundamental frequency or pitch in Hertz (Hz); v: speed of propagation of wave in m/s; L: scale length in metres (m); T: tension in Newtons (N), approx. mass (kg) × 9.81 (m/s); μ: linear density in kg/m.

Let's solve the equation for μ for the A string in standard tuning. From Table 4.1, we know that f for the A string is 110 Hz. Scale length L is 25.5" (≈ 0.65 m). T is 16 lb (≈ 7.26 kg).[3] Converting all numbers to the correct units, we obtain $\mu \approx 0.0035$ kg/m ≈ 0.0002 lb/in (i.e., string weighs about 2.3 g). For each string, f is defined by the tuning, L is set for the guitar on hand, μ is a property of the string, T solves the equation.

Pitch is inversely proportional to wavelength: as pitch rises (a point on the string moves up and down quicker along the y-axis), the wavelength decreases (nodes get closer to one another along the x-axis). So there is a relationship between space (distance) and time. You can't slow down the vibration of the string (reduce pitch) and keep the same vibration pattern along the string (same wavelength).

Equation (11.1) is somewhat incomplete but enough for our purposes. Other factors affect pitch like temperature or the guitar body's mechanical characteristics. An important factor is string stiffness (elasticity). A stiffer string will be more difficult to bend and made to oscillate like a sine wave, especially when nodes are

---

3. These figures are for Elixir Nanoweb Super Light strings (the A string is 0.032" in diameter); data from the manufacturer.

very close to each other, resulting in poor higher order harmonics. Another effect of stiffness is *inharmonicity* where harmonic frequencies slightly depart from their ideal frequency (multiple of the fundamental).

DID YOU KNOW? The low E, A, and D strings are *wound* strings: a metal/alloy wire is wrapped around a core material (e.g., metal, nylon), like a coil. This raises the linear density μ of the string while keeping the string relatively flexible. In raising μ, the purpose is to lower the pitch of the string, as expressed by Equation (11.1).

PITCH AT FRET N

In equal temperament, the octave is divided into 12 semitones. Since an octave doubles the frequency, the frequency of a note at fret N is given by:

$$f_N = f_0 \times 2^{\frac{N}{12}} \tag{11.2}$$

where f_N: frequency of the note at fret N; f_0: frequency of the note at fret 0. The reference fret can be any fret and N can be positive or negative (N steps above or below the reference fret, which isn't necessarily fret 0).

FRET SPACING

Fret spacing is derived as a sequence, with fret N's position being determined from the previous fret's position:

$$S_N = \frac{L - S_{N-1}}{\left(1 - 2^{-\frac{1}{12}}\right)^{-1}} + S_{N-1}$$

$$S_N \approx \frac{L - S_{N-1}}{17.817} + S_{N-1} \tag{11.3}$$

$$S_0 = 0$$

where S_N: distance from fret N to the nut; L: scale length.

NOTE We always change tunings and assume that tonal distance between neighbouring frets remains a half step. Is it so? Or do we need to reposition the fretwire to restore the half-step spacing? No, luckily, we don't need to. These equations tell us that changing string tension doesn't affect the half step between neighbouring frets.

CENT

In music, the cent is a unit measuring sound frequencies, particularly useful for small quantities due to its logarithmic scale. It is preferred over Hertz when fine-tuning…a tuning (adjusting intonation). In the field of acoustics, perhaps you are more familiar with a similar unit measuring sound amplitude: the decibel (dB).

$$f_{cent} / f_{ref} \text{ as a ratio of 1 cent} = 2^{\frac{1}{1200}}$$

$$f / f_{ref} \text{ in cents} = 1200 \times \log_2\left(\frac{f}{f_{ref}}\right) \tag{11.4}$$

where frequency f_{cent} is 1 cent higher than reference frequency f_{ref}; frequency f is compared to frequency f_{ref}; $\log_2$ is the logarithm to the base 2. Frequency f_{ref} is chosen as desired.

11.2 The harmonic series

The *harmonic series*, also known as the *overtone series*, forms the basis for several topics in music: harmonics, stability, consonance/dissonance, tuning, etc.

In the equal temperament system, an octave is divided into 12 equal intervals of a semitone each (or half step). Each semitone measures 100 cents. Thus the octave measures 1200 cents. Everything we discuss in this book and on the guitar is in an equal-tempered tuning system.

Now we understand that a vibrating string generates a sound made of a fundamental frequency and multiples of that frequency (harmonics). We know that a frequency f_b is an octave higher than a frequency f_a if it is twice that frequency: $f_b = 2f_a$. The octave doubles the frequency. We know that each harmonic component of a sound is a multiple of the fundamental frequency ($f_N = Nf_{fundamental} = Nf_1$). In particular, the 2nd harmonic is twice the fundamental frequency, the 4th harmonic is twice the 2nd harmonic's frequency, and so on.

Suppose we play note A2 (open A) on the guitar's 5th string. That note's 2nd harmonic is an octave above, it's A3; its 4th harmonic is an octave above A3 (or two octaves above A2), it's A4; and so on. In the octave between A5 and A4, there are 12 music notes (12 semitones). Since A5 is A2's 8th harmonic and A4 its 4th harmonic, between A5 and A4, there are also harmonics 5, 6, 7 of note A2. Do the notes relate to the harmonics? Yes, they do! Enter the harmonic series.

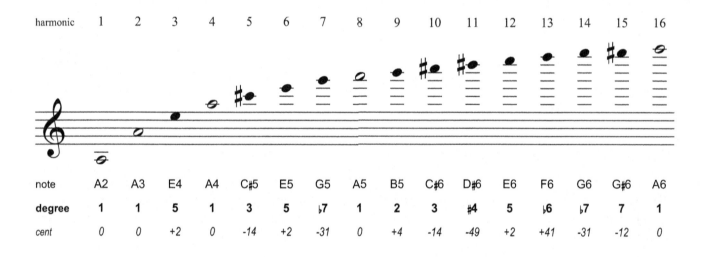

harmonic	1	2	3	4	5	6	7	8	9	10	11	12	13	14	15	16
note	A2	A3	E4	A4	C#5	E5	G5	A5	B5	C#6	D#6	E6	F6	G6	G#6	A6
degree	1	1	5	1	3	5	♭7	1	2	3	#4	5	♭6	♭7	7	1
cent	0	0	+2	0	-14	+2	-31	0	+4	-14	-49	+2	+41	-31	-12	0

Figure 11.14 *Harmonic series of note A2 up to the 16th harmonic*

Figure 11.14 is the harmonic series for A2. It shows how each harmonic corresponds to a note in the equal-tempered system. The fundamental 1 and its octaves (harmonics 2, 4, 8, ... , 2^N) match exactly the fundamental note A2 and its octaves [A3, A4, A5, ... , A(N+2)]. Other harmonics, however, do not precisely match a note on the staff. The closest note to each harmonic is written below the staff; the delta (or error) is specified in cents. For example, the 3rd harmonic of A2 is at frequency 330 Hz (3 × 110 Hz) and it is +2 cents above the closest note E4. The 7th harmonic of A2 is at frequency 770 Hz (7 × 110 Hz) and it is −31 cents below the closest note G5—if you listen to the 7th harmonic and G5, you will hear that they are slightly off. Octaves of A2 match exactly the note on the staff, the error is 0 cent. Figure 11.14 also shows the degree of each note, referenced to the A major scale.

A few observations on the harmonic series:

- The principles we just discussed apply to any note. The scale degree and error in the harmonic series of another note (like C2) are the same as for A2.
- The figure only shows the first 16 harmonics. The 5th and the 3rd scale degrees occur within the first 5 harmonics while the 7th's first appearance is at harmonic 15. But the 4th and the 6th do not appear at all within the first 16 harmonics! If you extend the staff, the 4th eventually appears at harmonic 21 (−29 cents below D) and the 6th appears at harmonic 27 (+6 cents above F♯). These findings have been linked to the stability charts of the Intervals chapter.
- One important note is markedly absent from the first 16 harmonics: ♭3rd.
- At a glance, you can see that notes undergo a logarithmic progression as a function of frequency (the curve described by the series follows that of a logarithm).
- In other publications, the harmonic series is often shown starting on the note C2 in the bass clef 𝄢 and spilling over to the treble clef 𝄞. Here, I chose to show it for the note A2 for several reasons: A2 is the open A string on the guitar, its 4th harmonic A4 is a standard reference pitch (A440), and its frequency is a nice round number 110 Hz. Also recall that the guitar being a transposing instrument, its notation is one octave above actual pitch. So the bass clef is not necessary, the downside is that many ledger lines are.

DID YOU KNOW?   Unlike strobe tuners, standard tuners are not precision devices and at best, they offer resolutions down to ±1 cent. Still, you can observe large deviations between the harmonic and its corresponding note on those devices. For example, first tune your G and B strings. Then, on the G string, strike the 5th harmonic, right behind fret 4. It's the 3rd (B5) and should be quite flat (error: −13.69 cents). Check the same note on the B string at its 4th harmonic on fret 5. It's the octave (B5) and should be spot on (error: 0 cent).

11.3   The harmonics map

▬▬▬ *Reference tables*

The following tables give you the numeric data behind the maps. All equations necessary to create these tables are provided in this book. You can go back to those equations if you need to extract further data or precision beyond two decimal points.

Octaves are highlighted in darker shaded rows. Pay close attention to the relationship between the harmonic number and the scale degree.

Scale length 24.75" is typical of the Gibson Les Paul and scale length 25.5" is typical of the Fender Stratocaster.[4] These two scale lengths are common amongst electric guitars. Scale length 650 mm (25.6") is common for classical guitars. By comparison, the scale length of a Fender Precision Bass is 34".

Table 11.2 indicates that the section of the fretboard between frets 12–24 is half the size of that from the nut to fret 12. Going towards the bridge, every time you divide the string length by two, you go up an octave in pitch. And if you were to extend the neck of the guitar behind the nut in order to drop one octave below the current open strings, with the same string gauge, you would need to add double the length of frets 0–12 to the neck. For a 25.5" scale guitar, that would be an extra…25.5"! Instead, it's more practical to add a thicker string to extend the range (hence the 7-string guitar).

---

4. Reports suggest that what is known as the 24-3/4" scale has evolved over the years to 24-9/16" (since 1969 in the Kalamazoo and Nashville plants) and 24-5/8" (since 1992 in the Montana plant), due to changes in production equipment at Gibson. *Source:* Stewart-MacDonald.

Table 11.1 *Harmonics mapping data*

NOTE				HARMONIC						
Interval from open A (cent)	Interval from open A (Hz)	Note	Scale degree simple / (compound)	Closest harmonic (Hz)	Interval from open A (cent)	Delta: $f_{harmonic} - f_{note}$ (Hz)	Delta: $f_{harmonic} - f_{note}$ (cent)	Proximity of harmonic with note	Harmonic number	Distance between nodes (× scale length)
0	110.00	A2	1	110	0.00	0.00	0.00	right on	1	1
100	116.54									
200	123.47	B2								
300	130.81	C3								
400	138.59									
500	146.83	D3								
600	155.56									
700	164.81	E3								
800	174.61	F3								
900	185.00									
1000	196.00	G3								
1100	207.65									
1200	220.00	A3	1 (8)	220	1200.00	0.00	0.00	right on	2	1/2
1300	233.08									
1400	246.94	B3								
1500	261.63	C4								
1600	277.18									
1700	293.66	D4								
1800	311.13									
1900	329.63	E4	5 (12)	330	1901.96	0.37	1.96	near	3	1/3
2000	349.23	F4								
2100	369.99									
2200	392.00	G4								
2300	415.30									
2400	440.00	A4	1 (15)	440	2400.00	0.00	0.00	right on	4	1/4
2500	466.16									
2600	493.88	B4								
2700	523.25	C5								
2800	554.37	C♯5	3 (17)	550	2786.31	−4.37	−13.69	far	5	1/5
2900	587.33	D5								
3000	622.25									
3100	659.26	E5	5 (19)	660	3101.96	0.74	1.96	near	6	1/6
3200	698.46	F5								
3300	739.99									
3400	783.99	G5	♭7 (♭21)	770	3368.83	−13.99	−31.17	very far	7	1/7
3500	830.61									
3600	880.00	A5	1 (22)	880	3600.00	0.00	0.00	right on	8	1/8
3700	932.33									
3800	987.77	B5	2 (23)	990	3803.91	2.23	3.91	near	9	1/9
3900	1046.50	C6								
4000	1108.73	C♯6	3 (24)	1100	3986.31	−8.73	−13.69	far	10	1/10
4100	1174.66	D6								
4200	1244.51	D♯6	♯4 (♯25)	1210	4151.32	−34.51	−48.68	very far	11	1/11
4300	1318.51	E6	5 (26)	1320	4301.96	1.49	1.96	near	12	1/12
4400	1396.91	F6	♭6 (♭27)	1430	4440.53	33.09	40.53	very far	13	1/13
4500	1479.98									
4600	1567.98	G6	♭7 (♭28)	1540	4568.83	−27.98	−31.17	very far	14	1/14
4700	1661.22	G♯6		1650	4688.27	−11.22	−11.73	far	15	1/15
4800	1760.00	A6	1 (29)	1760	4800.00	0.00	0.00	right on	16	1/16

Table 11.2 *Fret spacing: 1- normalised to scale length L; 2- for L = 24.75" and L = 25.5"*

fret number	fret position (normalised to scale length)	interval from open string (cent)
0	0.00	0
1	0.06	100
2	0.11	200
3	0.16	300
4	0.21	400
5	0.25	500
6	0.29	600
7	0.33	700
8	0.37	800
9	0.41	900
10	0.44	1000
11	0.47	1100
12	0.50	1200
13	0.53	1300
14	0.55	1400
15	0.58	1500
16	0.60	1600
17	0.63	1700
18	0.65	1800
19	0.67	1900
20	0.69	2000
21	0.70	2100
22	0.72	2200
23	0.74	2300
24	0.75	2400

fret number	fret position for scale length (in) 24.75"	fret position for scale length (in) 25.5"
0	0.00	0.00
1	1.39	1.43
2	2.70	2.78
3	3.94	4.06
4	5.11	5.26
5	6.21	6.40
6	7.25	7.47
7	8.23	8.48
8	9.16	9.44
9	10.03	10.34
10	10.86	11.19
11	11.64	11.99
12	12.38	12.75
13	13.07	13.47
14	13.73	14.14
15	14.34	14.78
16	14.93	15.38
17	15.48	15.95
18	16.00	16.48
19	16.49	16.99
20	16.95	17.47
21	17.39	17.92
22	17.80	18.34
23	18.19	18.75
24	18.56	19.13

Fretboard maps

The diagrams only show the nodes of the first 16 harmonics (except the fundamental). Only the harmonics on the A string are pictured. All strings having the same scale length, harmonics on other strings are located exactly in the same position along the neck as on the A string. The scale degree each harmonic is based on is referenced back to the open string, so you can work out the approximate note the harmonic sounds like for each string. For example, if we were to draw the same diagrams for the E string, harmonics would be E (1), B (5), E (1), G♯ (3), B (5), D (♭7), and so on.

As we saw in Section 11.1, the harmonic of order N has $N-1$ nodes, equally spaced. In the diagrams of Figure 11.15, some nodes are "missing." We will see why that is in the properties of harmonics.

Figure 11.16 shows the harmonic number, the corresponding scale degree (for the A string, this refers back to the A major scale), the note the harmonic is closest to, and the fret number where that note can be found. The fret number is chosen within frets 0–11 on the same string and the note's pitch is one or several octaves below the harmonic. For example, harmonic #6 near fret 3 is the 5th of the scale (note E) which can be found on fret 7, but that note on fret 7 is two octaves below the harmonic!

Next page:
Figure 11.15 *Harmonics 2 through 16*

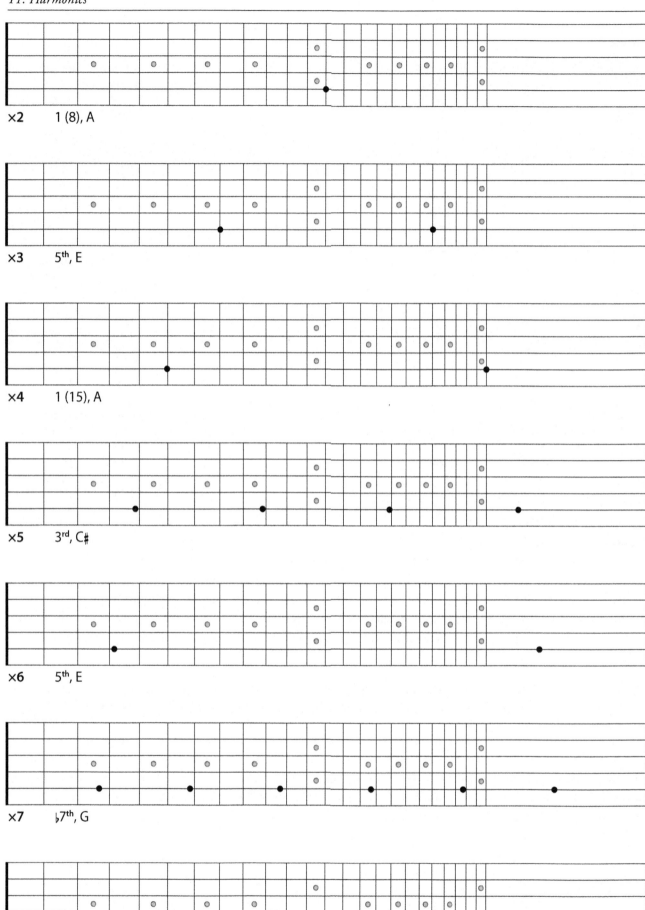

×2   1 (8), A

×3   5th, E

×4   1 (15), A

×5   3rd, C♯

×6   5th, E

×7   ♭7th, G

×8   1 (22), A

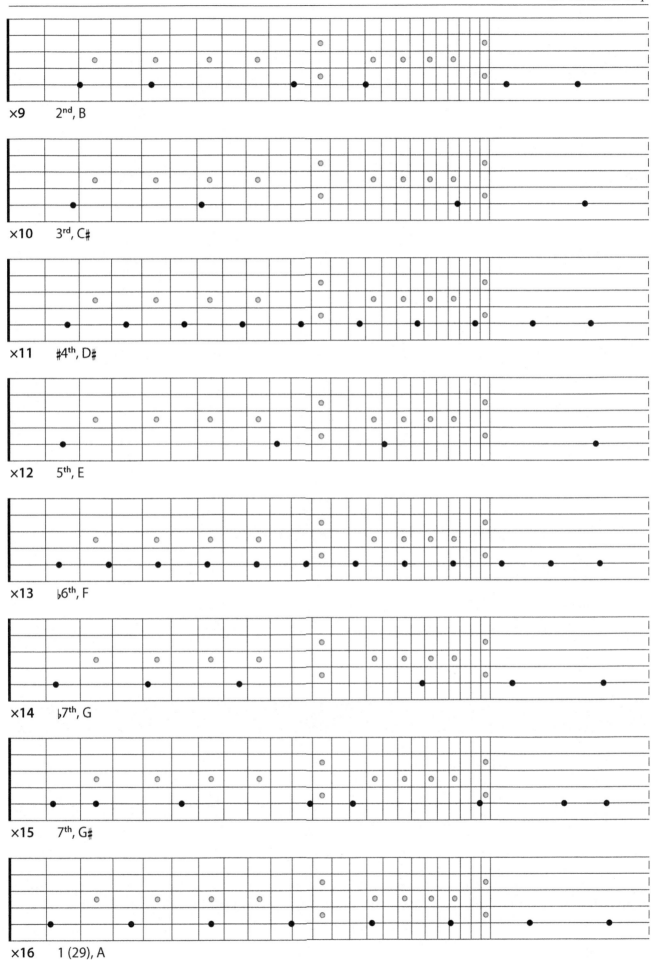

×9   2nd, B

×10   3rd, C#

×11   #4th, D#

×12   5th, E

×13   b6th, F

×14   b7th, G

×15   7th, G#

×16   1 (29), A

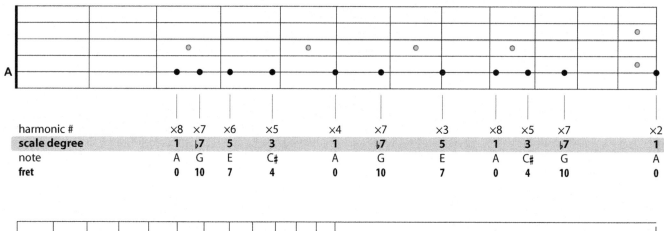

harmonic #	×8	×7	×6	×5	×4	×7	×3	×8	×5	×7	×2
scale degree	1	♭7	5	3	1	♭7	5	1	3	♭7	1
note	A	G	E	C♯	A	G	E	A	C♯	G	A
fret	0	10	7	4	0	10	7	0	4	10	0

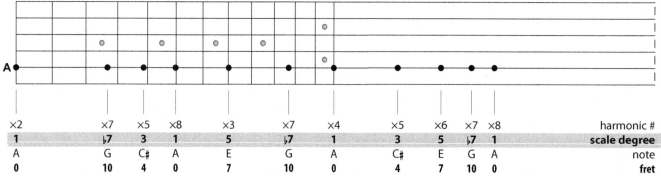

×2	×7	×5	×8	×3	×7	×4	×5	×6	×7	×8	harmonic #
1	♭7	3	1	5	♭7	1	3	5	♭7	1	**scale degree**
A	G	C♯	A	E	G	A	C♯	E	G	A	note
0	10	4	0	7	10	0	4	7	10	0	**fret**

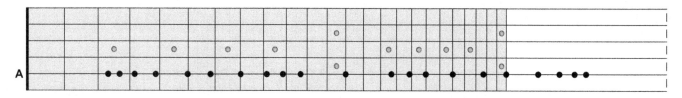

Figure 11.16 *Harmonics 2 through 8 within frets 0–12, fret 12–bridge, and over the neck*

11.4 Properties of harmonics

▬▬ *General properties*

These simple properties allow you to eyeball the location of a harmonic you may not be familiar with and understand what to expect when dealing with harmonics on the guitar. By the way, on guitar, we generally speak of "the harmonic at fret so-and-so" when in fact we refer to a harmonic node.

As evidenced by the diagrams, harmonics do not stop at the fretboard, they extend all the way to the bridge.

Fret 12 is an axis of symmetry for all harmonics. A harmonic of order *N* on one side of fret 12 is also available symmetrically on the other side of fret 12. Or put differently, the harmonic at distance D from fret 12 is also available at distance D from fret 12, on the opposite side.

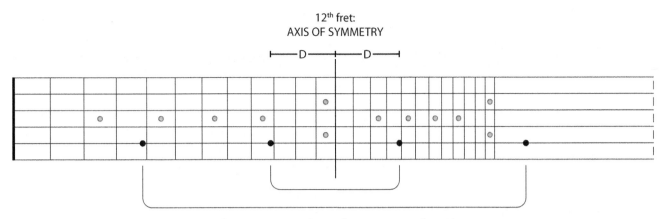

Figure 11.17 *Axis of symmetry at fret 12*

Unlike fretted notes, harmonics make no distinction between the nut and the bridge—these are just two ends of the same string! A harmonic of order N located at distance D from the nut is also available at an equal distance from the bridge. This and the previous property are two sides of the same coin (fret 12 symmetry). When locating a node near fret 12, you can rely on the former, and when locating a node near the nut or the bridge, you can rely on the latter.

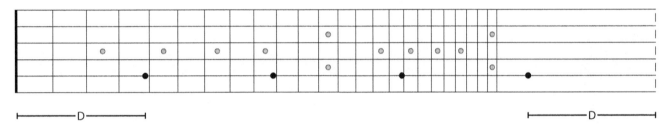

Figure 11.18 *Equidistance from nut and from bridge*

Harmonics are placed according to a linear scale and frets are placed according to a logarithmic scale. Therefore, relating harmonics' location to frets is difficult and inaccurate except at specific points like octaves.

As a rule of thumb, lower order harmonics are louder than higher order harmonics. In fact, harmonic N is likely to sound louder than harmonic $N+1$. For this reason, only the first few harmonics are of practical use (e.g., the 16th harmonic is probably difficult to hear). This is not always the case; we saw in the example of Figure 11.13-1 that harmonic 4 is not audible (always equal to zero), but harmonic 5 is audible.

In theory, a harmonic of order N has at most $N-1$ available nodes (the two nodes corresponding to the nut and bridge are not available). Nodes are spaced at every $\lambda_N/2$, starting from the nut or the bridge, BUT the sound for some of these nodes may be drowned out by lower order harmonics. This leads to the next point.

A node of harmonic N must be the lowest order harmonic node at that location in order to sound at frequency f_N (Table 11.3).[5] If not, the sound of harmonic N will be drowned out by some lower order harmonics which f_N is a multiple of. In Figure 11.19, the 4th harmonic has three nodes but one node is shared with the 2nd harmonic (sounds at f_2) so only two nodes will sound at f_4. This is the reason why there are *missing nodes* on the neck diagrams of Figure 11.15. This also means that a harmonic of order N contains harmonics of order $k \times N$ (where k is an integer) so it is not a pure sine wave. For example, the harmonic of order 3 on fret 7 contains not only the 3rd harmonic but also multiples of that harmonic: 6th, 9th, 12th, 15th, etc.

---

5. A short computer program can determine the number of harmonic nodes sounding at f_N for a given N. It involves prime numbers.

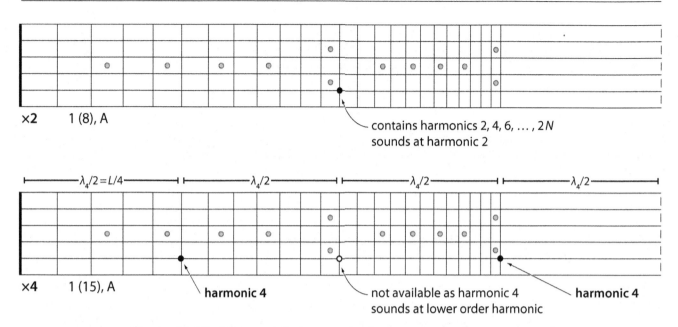

contains harmonics 2, 4, 6, … , 2*N*
sounds at harmonic 2

×2   1 (8), A

×4   1 (15), A

harmonic 4

not available as harmonic 4
sounds at lower order harmonic

harmonic 4

Figure 11.19 *Missing node: lower order harmonic is the dominant sound*

Table 11.3 *Number of dominant nodes of Nth harmonic (N is the lowest order of harmonics at these nodes)*

Order *N* of harmonic	1	2	3	4	5	6	7	8	9	10	11	12	13	14	15	16
Number of nodes sounding at frequency f_N	0	1	2	2	4	2	6	4	6	4	10	4	12	6	8	8

Depending on the initial conditions (such as the way or the location the string is plucked), some harmonics may be very quiet or even absent. See Figure 11.13.

Since the string length can be divided at will, there is an infinite number of harmonics available. But higher order harmonics are faint, and at some point beyond the audible range. There is a harmonic node literally anywhere on the string (as shown in Figure 11.20, and that's only the first 16 harmonics)!

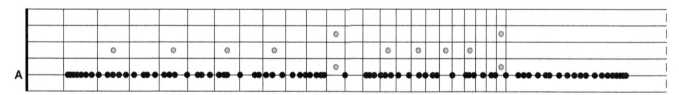

Figure 11.20 *A harmonic node anywhere: harmonics 2–16*

▬▬ *Transposing harmonics*

The harmonics maps shown so far are for the open string. What happens to those harmonics if we fret a string? Are the harmonics still available? Do they remain at the same location on the fretboard? Where can we find the nodes?

The harmonics map for the open string is based on the guitar's scale length (length of the open string). By fretting a string at fret *N*, the string length is reduced and the new effective scale length is the distance from fretwire N to the bridge. So the harmonics map is shifted towards the bridge and its spacing is compressed, just like frets. The new harmonics map is the same with fret N now acting as fret 0: simply shift all natural harmonics by N frets towards the bridge. The example in Figure 11.21 shows how harmonics shift two frets up towards the bridge when fretting the string at fret 2.

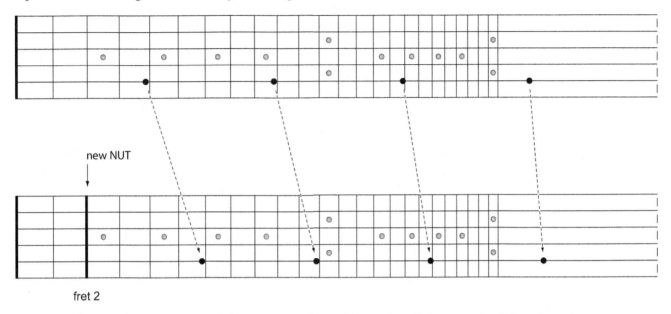

Figure 11.21 *Transposing harmonics to fret 2 (shown for 5th harmonic): shift nodes 2 frets up*

11.5 How to produce harmonics

Since you now understand the mechanism behind harmonics, you know that frets are not involved in generating them. All you need is the string and two posts—the nut (or fret subbing as nut) at one end of the string and the bridge at the other end. You simply need to know the specific points on the string to reach for to get a harmonic (like acupuncture!). Harmonics generated with an open string are called *natural harmonics* and harmonics generated with a fretted string (stopped note) are called *artificial harmonics*.[6] This distinction is only one of terminology and the underlying method to generate the harmonic is identical in both cases.

▰▰▰ *Isolating a harmonic*

What do we mean when we talk about harmonics on guitar? So far, we have defined harmonics and we know that the waveform of a vibrating string is the superposition of an infinite number of harmonic waveforms. We have located where, along the string, each harmonic has its nodes, and have characterised several properties of harmonics (frequency, associated note, etc.). But can we extract a particular harmonic and hear its sound? By performing a specific manoeuvre on the vibrating string, it is possible to isolate the harmonic of order N, and all its multiples (harmonics of order $2N$, $3N$, $4N$, ... , $k \times N$, where k is an integer). This manoeuvre doesn't discriminate between harmonic N and its multiples: we get them all! But amongst all these harmonics, the sound of the lowest order harmonic is usually dominant—what we mostly hear—and we simply talk of the Nth harmonic, ignoring the higher order multiples that also make up the sound.

---

6. There is nothing "artificial" about artificial harmonics. They are bona fide harmonics, just like natural harmonics.

In the example of Figure 11.22, we have a vibrating string on a guitar of scale length *L*. That vibrating string, at any time *t*, is made of the superposition of the fundamental and its harmonics.[7] We want to extract the 3rd harmonic (h3). That harmonic has two nodes, where at all times, the associated waveform stands still (does not swing up and down). Let's focus on the node marked by a dot in the figure. We see that all other harmonics are moving up and down at that node, except for multiples of the 3rd harmonic (6th, 9th, 12th, *k* × 3 harmonics). By placing a finger on the string at that node and quickly removing it, we choke all vibrating harmonics, except those with a node (a zero) at that location. The harmonics with a node at that location stand still at the node anyway, whether we poke the string or not. Therefore, those harmonics will keep vibrating after we poke the node with our finger. The resulting waveform is only made of harmonic 3 and its multiples *k* × 3 (usually sounding a lot weaker). This is how we can manually extract the 3rd harmonic.

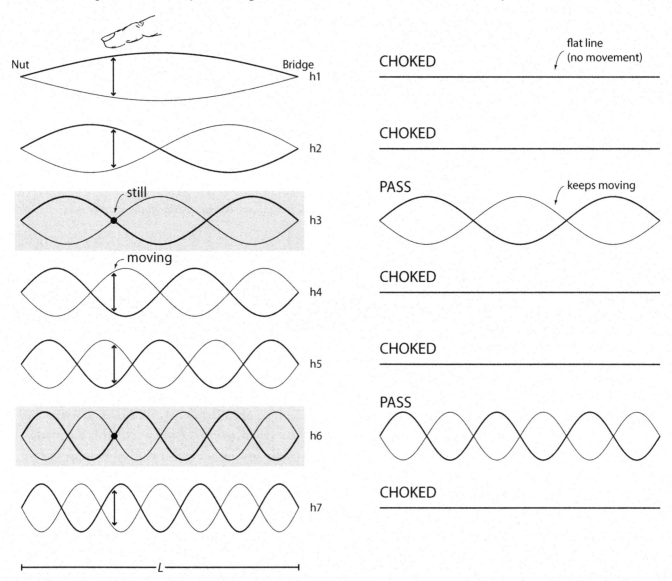

Figure 11.22 *Generating the 3rd harmonic*

The flesh of the finger makes contact with the string not just at the node but on a tiny stretch of string around the node too. So the string's vibration will be choked at the node and dampened on that stretch. This is another reason why higher order harmonics (shorter wavelength) sound weaker.

---

7. To better show each harmonic, the amplitudes are not to scale and are shown at their maximum swing

You have to remember that when you first pick the string, all these harmonic waveforms coexist at the same time within the string's motion. You don't "see" each individual harmonic as shown on the graphs. Think of them as riding on top of the fundamental. Consequently, all the nodes for the harmonics are in fact moving up and down over time, even though we say they stand still. They stand still relative to their own swing.

Figure 11.23 shows the fundamental (h1) and harmonic 5 (h5) on their own. If the vibrating string was only made of h1 and h5, the resulting waveform h1 + h5 at that moment would look as if h5 was riding on top of h1! You can see that the nodes of h5 would be moving up and down as h1 moves up and down.

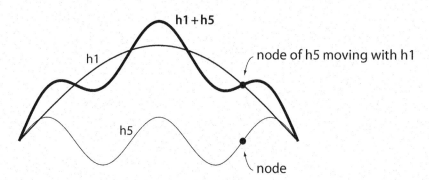

Figure 11.23 *Harmonics ride on top of each other*

Be it for natural or artificial harmonics, the most commonly played harmonic is hands down the octave at fret *N* + 12. It's easy to find, is quite loud, and is the same note as the fundamental note (open or fretted at fret *N*). But you can see that there are plenty more harmonics up for grabs!

DID YOU KNOW?   Other instruments produce harmonics too (e.g., strings, horns). The sound of a note any instrument produces is made up of the superposition of harmonics. So all instruments are capable of generating harmonics, but not all instruments offer a practical means to isolate "individual" harmonics (like the piano).

▬▬ *Natural harmonics*

Natural harmonics are based on the full scale of the guitar (string length is from nut to bridge) and are at fixed locations according to the maps shown earlier. Here are several ways to generate natural harmonics:

Harmonic node struck by left hand finger:
- Lightly touch a node with a left hand finger, then pluck/pick the string with the right hand and immediately let go of the string with your left hand finger. You can also pluck the string with the right hand first and then touch the node with the left hand finger. As seen in the previous section, by placing your left hand finger on a harmonic node, your finger does not affect the string vibrations caused by that particular harmonic (pass). Yet, your finger kills the string vibrations caused by other harmonics (choked). Remember that the string's vibration is made of the superposition of several harmonic waveforms.

Harmonic node struck by right hand finger:
- Lightly touch a node with a right hand finger (usually index or middle) and pluck the string with another right hand finger (e.g., thumb, middle, ring, pinkie) or the pick. Immediately remove the right hand finger from the node. A popular pairing is index (poke/choke) + thumb (pluck). We'll call this technique *pluck 'n' poke*.
- Pick the string and in the same pick motion, immediately choke it with the side of the thumb at a node. This technique is called *pinch harmonic*. The right hand sets the string in motion (pick) and chokes it

(side of thumb). This method usually brings out harmonic nodes located in the picking area.

- With a right hand finger (e.g., index or middle), tap on the string over a harmonic node. Your finger will set the string in motion and choke it at the same time. This technique is coined *tapped harmonic* (or the grittier slapped harmonic). Unlike the other methods, the string bounces off the fretwire near the node. As a result, this is most effective at harmonic nodes located right over a fretwire (like frets 5, 7, 12). When tapping on the string, keep the tapping finger loose and bouncy for best result (don't stiffen it up).

NOTE In tapped harmonics, the fleshy part of the finger sets the string in motion and chokes it by acting as a cushion on the string near the harmonic node. Try doing this with the edge of your pick (narrow and hard material). The edge will strike only the node and won't choke the string nearby; you will hear more of the fundamental and less of the harmonics.

Artificial harmonics

Artificial harmonics are produced with a fretted string. The string is effectively shortened and the new scale length is the distance between the fretted fret and the bridge (as opposed to the nut and the bridge for natural harmonics). The harmonics map is transposed accordingly, with the fretted fret acting as the new nut.

The left hand is no longer available since its job is to fret the string. The harmonic must come from the right hand which plucks and chokes the string. This can be done through the same right hand methods already discussed.

Artificial harmonics allow you to play harmonics for various scale lengths and to add effects on top such as string bends or vibratos. For example, a pinch harmonic (of order N) followed by a left hand string bend raises the pitch of the harmonic: the string keeps vibrating in its harmonic mode N (and its multiples) while the string is bent. Another variant involves continuously hammering on and pulling off a string (open or not) with the left hand and sliding the flesh of the right hand palm/finger (like the pinkie) on the string, lightly brushing it. The hammer-on/pull-off sets and keeps the string in motion while the right hand flesh rakes random harmonics along the way. Another dazzling effect is the luscious sound of *harp harmonics* where a chord grip is arpeggiated through a cascade of regular notes (plucked) and harmonics (pluck 'n' poke).

DID YOU KNOW? Since for harmonics, there is no distinction between the nut and the bridge (two ends of the string), you can pluck the string behind or in front of the node you choke the string at. For instance, you can choke the string at fret 12 and pluck it anywhere between the nut and fret 12, or you can pluck it between fret 12 and the bridge—it doesn't matter, you still get the 2nd harmonic. Try it!

A real-life example of plucking the string behind the harmonic node (between nut and node) is the left hand hammer-on/pull-off and right hand palm/finger sliding harmonics, just described. Another example is to use the pluck 'n' poke technique with the left hand. If you feel adventurous, you could play harmonics with both hands at the same time, using pluck 'n' poke for the left and the right hand!

Ghost harmonics

Earlier, we pointed out missing nodes on the harmonics maps. They are missing because at those nodes, the sound of a lower order harmonic prevails. Despite being drowned out, higher order harmonics sharing those nodes are in fact present in the resulting harmonic sound. But is there a way to isolate these higher order harmonics? Now that we know how to generate harmonics, let's take a closer look through an example.

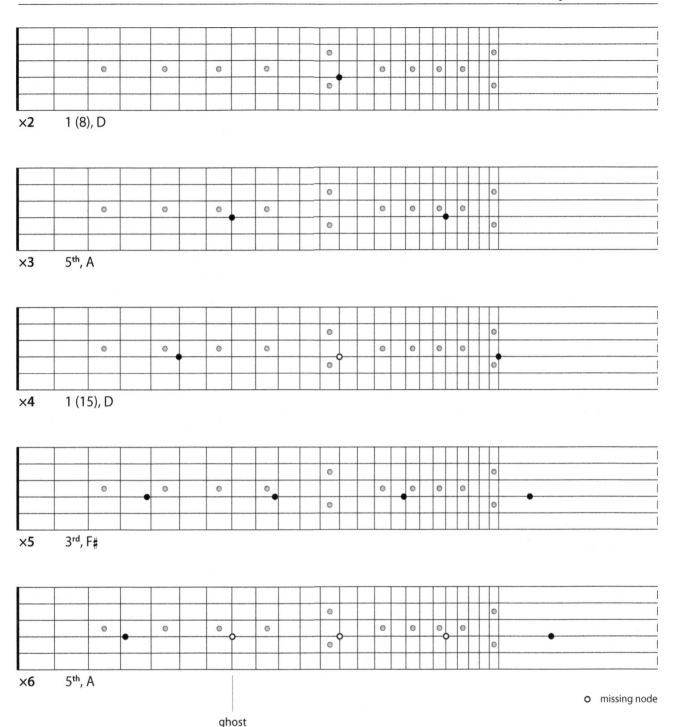

× 2   1 (8), D

× 3   5th, A

× 4   1 (15), D

× 5   3rd, F♯

× 6   5th, A

ghost

○   missing node

Figure 11.24 *How to generate ghost harmonics at missing nodes*

Figure 11.24 shows all the nodes, including missing nodes, for the 2nd, 3rd, 4th, 5th, and 6th harmonics of the open D string. **Prep step:** strike the 2nd harmonic (h2) on the D string at fret 12 (pluck the string with the right hand and lightly touch the string above fret 12 with your left hand finger) and let it ring. The sound you hear is mostly that of h2 but also contains all its multiples h4, h6, h8, h10, etc.

- While the string is still ringing at h2, with your left hand finger, lightly touch the string above fret 5 (that's a node for h4). You now hear h4. Double-check this by striking the harmonic at fret 5 from scratch. You hear the same pitch: h4.

- Repeat the prep step. While the string is still ringing at h2, lightly touch the string above fret 7 (that's a node for h3 and a missing node for h6). <u>You now hear h6</u>. You don't believe it? Strike the harmonic on fret 7 again from scratch, you will hear that it sounds different! It sounds at h3. You can cross-check for the sound of h6 by striking the harmonic near fret 3 from scratch.

- Repeat the prep step again. While the string is still ringing at h2, lightly touch the string above fret 9. Under normal circumstances, fret 9 is a node for h5. However, no sound comes out of the guitar anymore and the string is mute. Why? Harmonic h5 is not a multiple of h2 so the vibrating string at h2 does not have a node at fret 9. When touching the string above fret 9, you choked h2 and its multiples, leaving nothing else to ring.

I like to call the harmonic you got out of the missing node a *ghost harmonic*, because it is available but you have to know how to let it out of the closet! While it is possible to isolate those harmonics with missing nodes, it is not always practical in a playing situation (it's a multi-step process).[8]

DID YOU KNOW? *Ghost notes* are produced by lightly depressing the string with the left hand—but not fully to fret the note—and then plucking the string. The string is almost muted but not quite: you get a quick-decay sound out of it (it doesn't ring for long). The pitch that is produced is a mix of choked string at a nondescript pitch and some high-pitch component, making for an overall metallic sound. If you listen carefully, that high-pitch component is in fact a harmonic. Therefore, in the methods outlined to generate a harmonic, if you leave the finger on the node, you get a ghost note. Try it with the A string: brush the string with your left hand finger, and move it up and down the string, all the while you're picking.

Harmonics and pickups

When a magnetic pickup is used to capture the string's vibrations, the location of the harmonic node with respect to the pickup matters. If the harmonic node is located right atop the pickup (especially the narrower single-coil pickup), little sound will come out of that pickup. This is because the string is still and does not vibrate at a harmonic node. All of a sudden, a harmonic you hear unplugged will sound faint when plugged in. Unplugged, you hear vibrations over the entire string; plugged in, you only hear vibrations over a narrow section of the string located above and near the pickup. Switch to another pickup or a combination of pickups to avoid this situation. This phenomenon never occurs for the open string or the fretted note because the nodes of the fundamental (h1) are always at the nut / fretted fret and at the bridge, never over the pickups. Note that a piezoelectric pickup, frequently found in acoustic guitars, senses variations in pressure rather than magnetic field and is therefore immune to this issue.

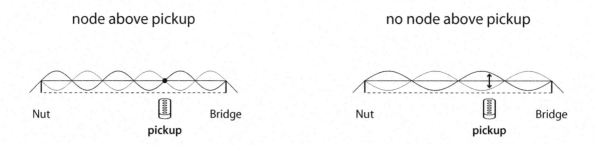

Figure 11.25 *Harmonic node and pickup placement*

---

8. The ghost harmonic $hk \times N$ is a multiple of the regular harmonic (i.e., sounding) hN because they share the missing node. The way to get to the ghost harmonic is to set the string in motion at harmonic hk, then stun the string at the missing node. In the example, $N = 3$, $k = 2$.

▬▬▬ *Harmonics and amplifiers*

An ideal amplifier is a *linear system*: a pure tone (sine wave) at its input produces the same pure tone at its output, only stronger in intensity. So if we plug into an ideal amplifier, the note coming out of our guitar—the fundamental with its harmonics—will come out of the amplifier sounding exactly the same, just louder. An amplifier in saturation is a *non-linear system*: a pure tone at its input produces the same pure tone at its output but also adds harmonics of the pure tone at the output. The ouput is no longer a replica of the input: it's *distorted*. This is what an overdriven guitar amplifier or a distortion pedal does. As a result, if we plug our guitar into such non-linear system, the sound of a note (which is a pure tone + its harmonics) will come out stronger but the harmonics are further boosted by the amplifier. This doesn't change the sound coming out of the guitar (its harmonics included); the change occurs afterwards, once the signal goes through the overdriven amplifier or the effects pedal. So with distortion, you can enhance your ability to get harmonics.

11.6 Applications of harmonics

Not only can you use harmonics in a musical context, you can also use them to set up your guitar. We look at a few use cases here.

▬▬▬ *Tuning the guitar*

There is a widespread idea that tuning with the help of harmonics is very accurate, if not more accurate than other tuning methods. Let's look into that more closely. One such method is through the harmonics found at (near) frets 5 and 7. Here is how it goes (Figure 11.26).

1. We need a reference pitch, such as that given by a tuning fork (the most common tuning fork generates A4 = 440 Hz). We will first start with the 5th string A, which should be tuned to A2 = 110 Hz. Even though the tuning fork's pitch is two octaves higher, adjust the tuning gear on the guitar so that the sound from the string and the pure tone from the tuning fork match. They will be octaves apart but you can't mistakenly tune to any other A than A2 because the string would either be extremely loose or extremely tight. So you would know if your ear locked to the wrong octave. That being said, with your knowledge of harmonics, you can get hold of A4 (4th harmonic) near fret 5. Strike the tuning fork and while it resonates, tune the A string so that the harmonic at fret 5 matches the tuning fork. When you get close, you will hear a *beat*—a pulsating sound or warble—which corresponds to the error in pitch between the A string and the tuning fork: **error** = $f_A - f_{ref}$.[9] Finely adjust the tuning gear until you no longer hear the beat. As you turn the tuning gear to adjust string pitch: if the beat becomes "quicker," the error is increasing; if the beat becomes "slower," the error is decreasing. Once this error reduces to zero and you no longer hear the beat, the A string is in tune at A2 = 110 Hz. Next, we tune the 6th string E.

2. The 6th string E is down a P4 interval from the 5th string A, tuned to A2. The 6th string should therefore be tuned to E2.[10] Since each string has the same harmonics pattern, once in tune, the E string will have its 4th harmonic E4 over fret 5. The A string, which is already in tune, has its 3rd harmonic E4 (5th degree of A major scale) over fret 7. So generate these harmonics on strings 6 and 5 and let them ring, then simply adjust the E string for the beat sound (error) to disappear. The E string is now tuned to E2. But if you look closely at Table 11.1, E2 is not exactly E2! The 3rd harmonic E4 over fret 7 on the A string is +1.96 cents above the note E4 in equal temperament. This trickles down to E2 which is also

---

9. The strobe tuner turns this audible beat signal into a visual signal you can see, making for precise tuning to a reference signal.
10. The tipping point for the numbering of octaves is the note C. It goes like so: **C1** D1 E1 F1 G1 A1 B1 **C2** D2 E2 F2 G2 A2 B2 **C3** D3.... The lowest C on the piano is C1 and the middle C on the grand staff is C4.

+1.96 cents sharp. So our E string is almost in tune, it is +1.96 cents sharp. *Read this paragraph again and make sure it is understood before moving on.* Next, we tune the 4th string D.

3. The 4th string D is up a P4 interval from the 5th string A, tuned to A2. It should therefore be tuned to D3. We proceed in a similar fashion as in step 2. The A string has its 4th harmonic A4 over fret 5. Once in tune, the D string will have its 3rd harmonic A4 (5th degree of D major scale) over fret 7. So generate these harmonics on strings 5 and 4 and let them ring, then simply adjust the D string for the beat to disappear. The D string is now tuned to D3. But again, D3 is not exactly D3! The 3rd harmonic A4 over fret 7 on the D string is +1.96 cents above the note A4 in equal temperament. This trickles down to D3 which is –1.96 cents flat. Be careful with the error sign: unlike the low E string tuning, the error sign here is negative.[11] So our D string is almost in tune, it is –1.96 cents flat. Next, we tune the 3rd string G.

4. Same as in the previous step. We end up with the G string being almost in tune: it is tuned to G3 but is –1.96 cents flat compared to the D string, which is already –1.96 cents flat compared to the A string, which is in tune. So the G string is a cumulative -2×1.96 cents ≈ -3.91 cents flat.

5. Now, we tune the 2nd string B. We can't proceed like before because the 2nd string B is up a M3 interval from the 3rd string G, tuned to G3—it is no longer a P4 interval. The 2nd string should therefore be tuned to B3. **One alternative is to seek the 3rd harmonic B3 on the 6th string E, fret 7.** So generate that harmonic on the low E string and pluck the open B string, then simply adjust the B string for the beat to disappear. The B string is now tuned to B3. But hang on, the E string was tuned +1.96 cents sharp and looking at Table 11.1, its 3rd harmonic is also +1.96 cents above B3. So we just tuned the B string $+2 \times 1.96$ cents $\approx +3.91$ cents sharp. Our B string is almost in tune, it is +3.91 cents sharp. Last, we tune the 1st string E.

6. The 1st string E is up a P4 from the 2nd string B, tuned to B3. It should therefore be tuned to E4. We can use the same method as in step 3, tuning the high E string with the help of the B string and harmonics on frets 5 and 7. This would result in the high E string being +1.96 cents sharp. But with several intermediate tuning steps separating the B string and our reference A string, there is the possibility we introduced additional error. There is a better way. In step 2, we used the A string's 3rd harmonic E4 over fret 7. We use that again to tune the high E string. Generate the harmonic on string 5 and pluck the open high E string, then simply adjust the high E string for the beat to disappear. The high E string is now tuned to E4, with a +1.96 cents error.

In step 1, if you don't have a reference pitch available to you, you can tune the A string to how your ear remembers that string should sound like, and proceed with the rest of the method. The guitar will be in tune with itself (relative tuning) but probably out of tune with standard tuning: strings will be all flat or all sharp. You can fret harmonics on frets 5 and 7 at once with fingers 1 and 3 or better, 1 and 4. In steps 5 & 6, pluck the open string softly so as not to overpower the harmonic on the other string. The choice of harmonics for tuning is limited because some introduce significant error ($\times 5/3$, $\times 7/\flat 7$) or are difficult to bring out ($\times 9/2$).

The table summarises the results. For comparison, the small table on its right shows the results achieved by the most common tuning method for guitar, using the 5th fret / open string combination, except for strings 3 & 2 where the 4th fret / open string combination is used. In this method of tuning, the lower string is fretted at fret 5 and the next string up is tuned open to match the lower string. By depressing the string against the fret, string tension slightly increases compared to the open string, thereby introducing an error in the tuning. So the table on the far right ought to be edited by indicating an error in all cells in the delta column except for the A string tuned open to the tuning fork. Each string is slightly sharp, except A which is spot on, and the low E string which is slightly flat.

---

11. Once in tune, error (actual – ideal): open A (A2) = 0, A string fret 5 harmonic (A4) = 0, D string fret 7 harmonic (A4) = 0, open D (D3) = –1.96.

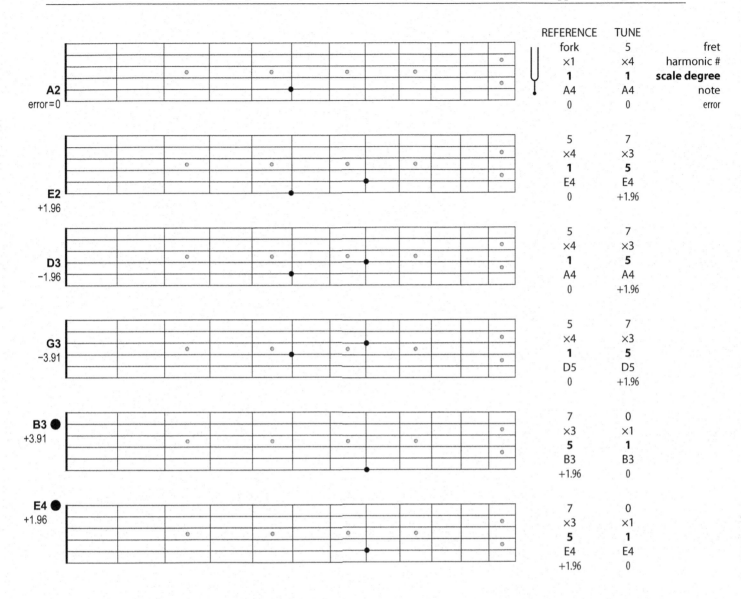

Tuning with harmonics					Tuning with 5th fret / open string		
string / standard tuning	frequency in standard tuning (Hz)	tuning to note*	frequency of resulting tuning (Hz)	delta: $f_{tuned} - f_{standard\ tuning}$ (cent)	tuning to note	frequency of resulting tuning (Hz)	delta: $f_{tuned} - f_{standard\ tuning}$ (cent)†
6　E2	82.41	E4	82.50	1.96	A2	82.41	0.00
5　A2	110.00	A4	110.00	0.00	A2	110.00	0.00
4　D3	146.83	A4	146.67	−1.96	D3	146.83	0.00
3　G3	196.00	D5	195.56	−3.91	G3	196.00	0.00
2　B3	246.94	B3	247.50	3.91	B3	246.94	0.00
1　E4	329.63	E4	330.00	1.96	E4	329.63	0.00

* Tuning is to a harmonic and approximately corresponds to the note in column 3.	† In reality, error is ≠ 0.

Figure 11.26 *Tuning with harmonics (5th/7th fret method)*

So the accuracy of this harmonics tuning method is a myth but there are some advantages:

- No string is depressed, therefore no extra string tension is skewing the tuning process. We are either dealing with harmonics or open strings.
- Once the two harmonics on the strings are produced, the left hand can start adjusting the tuning gears while the two notes keep ringing. This is not the case with the 5th fret / open string method where the left hand must depress a string at all times.
- By "purifying" the tone (no other component of the string's sound is ringing except those harmonics with a node on frets 5 and 7), we are now comparing two signals closer to a pure tone and the difference (i.e., the error or beat) is clearer to the ear. This is an extra prop to help us tune. The beat is still there if the open string and fretted string are compared, but not as clear because it drowns in other harmonic components.
- The error is at a more noticeable frequency. Assume f_{ref} is the tuned frequency of the open string and f_{open} is the current/untuned frequency of the open string you are tuning. When tuning at the open string frequency (low frequency), the error is $f_{ref} - f_{open}$. When tuning at the Nth harmonic of the open string (higher frequency), the error is multiplied $N \times (f_{ref} - f_{open})$ and is still detectable even if $f_{ref} - f_{open}$ is very small. It's like "hearing" the error under a magnifying glass!

We could have saved ourselves the entire analysis by simply looking at Table 11.1 and taking stock of the fact that the only note that A and any of its harmonics are perfectly in tune with is A (and its octaves). With all the other 11 notes in the equal-tempered system, there is some error. Therefore, the only note we can hope to tune the guitar to with a reference pitch of A and harmonics…is the note A.

▬▬ *Intonation*

You can sometimes read in the guitar manufacturer's setup guide or owner's manual to check the *intonation* of your guitar at fret 12. Intonation is a fine measure of pitch accuracy. Look at Table 11.1 & Table 11.2-1. On a tuned string, you see that the 2nd harmonic coincides exactly with fret 12 (1200 cents above open string), both for location and for pitch. Remember that fret 12 must be the midpoint of the string length. If you bring out the harmonic right above fret 12 and then fret the string at fret 12, the two notes should sound identical. If not, the intonation of the guitar is off and needs correcting. What this means is that the string length (scale length L) is not exactly what the fret spacing was designed for (e.g., scale length $L_{design} = 25.5"$). You can't do anything about fret spacing but on most guitars (except acoustic guitars), you can adjust the string length. You do this by slightly moving the bridge saddle for that string—you'll need a few iterations to get it right:

- Move the saddle back towards the bridge if the fretted note was sharp compared to the harmonic (L increases so f drops). See Equation (11.1).
- Move the saddle forward towards the nut if the fretted note was flat (L decreases so f rises).

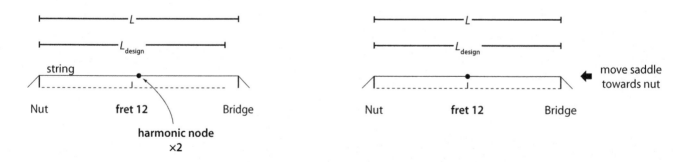

Figure 11.27 *Correcting intonation: fretted note flat, reduce L*

Feedback

Have you ever noticed situations when your guitar is plugged into an amplifier, you hold a note, the note keeps ringing and at some point may gradually shift to a higher pitch, sustain itself, and become louder? Or, perhaps you are holding your electric guitar minding your own business, not even playing, and a string or a group of strings starts to vibrate, gradually sounding louder and louder? These are symptoms of *feedback*. Feedback requires two ingredients: 1- an energy source, 2- a means for the output signal (from the speaker) to reinforce the input signal (from the pickup): a loop. When the string is vibrating, it usually contains more than one frequency component. The energy source (mains powering the amplifier) helps amplify the signal. The amplified signal further excites the string at the resonance frequency and the signal to be amplified gets stronger, in turn producing an even stronger output from the amplifier, which further excites the string, and so forth. This snowballs and could go on forever if it weren't for the saturation boundaries of the system. Whether this happens to an open string or a fretted string, the system naturally leans towards a harmonic frequency. This is why the initial note may gradually shift towards a higher pitch.

If the guitar isn't plugged in or on an acoustic guitar, there is no chance for feedback because there is no energy source fuelling the string's vibration. If the guitar is plugged in and you add a filter within the loop, like a soundhole cover for an amplified acoustic guitar, you are reducing the gain at the resonance frequency and feedback won't set in. Think of it as breaking up the loop.

The block diagram in Figure 11.28 conceptually represents the feedback loop. It is made of the guitar pickup (converting sound to electricity), the amplifier (acting as the energy source, making the signal larger), the speaker (converting electricity back to sound). The loop is closed by a filter, made of the joint action of the medium separating the speaker and the pickup (air/ether, distance, orientation, etc.) and the guitar body and string (with their acoustic properties). The system senses the string's motion above the pick (over time), reinforced by the feedback signal $w_{feedback}(t)$, and amplifies it. w: open loop string vibration (no feedback), $w_{feedback}$: reinforcement of string vibration through feedback, w_{string}: actual string vibration sensed by pickup.

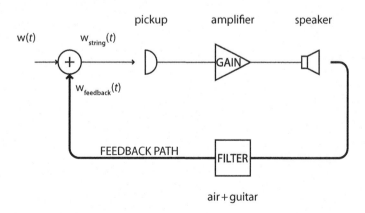

Figure 11.28 *Audio feedback loop*

A | INTERVAL SHAPES

This collection of diagrams is an interval "eye chart" and judging by the sheer number of intervals shown, you don't want to memorise this (not in one sitting anyway!). It's only for reference. To limit the number of diagrams, I have deliberately put constraints on selected interval shapes:

- Intervals range from unison (1) to two octaves (15).
- Only intervals spanning 6 frets or less are shown (6 frets is the size of an extended left hand position).
- Only perfect and major intervals are shown.
- Gap intervals (five ♯/♭ intervals, noted as ♭) are provided separately and restricted to ♭2–♭7 range only.

Shapes are shown in the order of increasing string separation: the notes of the interval are on the same string, one string apart, two strings apart, etc. Occasionally, a shape is skipped in a particular sequence; that's because it spans more than 6 frets.

Many shapes repeat from string to string. Watch for shapes that incorporate strings 3–2 (half-step shift). An interval on a pair of strings of separation N has the same shape regardless of the strings as long as the pair does not include strings 3–2.[1] If the pair includes strings 3–2, the interval shape becomes one fret narrower or wider. This is much easier to understand through an example. Look at the interval of a 5th on pairs of strings of separation 2 (the last four interval shapes in the 5th's row). The 5th on string pairs 6–4 and 5–3 is four frets wide. But the 5th on string pairs 4–2 and 3–1 is only three frets wide, because the pair includes strings 3–2. Recognise repeating shapes and their string 3–2 transformation so there is less to learn.

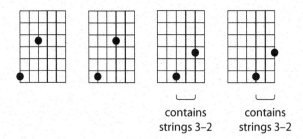

contains strings 3–2   contains strings 3–2

Figure A.1 *Interval containing strings 3–2 is one fret narrower*

Each shape is made of scale degrees 1 (bottom note) and X (top note), but also $\overline{X}$ (bottom) and 1 (top), thanks to the inversion rule. Keep this in mind as these "inversions" come for free.

A progressive way to familiarise yourself with these shapes is to concentrate on one interval at a time. For instance, take those you encounter the most, like the ♭3rd, 3rd, 4th, 5th, ♭7th, or the octave, and practise "seeing" them and playing them on the guitar. With time and experience, you learn to immediately recognise the shapes of the intervals you use most often and can quickly work out any other.

---

1. Separation of a pair of strings is 0 for the same string, 1 for adjacent strings, 2 for a pair of strings skipping one string, etc.

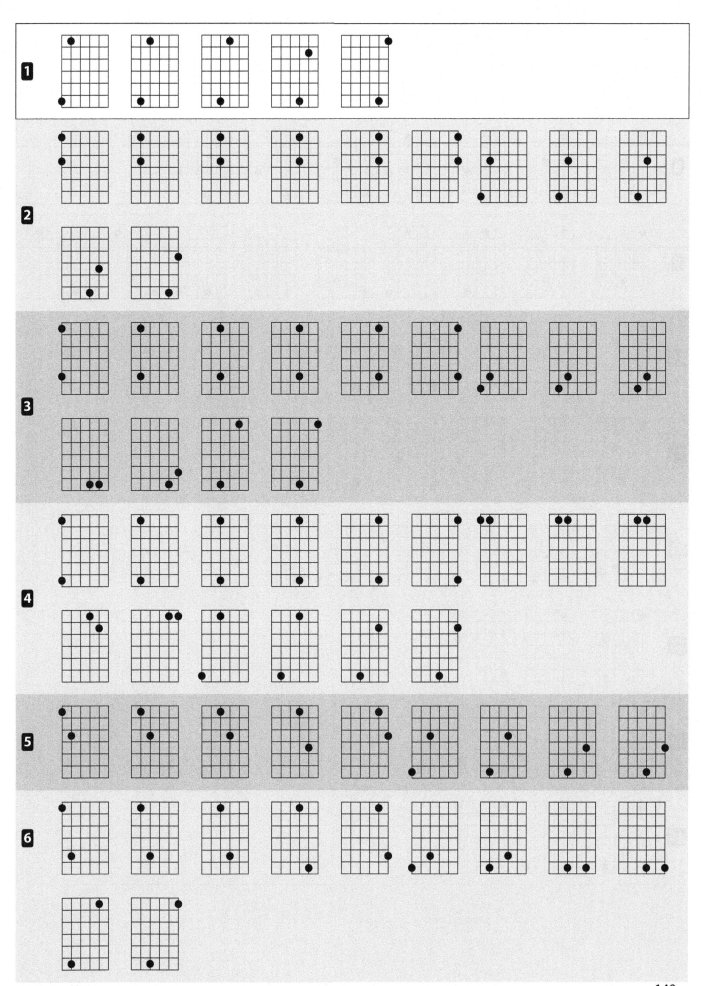

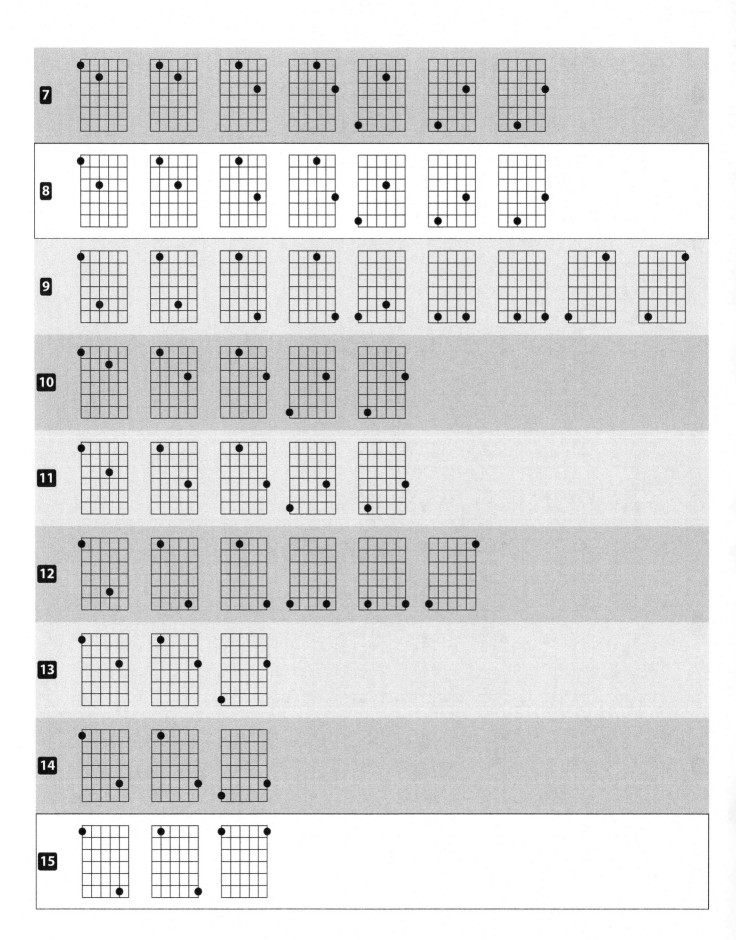

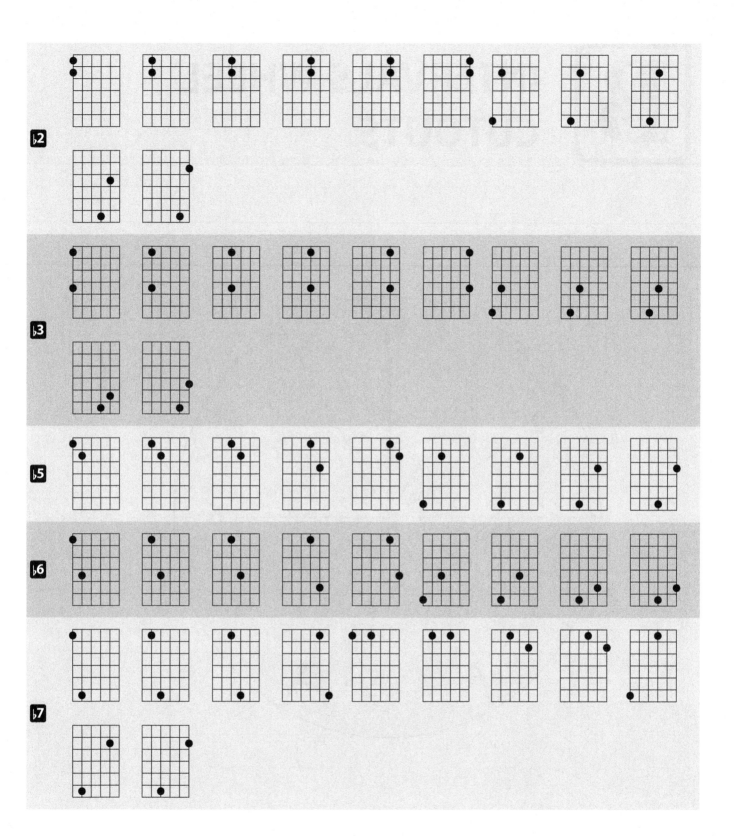

Table A.1 *Inversions: perfect and major intervals + TT*

Interval ↕	1	2	3	4	#4	6	7
Inversion	8	♭7	♭6	5	♭5	♭3	♭2

INTERVALS WHEEL
CUTOUTS

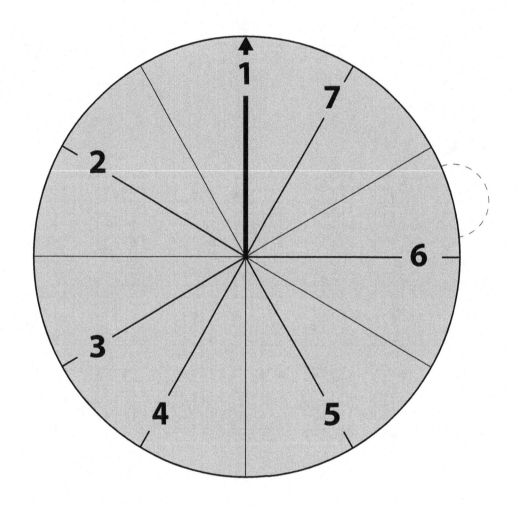

INTERVALS WHEEL
small wheel

🚫 *DO NOT tear or cut out*

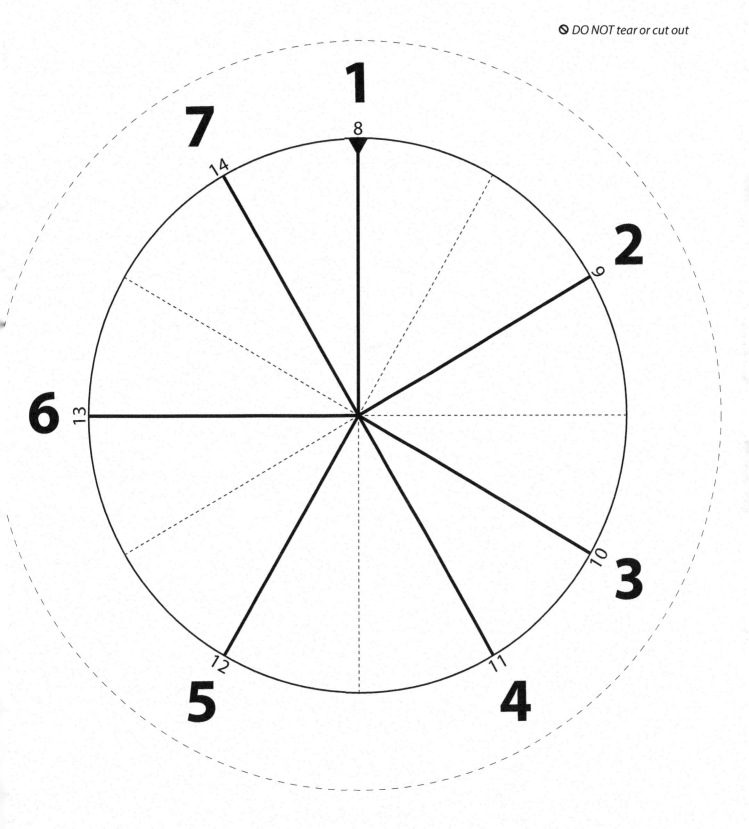

FRET MARKERS

The vast majority of electric and acoustic guitars come with *fret markers*, classical guitars notably don't. All guitars typically have side dots. The most widespread embodiment of fret markers is in the form of dot inlays, placed at frets 3, 5, 7, 9, 12, and repeating at frets 15, 17, 19, 21, 24. All are single dots except for frets 12 and 24 that carry two dots. No doubt fret markers are useful landmarks to help find your position on the fretboard. But perhaps you have wondered why dots are placed on those frets, why there aren't more or fewer, and if their position is related to the construction of the guitar, to the tuning, to playing habits (e.g., open position), or anything else. Though I haven't found a definitive answer as to the origins of these markers, I will expose some personal thoughts on this topic.

Some pretend the placement of dot inlays is related to the location of harmonics on the guitar. I believe this isn't so. We saw that lower order harmonics are not exactly located above the fretwire. But what definitively dispels this belief is that dot inlays repeat at the octave on frets 15, 17, 19, etc., and therefore follow the logarithmic placement of frets. And we know that harmonics follow a linear arrangement on the strings.

Are dots linked to the tuning or to a scale pattern that forms on the fretboard? Looking at the layout of notes on the fretboard, string by string, I don't see a convincing relationship between any one string and the dots that stands out. Besides, one would expect any such relationship to apply to all strings, not just one string. The intervallic pattern between markers, from the nut to fret 12, is: 1½–1–1–1–1½, or 1---♭3--4--5--6---8. That's a pentatonic scale but is neither the major nor the minor pentatonic we are most familiar with.

The most likely rationale behind dot inlays is the role of a visual cue. Are there too many or too few? 3, 5, 7, 9, is an odd pattern and 1 and 11 could be part of the set but were dropped. This makes sense because 1 is right next to 0 (nut) and 11 is right next to 12 (octave) and 0 and 12 already provide a visual cue in those areas. Why was an even pattern like 2, 4, 6, 8, 10, not selected (0 and 12 would be part of this set)? Well, that's one additional marker compared to the odd set. Maybe that's too crowded. If a single marker had to stay, it would be that on fret 12.

Besides serving as a visual aid for the player, fret markers also share this purpose when teaching or showing something on the fretboard. Another purpose of fret markers is purely decorative and an outlet for luthier creativity, to the point where fret markers can become a distinctive part of a guitar or a brand's identity.

If you have any insight into the origins of fret inlays, from luthiers, manufacturers, or from a historical perspective, I would love to hear it.

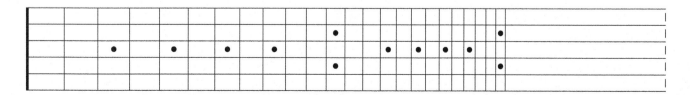

[**pelemeleworks**.com]

- **MUSIC PAPER**, the manuscript paper series.
  a range of blank manuscript paper designs for guitar and other instruments, available in pocketbook and notebook formats.

  pelemeleworks.com

- **CHEATSHEET Music**, the music cheatsheet series.
  a series of practical cheatsheets on key music topics for the musician, teacher, and student.

  cheatsheetmusic.com

- **INTERVALLIC FRETBOARD** – *Towards Improvising on the Guitar*.
  a thought-provoking book on fretboard visualisation, using intervals to understand its geometric properties and navigate its layout.

  intervallicfretboard.com

- **GUITAR FINGERS** – *Essential Technique in Pictures*.
  an in-depth tutorial on left hand and right hand technique for guitar, through pictures and short exercises.

  pelemeleworks.com

- **GUITAR NOTE FINDER** – *Learn the Notes on the Fretboard*.
  a handy aid to help memorise the notes on the fretboard and map them to the music staff.

  pelemeleworks.com

- **FRETBOARD PhD** – *Master the Guitar Fretboard through Intervals*.
  a most unique and comprehensive, borderline obsessive study of the guitar fretboard, with an emphasis on intervals. From basics…to harmonics!

  pelemeleworks.com

CPSIA information can be obtained
at www.ICGtesting.com
Printed in the USA
BVOW09s0838160217

476314BV00027BA/472/P

9 781939 619082